Four years after the publication of Wittgenstein's *Investigations*, Rush Rhees began writing critical reflections on the masterpiece he had helped to edit. In this edited collection of his previously unpublished writings, Rhees argues, *contra* Wittgenstein, that although language lacks the unity of a calculus it is not simply a family of language games. The unity of language is found in its dialogical character. It is in this context that we *say* something, and grow in understanding, notions not captured in Wittgenstein's emphasis on language games, following rules, and *using* language. Rhees develops Wittgenstein's notion that to imagine language is to image a form of life, without suggesting that we are all engaged in an all-inclusive conversation. The result is not only a major contribution to Wittgenstein scholarship, but an original discussion of central philosophical questions concerning the possibility of discourse.

WITTGENSTEIN
AND THE POSSIBILITY OF DISCOURSE

WITTGENSTEIN AND THE POSSIBILITY OF DISCOURSE

RUSH RHEES

EDITED BY

D. Z. PHILLIPS

Rush Rhees Research Professor
University of Wales, Swansea
and
Danforth Professor of the Philosophy of Religion
Claremont Graduate University, California

CAMBRIDGE
UNIVERSITY PRESS

PUBLISHED BY THE PRESS SYNDICATE OF THE UNIVERSITY OF CAMBRIDGE
The Pitt Building, Trumpington Street, Cambridge CB2 1RP, United Kingdom

CAMBRIDGE UNIVERSITY PRESS
The Edinburgh Building, Cambridge CB2 2RU, United Kingdom
40 West 20th Street, New York, NY 10011–4211, USA
10 Stamford Road, Oakleigh, Melbourne 3166, Australia

First published 1998

Printed in the United Kingdom at the University Press, Cambridge

Typeset in Baskerville 11/12½ pt [CE]

A catalogue record for this book is available from the British Library

Library of Congress cataloguing in publication data
Wittgenstein and the possibility of discourse / Rush Rhees; edited by D. Z. Phillips.
p.   cm.
Includes bibliographical references and index.
ISBN 0 521 62261 1 (hardback)
1. Language and languages – Philosophy.   2. Discourse analysis.
I. Phillips, D. Z. (Dewi Zephaniah)   II. Title.
P106.R47   1998
121'.68 – dc 21   97–25416   CIP

ISBN 0 521 62261 1 hardback

5-12-98

Contents

2.6.57.

The whole conception of the growth of understanding was one which the sophists would have questioned.

For them, the growth of understanding could only mean the growth of skill (efficiency, I suppose), or the multiplication of skills (so that there is nothing he does not know).

The distinction between the growth of understanding and the growth of skill may be hard to draw. Growing wiser, and gorwing more efficient or more same competent.
Once again, we have the question of the kind of unity. A skill would have the sort of unity that a calculus does. The sort of unity that is fostered by motion study.

Incidentally, we could hardly find the connexion between the growth of one skill and the growth of another, which would be anything like the connexion between the growth of understanding in one field and in another, as Plato thought of that.
(This may be at the root of some of the disputes about "transferred training". The acquiring of competence or skill in one field, need not make you any better fitted to become competent in another.
But if we talk about the growth of understanding, it is a different matter.

Has this anything to do with what is meant by saying that philosophy is contemplative? I expect Plato thought it had.

Anyway, it looks as though the two issues hang together:
1) whether understanding is just competence;
2) whether one xxix can talk in a ganeràl way about understanding, or the growth of understanding.

Certainly we must agree that there could be no sense in speaking of the growth of understanding xa as Plato might have wished to, if understanding is just a matter of competence.

The pursuit of understanding would act as a counter weigh to the pursuit of competence.

The question whether language is a skill. That is rsally the same thing. Xxxixxxxxxxxxxxx
Whether speaking it as a technique.

And so: whether thinking is a technique. (Socrates's method was opposed to this.)
And whether living is.
Once again: whether life has or can have the unity of a skill.

A sample page from Rhees' notes.

Editor's note

Rush Rhees' notes, which make up the present work, are part of the Rush Rhees Archive purchased by the Department of Philosophy, University of Wales, Swansea, after his death. The purchase was made possible by a memorial fund to A. E. Heath, foundation professor of philosophy at Swansea, the generous gift of Heath's widow. The Archive amounts to sixteen thousand pages of manuscript.

Rush Rhees began writing his notes on Wittgenstein's later views on language on 26 May 1957. The last notes on the topic are dated 19 February 1960.

What confronted me, initially, as editor, was a large pile of pages. Apart from the dates on the notes, there were no divisions in Rhees' material. It took a year and a half of reading and re-reading before I could see the wood for the trees, and appreciate the developments in Rhees' arguments. The result is that all titles in the present work, those of the chapters and the title of the book, are mine. I am also responsible for the divisions within the chapters.

It was clear from the outset that it was impossible to publish the notes as they stood. Most of the notes (often daily notes) are no more than five pages long. Rhees often recapped the argument of the previous day or days, so the notes contained a great deal of repetition. On the other hand, it would have been foolish to eliminate all repetition in a mechanical way. Rhees approaches the same point from a number of different directions, and what seems like repetition often includes a striking remark which brings new insight to the point being discussed. Rhees' arguments have a cumulative effect which I have tried to preserve.

Rhees' notes are written in his highly distinctive style. Many, if not most, of his paragraphs consist of no more than one to three sentences. Such paragraphs are themselves written in clusters with wider gaps between each cluster. This style, as indicated in the sample page preceding this note, should not be confused with Wittgenstein's numbered paragraphs, and the decision which faced me was not at all like the one which would be involved in deciding to omit some of Wittgenstein's paragraphs. It was simply that Rhees' organization of his small pages, one which allows the reader to concentrate on some of his arresting sentences, as in the short essays in his *Without Answers*, became a positive disadvantage when the length of the present book became obvious. It broke up the continuity of the argument in a way which made it extremely difficult to follow. It was necessary to bring the paragraphs together in a more orthodox way, eliminating the more obviously superfluous repetitions and asides in doing so. But this is not the end of the story. Rhees did not take himself to be developing a single text. Most days his notes showed progress as he wrestled with Wittgenstein's and his own thoughts, but he often went forwards and backwards between various topics, even within a single set of notes. The notes could not have been published in the sequence within which he wrote them. The sequence I have chosen is the one which, in my opinion, reflects best the developments in his argument. I have indicated, however, dates of the notes which make up the chapters. Needless to say, Rhees' notes will remain in their original sequence in the Archive.

The editorial problems which confronted me were formidable, and since I think with a pen in my hand, rather than a finger on a word-processor or even a typewriter, the re-organization involved arriving at a handwritten manuscript of 350 pages.

Rhees' reflections on these topics, it seems to me, have the depth and originality which characterized most of his work. I only hope that after my editorial endeavours the spirit of the original has been preserved.

I am extremely grateful to Mrs Helen Baldwin, secretary to the Department of Philosophy at Swansea, for preparing the typescript for publication, and to my colleague Timothy Tessin for help with the German phrases in the text and with proof-reading.

Editor's introduction

Four years after the publication of Ludwig Wittgenstein's *Philosophical Investigations* in 1953, Rush Rhees, one of Wittgenstein's literary executors and closest friends, began writing critical reflections on the masterpiece he had helped to edit. Wittgenstein visited Swansea frequently for discussions with Rhees. *Discussion* should be emphasized, since it is hard to imagine Rhees as a passive listener. Norman Malcolm told me of occasions with Wittgenstein when, while he and others would listen, Rhees would ask probing questions. Perhaps the present work is the cumulative result of those discussions. It represents an extension of Wittgenstein's investigations in a philosophical spirit of which Wittgenstein would have approved.

I

Rhees had written: 'There are certain problems which come up again and again from the time of the early Greeks right down to the present; and I should maintain that the other problems generally centred around them.'[1] He had in mind questions concerning the relation of logic to reality, the relation of language to reality, and what it means to *say* something. These questions cannot be treated separately, although there are important differences between them. They have involved philosophers, ever since Parmenides and his predecessors, in speculation about the unity of discourse and the unity of the world:

What is the difference between saying something and making a noise ...? This includes the question of the relation of language to reality. And it is the same sort of thing which people have discussed in recent times when

---

[1] 'The Fundamental Problems of Philosophy', ed. by Timothy Tessin, *Philosophical Investigations* vol. 17, no. 4 (October 1994), p. 573.

they have asked what a proposition is, or when they have asked what understanding is – ... (Wittgenstein in a reply to Joad insisted that 'the questions we are discussing, are the same questions which Plato discussed'.) But I would maintain that the same can be shown in the discussions of Descartes and right on through Kant and Hegel.[2]

In the first two parts of the present book, Rhees shows how there are parallels between Plato's and Wittgenstein's treatment of these central questions. Plato asks whether 'understanding' is a matter of competence, and whether a criterion can be found to distinguish 'understanding' from what is 'not understanding'. He is clear that language is not simply a collection of skills, as the sophists claimed. On such a view, the only criterion for saying or doing one thing rather than another is the success that the saying or doing bring. In that case, Plato argued, there can be no such thing as growth of understanding. We do not simply want to know the answer in mathematics, or the verdict in the Assembly. We want to understand how these outcomes are arrived at. That goes with understanding *the kind* of outcomes they are. Further, Plato argued, such answers and verdicts are not isolated from what surrounds them; they have their significance in a language and in lives which people share with each other. The answers and verdicts hang together with other things. Rhees' central question is: how do things 'hang together' in language, what kind of unity does language have?

' "Understanding" makes sense if living makes sense.' Rhees realizes that this sounds empty, said just like that, and he endeavours from different directions, throughout the book, to bring out why he thinks the remark is so important. He thinks that searching for justifications of the sense which living has is futile. Plato, however, searches for such a justification. For him, to say that 'understanding' has sense if living makes sense would seem arbitrary. Plato would not be content to say, for example, that there are distinctions between right and wrong within the sciences. He would want to ask whether the sciences themselves are right or wrong. His own answer is to say that 'understanding' has sense because all discourse is about reality. But, interestingly enough, Plato never tells us what this 'relation to reality' amounts to. In this respect, the conclusions of his dialogues are, in the main, negative: they tell us what the relation is not. On the other hand, Plato still insists that if language, discourse, is to be

---

[2] Ibid.

more than a collection of skills, it must have *some* kind of unity. Should one not endeavour, then, to say what this unity consists in?

One of Rhees' main themes in the book is to argue that we need not embrace Plato's conclusion. Protagoras denied that a common measure can be found for what is to count as discourse. Plato thought that the consequence is that language is a collection of absurd games. And if *that* is what language is, there can be no growth of understanding. Rhees wants to argue that 'growth of understanding' *does* depend on the unity of language, but that the unity language has does *not* depend on there being a common measure of what makes discourse discourse. What kind of unity, then, does language have? That is the theme of Rhees' discussions.

II

Many philosophers will be surprised by Rhees' comparison of Plato and Wittgenstein. They will say that Wittgenstein, in his later work, gave up worrying about the conditions of the possibility of discourse. Rhees denies this. From first to last, he insists, Wittgenstein's chief concern is with 'what it means to say something'. Rhees claimed that his last work, *On Certainty*, is an essay about logic.[3] Wittgenstein did not turn his back on the central questions of philosophy. What changed, radically, was the way in which he treated these questions.

In his early work, Wittgenstein wanted to determine the nature of a proposition, to find out its general form. What 'saying something' amounts to, he argued, cannot vary from context to context. If it did, 'sense' would not be determinate. The determination of sense makes it necessary to arrive at some kind of criterion for what *can* and *cannot* be said.

By the time Wittgenstein wrote the *Investigations*, he had moved away from this position. Instead of claiming that logic determines what *can* and what *cannot* be said, he asks us to look at the logic, or the grammar, as he puts it, of what *is* said. When we do this, we see that 'saying something' does not come to the same thing in every context. Wittgenstein brings this out by an analogy between games and language. We play a variety of games, but we do not assume that all games must have something in common. Given the variety of

---

[3] See Rush Rhees, *There Like Our Life: Discussions of 'On Certainty' and Related Issues*, ed. D. Z. Phillips, hitherto unpublished (provisional title).

language games we play, why assume that every language game must have something in common? Instead of assuming that this *must* be the case, why don't we look to see *whether* it is the case? Just as we can be content with saying that we play a variety of games, so we can be philosophically content with saying that we play a variety of language games.

Rhees thinks that that philosophical contentment is premature. In fact, concentration on what Wittgenstein has to say about the variety of language games we play can lead us to ignore the central issue that the analogy between language and games subserves: 'What does it mean to say something?' It can also lead to an inadequate and impoverished conception of philosophy.

Wittgenstein draws attention to ways in which the grammars of different language games may become confused in our thinking. So it is tempting to conclude that philosophy is no more than the battle against such confusion; a matter of skill in clearing away our conceptual muddles. As Rhees points out, we can be puzzled by the differences between language games without being puzzled by the question of whether discourse is possible at all; whether we really do say anything to each other. That question need not even be raised. For some philosophers, this is all to the good, since the question itself, they would say, is a confused one. We should put it aside, since it is a question well lost.

Rhees insists that Wittgenstein did *not* put this question aside. To repeat: his talk of language games and grammatical confusion is part of his effort to tackle it, and Rhees is not denying the importance of the contribution. But he is saying that, sometimes, such talk makes it harder to appreciate the larger issue it is meant to subserve.

Wittgenstein, in showing that our language games do not have a common form, wanted to show that language does not have a formal unity like the unity of a calculus. 'Speaking' is not one thing, it is doing many things. But, again, if we concentrate only on particular language games, and the particular confusions they can occasion, we shall not see how there can be more general confusions about language and the possibility of discourse. And if philosophers object to general observations about language, it must be remembered that it is not as though Wittgenstein himself did not make general observations about language. He talked not only of language games, but of a family resemblance between them, and concluded that this is the kind of unity language has, the unity of a family of games. Rhees wants to show that the deepest forms of confusion about language take a general form, and that calling language a family of games is one of them.

Rhees agrees with Wittgenstein that language does not have a formal unity like a calculus. It does not follow, however, that it makes no sense to talk of the unity of language. Rhees agrees with Plato that, unless language has a unity, there can be no such thing as growth of understanding. The issue is whether Wittgenstein's analogy between language and games helps or hinders our recognition of the kind of unity language has.

Rhees points out that if you explain a particular game to someone, you are already assuming that that person can speak. We cannot explain what 'speaking' is in the same way. You assume that a person is ignorant of a certain game, hence the need for an explanation, but what are you assuming if you said that a person is ignorant of what 'speaking' is? You may be puzzled about what a game is without being puzzled about discourse.

In the analogy with games, Wittgenstein wanted to avoid the temptation of looking for an ultimate explanation of language. He had moved away from the view that, by making explicit the structure of the symbolism, rules of logic can be arrived at which show what combination of signs are possible, what can and cannot be said. The emphasis in the *Investigations* is not on how language can and cannot be used, but on how language *is* used in a variety of ways. And that is why Wittgenstein places so much emphasis on 'that's how we do it' and 'that's what we call "going on in the same way"'; he wants to get away from the idea that there is a necessity underpinning our ways of speaking. Wittgenstein wants to show that the relation between words and things is not an external one. The connexions happen *in* the game. Rhees argues, however, that something of the older conception of logic survives in the *Investigations*. The 'structure' of the proposition is replaced by the 'structure' of the game: it is still a matter of 'doing things with words'.

Wittgenstein wanted to avoid a conception of 'teaching someone to speak' which presupposes that a person can speak already. He thinks the notion of 'training' helps him to do this. But since he emphasizes training people to use particular expressions, it is difficult to see how he is any further forward, since this seems to presuppose that a person can already use *other* expressions. Furthermore, as we shall see, the notion of 'training' creates far-reaching difficulties of its own. For the moment, it can be noted that a person may be trained in a certain use and yet have nothing to say. Someone might even be trained to detect the difference between one sound and another without learning to speak.

If we say that we are trained to apply rules, or to follow rules in the same way, Rhees' objection is that language is not a matter of applying rules, or of going on with anything; it is not a matter of *doing* anything in that sense. It is a matter of speaking to other people, whereas, in a game, nothing is said. A move in an imaginary game is just as brilliant *as a move*, as it is in a real game. The 'games analogy', with its proximity to mastering techniques and skills, leaves out 'understanding between people', and thus makes the relation to rules too external a matter. The Sophists, too, were happy to speak of language as a collection of techniques. For Plato, and for Rhees, the price of doing so is too high: the exclusion of the possibility of growth of understanding.

III

In the first two parts of the book, Rhees comes back, again and again, to the contention that language makes sense if living makes sense. If you speak of using language to do certain things, it makes it look as though doing those things were intelligible apart from language. If someone asked you what you had learned when you learned to speak, you would not reply, 'I have learned to use these propositions.' This is why Rhees thinks that the analogy with mathematics and the calculus continues to exercise a hold on Wittgenstein: *using* a calculus, mathematical *operations* – doing something. Rhees thinks there is no analogy between 'using a calculus' and 'using language', not because he seeks a better analogy for 'using language', but because he does not think that 'saying something' is a matter of '*using* language' at all.

If we want to appreciate the connexion between 'understanding' and 'living', Rhees thinks it more profitable to reflect on the conversations which people have with each other. Here, the disanalogy with games is evident. The kind of understanding one can have in a conversation is not like knowing the moves in a game or in a dance. It is not 'knowing one's way around' in that sense. The game or dance is self-contained in a way a conversation is not. A conversation is not taught as a game is taught. Rhees' point is not that it is taught in some other way, but that the notion of 'teaching' is out of place here. Promises to teach 'the art of conversation' turn it into a debate or a convention. You learn how to play a game, but not how to conduct a conversation or a discussion, and you do not follow the course of a conversation in the way you follow the course of a game. Again, that would make the 'following' too external a matter. Having enjoyed a game, you might decide to repeat it, whereas it would make no sense to repeat a conversation. One may decide to discuss certain matters further, but not to have the same conversation again. We may relate a conversation to someone else, or be directed to tell the jury the details of a conversation. But this is neither having the same conversation again, nor the repeated application of a technique.

What we can learn from a conversation depends on the fact that it is part of a dialogue which is connected with things outside the dialogue. This does not mean, of course, that what we learn from every conversation is the same. We must know the *logos* of the discussion, which is another way of saying that there is something to understand in it. And if we say that that understanding depends on connexions between the conversation and other things, we will be asked what that connexion is. To say that understanding the connexion is an understanding of life will seem hopelessly vague. So the vital question becomes: how do these things hang together? This is another way of asking what kind of unity language has. There is a generality involved, but of what kind?

Rhees argues that it is not the generality involved in a technique. The *Investigations* begins with training a child to speak, but one is not *trained* to do this. Later, in his work, Wittgenstein recognized a generality in language which is not the generality found in a game or technique. He said that to imagine a language is to imagine a form of life. Wittgenstein never makes very explicit what he means by a form of life. When he gives examples, they are often of 'ways of doing things': institutions or ways of working. For Rhees, this still makes 'speaking' too external a matter. The internal connexion between 'speaking' and 'living' he wants to emphasize is a matter of *understanding the language that is spoken*, seeing the sense of the ways in which people speak to each other. Knowing one's way around this is not a matter of mastering the meanings of expressions (cf. Plato's Forms), or of knowing one's way round a game or an institution.

Conversation is not simply a matter of mastering a vocabulary.

People may have the same vocabulary and yet be unable to understand each other. We bring something to a conversation, for example, when we say, 'In my opinion . . .' And others respond. Conversation and discussion is trying to understand, trying to get clear about something. This is what Plato was emphasizing in saying that discussion must be *about* something; its reality depends on that.

Rhees has wanted to emphasize: first, that a conversation is connected with things outside itself; second, that people must have something in common to have a conversation. He realizes, of course, that all language is not conversation. We may be ordering a coffee, writing an inventory, or doing a thousand other things which are not conversation. But in discussing the unity of language, Rhees thinks this can be clarified by using 'conversation' as a centre of variation which throws light on other aspects of language which are not conversation.

Scepticism is the *denial of the possibility* of understanding. Rhees argues that if we concentrate on clarifying confusions between different forms of language, neither the depth of the sceptical challenge, nor the anxiety it has created for philosophers, can be appreciated. We will not understand why great philosophers, including Plato and Wittgenstein, have been concerned about the possibility of discourse.

IV

Rush Rhees' paper, 'Wittgenstein's Builders', has become a classic.[4] It might be said that all the points made in Part Three of Rhees' book can be found in it. On the other hand, the paper is highly condensed, and what may seem to be occasional criticism there, is shown to be a more far-reaching and sustained critique in the book. Chapter 10 in the present work is the nearest to the published paper so, for that reason, I have called it a recapitulation. The discussion of Wittgenstein's example of the builders is ideal for Rhees' purposes, since it enables him, by reference to a single example, to raise the issues about language he has discussed in the first two parts of the book.

In Wittgenstein's example, a builder, on a building site, calls out

---

[4] *Proceedings of the Aristotelian Society* (1959–60). Reprinted in Rush Rhees, *Discussions of Wittgenstein* (London: Routledge, 1970).

'Slab' to a colleague, who then brings him a slab. Wittgenstein said that this order could constitute *the whole* language of a tribe. Rhees thinks this suggestion is unintelligible. His objection is not, as some critics of his paper have suggested, that the vocabulary of this language is too restricted. It is no answer to Rhees, therefore, to conjure up imaginative pictures of how the builders example can be made richer than it first appears. Rhees' objections are logical. If language involves saying something, Rhees is claiming that *nothing is being said* in Wittgenstein's example. Why does he say this?

When one builder calls 'Slab' and the other reacts, we seem to have no more than the reaction to a signal. The builder is reacting as a trained animal would. But Wittgenstein intends his example to be an example of a primitive *language*. That being so, the builders must be said to understand each other. If the builder is obeying an order, he understands the activity he is engaged in. Unlike the trained animal, the builder does not simply react correctly; he understands what he is doing. A house dog may respond to an order, but it does not know what the signal means.

Rhees brings out features of the situation which would be present if the builders understood each other, features absent from Wittgenstein's example. We could imagine the roles of 'giving an order' and 'receiving an order' being reversed between the two builders. There may be, at times, no sharp dividing line between a signal and a sign, but it is important to emphasize that the builder understands the sign as part of an operation, and that that remains the case even if we choose to call 'Slab' a signal. It is a signal he can be said to be waiting for, since a different signal could have been given. This is part of understanding it – an essential part. Further, it is a signal which may lead to discussion: 'Why did you give me that signal if you didn't want me to . . . ?' It is no accident that neither discussion nor conversation suggest themselves as having a natural place in Wittgenstein's example.

A dog may respond to a signal, but it does not *use* the signal itself; it does not use *this* signal as opposed to another. Wittgenstein's builders, if they understood each other, would be able to do that. It may seem pedantic to say that a horse doesn't understand 'Whoa', since, otherwise, why bother to give it the order? But then it is important to remember what is absent in this case. The horse does not understand what the signal means in the absence of the order. It does not tell you whether another horse is going to stop, or understand a question as to why it didn't. But all these considerations are part of the background when an order is understood; and to understand one needs to know the language. And knowing the language involves being able to do other things. The builder is not *just* in that position, in that job, giving the signal 'Slab'. Otherwise, he could be replaced by a machine, in which case the possibility of questions and discussions does not arise. We can have machines controlling machines, but one builder is not 'minding' another, as one might mind a machine or a horse. Even in the case of a game, a person is not set to play chess as a machine can be. The builder can go off and do things other than his job. The builder is not simply trained to react.

Rhees wants to emphasize that even if we call the builder's order a signal, it has its sense in a wider context. In this sense it can be thought of as part of a conversation. The same is true in simple matters, such as saying, 'How nice your hat is.' Life couldn't be entirely within an organization, since that organization is *about* something, and that means that it will be connected with things other than itself. So Wittgenstein's builders could not have a language which is spoken only in connexion with their building. Yet that is what Wittgenstein asks us to suppose. Building cannot be the only things in their lives. You may carry on a business in living, but living is no business at all.

If we are speaking a language in one connexion, we must speak it in other connexions as well. But why not just here? Rhees' reply: because language is a part of a way of living with other people. The child learns the language from people who are living it, and that is not a matter of training. The assumption that there could be a conversation which is the only one ever held is a logical absurdity. Rhees recognizes that there are difficulties to be avoided in showing this. Rhees wants to avoid saying, with Plato, that language constitutes one big all-inclusive conversation or dialogue, but he also wants to avoid saying that the only alternative is that language is a family of language games. Although Wittgenstein insists that language is not doing one thing, but doing many things, Rhees thinks that in the games analogy it is left too similar to matters of technique – a family of games. Despite the fact that Plato thought of the unity of language as the unity of a dialogue, Rhees thinks that his notion of the unity of discourse is more satisfactory than Wittgenstein's, since it emphasizes involvement in conversation and the growth of understanding that involves. When Wittgenstein, on the other hand, speaks of language as a family of games, he does not tell us whether, in these games, people would be speaking *the same* language. We have no idea what kind of life his builders have; what their institutions are like; their songs, their humour; their rituals, if any, and so on. Critics of Rhees' paper who have blandly filled in these details have not appreciated Rhees' logical point in relation to them: how the builder's 'Slab' would not be *saying* anything without them. Wittgenstein was nearer to these issues, Rhees argues, in some of his discussions of mathematics. Wittgenstein asked whether there could be a pure mathematics without any question of its application. If one thought that possible, he asks what the difference would be between pure mathematics and a wallpaper pattern.

Rhees points out, however, that the analogy between language and mathematics is a limited one. Wittgenstein said that if we want to understand a proposition we should look at what we do with it. But can we say that of language? Can we speak of the application of language in the way we can speak of the application of a rule in mathematics or in physics? Rhees suggests that, sometimes, Wittgenstein confuses a particular case of application, like a proposition in engineering, and other contexts where one wouldn't speak of the application of language at all.

Many philosophers would want to put aside questions about language as such. Asked, 'What is language?' they'd reply by giving examples and saying 'This sort of thing'. But, then, for Rhees, this avoids the central questions of philosophy. Both Plato and Wittgenstein are concerned with the possibility of discourse and want to bring the examples together in some way. They certainly want to say that 'understanding the language' and 'understanding what is said' have to be treated together. Rhees says that Plato regarded language as an extension of the understanding, and insisted that it is an extension in time; it cannot be grasped all at once. Wittgenstein's emphasis is the other way round: for him, 'understanding what is said' is to understand its role in the language game. For Rhees, Wittgenstein's emphasis, unlike Plato's, gets away from the role of 'what is said' *in the language.* For, in some sense, there *is* a language which is common to all the games.

And so we are back to the big question: how do the different games hang together in language? Rhees is inclined to agree with Plato in treating language as an extension of what is said. If this is left out, we can still clarify different roles and different grammars, but what we do not clarify is the place these have in a conversation. To include this in Wittgenstein's example of the builders, we would have to distinguish between the role of 'Slab' in this particular job, and its role in the language, the point being that the latter is not confined to this particular job, this particular language game. We do not say anything in a game. That is why Wittgenstein's analogy between language and games is so misleading: it suggests formal relations where it is inappropriate to do so.

Rhees wants to deny that language has the unity of a calculus, or the unity of a game. He wants to say that the unity language has is the unity of a common intelligibility. It is the unity of language which makes it possible for people to understand each other. Or, rather, we should put it the other way round: that people do understand each other is the unity that language has.

v

'Language has sense if living makes sense; the unity of language is the unity of a common intelligibility.' Rhees did not elaborate on this in his paper on 'Wittgenstein's Builders', but he does so in the fourth and final part of this book. He is taking up issues which arose in the discussion of his paper and his own further reflections on it.

The generality of language is not the generality which comes from applying rules. This is where the analogy with the distinction between pure and applied mathematics limps. Rhees thinks that for all the revolution in Wittgenstein's later philosophy, the analogy between mathematics and language continued to exercise a hold on him. Moreover, he argues, it did so in a way which led Wittgenstein to retain what is misleading in the analogy, and to let go its valuable aspects.

Wittgenstein, as we have seen, does not want to say that language is like a calculus, but he does not see any difference in principle between language and mathematics. Mathematics, for Wittgenstein, is a department of language, a kind of language game. Rhees finds this already misleading, since doing mathematics together is not like having a conversation together. His point is that, because this is not emphasized, it makes it easier for Wittgenstein to speak, sometimes, at least, of language as a family of games, and to make the resemblances between them look like resemblances between techniques.

In the *Brown Book*, Wittgenstein wanted to get away from thinking that we learn the meaning of a word by learning the rules for it. This is why he emphasises what we *do* with words. His idea was that we can begin with primitive examples and then say, 'and so on . . .'. Rhees thinks this is misleading, and that 'and so on . . .' belongs to later stages of language where you already have something like a notation. But because Wittgenstein was thinking of language by analogy with mathematics, it was natural for him to think this way. Further, by emphasizing the kind of understanding achieved in mathematics or in a notation, 'understanding' lacks the temporality involved in the understanding which comes from speaking with people living their lives.

On the other hand, although Rhees thinks Plato and Wittgenstein were right to say that the unity of language is not the unity of a system, and that Wittgenstein was right in his later philosophy, to turn away from the analogy between language and a calculus, Rhees thinks that there is something in the analogy which Wittgenstein and others saw. Rhees argues that that 'something' is lost in Wittgenstein's later emphasis on language as a family of games.

Wittgenstein wanted to contrast the completeness of a system with the 'incompleteness' of language. But with this went Wittgenstein's insistence on the independence of language games from each other; an insistence which loses their interlocking intelligibility which the previous analogy between language and a calculus emphasized, albeit in a misleading way. One of the big revolutions in Wittgenstein's thinking was the rejection of the idea that there is no such thing as a new proposition, that one should be able to deduce any 'new' proposition from those already known. But in the analogy with games, there is a danger of losing the common intelligibility of language. Rhees says that he wants to emphasize the unity of language in a way which, perhaps, Wittgenstein did not, by showing that the common intelligibility of language need not imply that one has to resort to the notion of a common form.

Wanting to avoid thinking of language like a calculus, Wittgenstein turned to the analogy between language and an institution, since, here, one can speak of rules without thinking of them as the formal rules of a calculus. Think of the rules of a legal institution. The analogy also seemed to provide a useful comparison between the growth of language and the growth of an institution. We can make up rules as we go along. Language is like a city to which new additions and extensions can be made.

The analogy influenced Wittgenstein's discussion of contradiction. Instead of thinking of the possibilities of contradiction as being determined by the structure of language, Wittgenstein says that contradictions are matters we deal with *when they arise*. Instead of saying that contradictions *must* arise, Wittgenstein says that whether they arise depends on our ways of doing things, as does our way of dealing with them. Rhees is not denying the fruitfulness of the analogy between language and institutions in some contexts, but thinks it extremely important to recognize its limitations in others.

Rhees says that although the common intelligibility of language is not that of a common form, it cannot be elucidated in terms of participation in an institution either. In banking, for example, it makes sense to talk of becoming an expert in one's field, but, despite some analogies, it is not like this when we come to speak. Our growth in understanding is not a matter of developing proficiency. It makes 'the understanding' too external a matter. One might say that a particular language, French or English, is an institution, but one cannot say this of *language*. Perhaps one could say that mathematics is an institution. Plato would have resisted this, because of the place he gave to mathematics in our understanding. The reason why Plato gave it this place is the very reason why Wittgenstein would not: a perceived need of an ideal measure for language. Rhees recognizes the importance of Wittgenstein's denial, but he does not think that the alternative is an analogy between language and institutions or games.

As we have seen, Rhees wants to avoid saying that the unity of language is the unity of a dialogue. He also wants to avoid saying that it is the unity of one big enterprise (doing one's bit), and speaking is not like having a function within it. But the alternative is not to say that 'speaking' is a matter of mastering different activities: business dealings, surgical operations, debates in parliament or law courts, religious worship, and so on. Rhees insists that they are connected with each other in the lives people lead, a connexion in time and history. Plato made it too institutional a matter by concentrating, too narrowly, on what you learn in trades and professions. But even these, Rhees insists, could not be what they are without connexions with the rest of people's lives.

Suppose someone asks what 'speaking a language' is like in those lives? Is it like mastering a technique, following a rule, working in an institution? Rhees does not object to saying 'yes' to all these suggestions within certain contexts. The danger, he insists, is in failing to recognize the limitations of these analogies, especially when we are discussing the central question of the unity of discourse, and of what 'saying something' is. Rhees has wanted to emphasize the 'common intelligibility' of language which is shown in the connexions between things which people make in their lives.

Philosophers may seek further justifications. They may ask how we know that the connexions people make in their lives, which Rhees refers to, aren't all mistaken. Rhees says that such questions are related to requests to show that the ways we calculate are not mistaken, or to demonstrate the logicality of logic. In Wittgenstein's early philosophy, the general form of the proposition was supposed to fulfil this function. An expression having a certain 'form' is a condition of its intelligibility. 'Belonging to language' would then be a matter of an expression's relation to that form. This would be like deciding whether an expression belongs to a calculus or not, or whether a proposition belongs to a formal system. This view ran into major difficulties. Can you decide, in the same way, whether a proposition is intelligible? How can one look to its logical relations without presupposing them? If the intelligibility of a statement in a calculus lies in its relation to others, how can that be reconciled with the view that its intelligibility is already present by virtue of its form? One of the big philosophical issues concerns this use of 'by virtue of its form'.

When Wittgenstein turned to the notion of language as a family of language games, he insisted that each language game is a complete system of communication. What he wanted to insist on, as shown in his discussion of elliptical remarks, is that a language game is not incomplete. But, Rhees argues, he could have shown that without making the claim that a whole language could consist of playing one language game and no other.

Any single conversation gets its sense from other conversations which circulate round and about it, and no single account can be given of this. There is still a need to distinguish between genuine and sham discourse, but that is now understood in terms of the growth of understanding which occurs in dialogue with other people, something which need not involve the claim that I understand every remark that is made to me. Rhees used to say in discussion: 'I did not learn to speak by speaking to everyone about everything.'

If we saw that a child comes to understand others in such a

context, there is no general answer to the question of what it is that it learns, despite the fact that any answer will not be purely personal. The child picks up what it does mainly from the ways in which its parents talk to it, and to each other. That is why one can give no general answer to the question of what its growth in understanding consists in. And that is also why saying a child knows its way around is so unlike saying one knows one's way around in mathematics. So if we say that a child can speak and someone asks, 'About what?', the answer will be: 'About things a child can be expected to understand at that age.' The understanding which a child picks up is not a matter of making correct responses; it shows itself, partly, in the way a child asks and responds to questions. The child grows in under-standing in dialogue with others.

There is, therefore, a personal element in learning to speak, not simply because of the importance of aspects of language such as sincerity and irony, but because growth in understanding is essen-tially a growth in *judgement*. Rhees insists on this, and it is something he finds in Plato. In this way, becoming familiar with what people say is closer to aesthetic judgements than we might suppose.

VI

To understand people, we must understand more than the language. We must understand what they talk about in discussion. It seems absurd to say that we can have something to say to others if we do not know 'the meaning of expressions'. But is it not equally absurd to say that we must first master 'the meaning of expressions' so that we may have something to say to each other? Plato emphasized that language is not prior to dialogue, and that 'growth of understanding' goes hand in hand with a common life and a common understand-ing. Rhees, too, emphasizes that people do not talk to each other because they want to make themselves intelligible. Rather, intellig-ibility is found *in* the ways in which people talk to each other.

If this is where intelligibility is to be found, doesn't it make the whole thing arbitrary? Rhees says that this is a very odd use of 'arbitrary'. Rhees calls Part Two: xii of the *Investigations* 'the most important short statement for an understanding of the book'.[5] In

---

[5] Rush Rhees, 'The Philosophy of Wittgenstein' in *Discussions of Wittgenstein*. Rhees is discussing George Pitcher's *The Philosophy of Wittgenstein*.

that statement, Wittgenstein says: 'Compare a concept with a style of painting. For is even our style of painting arbitrary? Can we choose one at pleasure? (The Egyptian, for instance.) Is it a mere question of pleasing and ugly?'

Understanding language is understanding the dialogues people have with each other. This involves appreciating their styles of speech, hence the analogy with aesthetics. It seems to many philosophers that language can be discussed quite apart from an understanding of the lives people live. For them, 'what is said' is one thing, 'the depth' of what is said is quite another. And so it may seem that 'understanding life' is a matter for art, rather than a matter for philosophy. Rhees disagrees. It may be said that an artist needs to be familiar with the way people live if he or she is to understand an individual subject. But it can also be said that art does not illustrate, but *contributes to*, what is there to understand.[6] 'What is there to understand' is richer than what it often becomes in 'the philosophy of language'.

Rhees has argued that the unity of language has to do with its common intelligibility. Philosophers have asked what this intelligibility depends on. They have insisted that certain things must hold fast if there is to be intelligibility at all. Plato argued that Forms or certain principles must hold fast, while others have argued that certain facts must be beyond question, if there is to be any intelligibility. Rhees says that this intelligibility depends on dialogue. The issue is not: how is language put together?, but: how does language hang together in dialogue? In this dialogue, in certain circumstances, some judgements will hold fast. In these judgements, the distinction between 'the factual' and 'the grammatical' is not a sharp one.[7]

Rhees has argued throughout that philosophy's concern with language, with the unity of discourse, cannot be divorced from dialogues in the lives people lead. He says, however, that this matter must be treated with care, since it can be easily misconstrued. Rhees emphasizes that he is not saying that philosophers have some special insight into 'the course of human lives', or into why human lives go in the ways they do. Education gives one no special superiority in that regard. Again, Plato thought otherwise because he discussed

---

[6] 'Art and Philosophy' in Rush Rhees, *Without Answers*, ed. D. Z. Phillips (London: Routledge, 1969), pp. 135 f.

[7] Rhees does not develop these points further here, but they are his major concern in *There Like Our Life*, his discussion of *On Certainty* (see f.n. 3).

education often in relation to crafts and professions. Given the temptation to extract didactic lessons about 'how to live' from the writings of Wittgenstein, seen in some philosophers, Rhees' cautions here are timely.

The problems Rhees discusses come from philosophy, and the kind of understanding of them he seeks comes from philosophy too. He is arguing that 'saying something' involves learning to speak among people who face certain problems, and who seek certain kinds of solutions. For example, people who face deep problems in science, in morality, or problems of other kinds. It is in lives such as these, unlike the lives of animals, that there can be growth of understanding. It is in lives such as these that people can speak; that they can say something.

VII

This introduction is not a summary of Rhees' book. I am conscious of how much I have not mentioned, and of how many philosophical connexions I have not attempted to bring out. Rhees' argument is complex and cumulative, approaching central questions from many different directions. I hope, however, to have provided a preliminary aid for readers. To achieve this, I have extracted points from Rhees' discussions, not hesitating to use his own language, and tried to bring them together in a way which gives some indication of some of the main themes in his arguments. Before concluding, however, I shall allow myself some speculation on the likely reception of Rhees' work.

First, the book will be ignored by many, since an interest in Wittgenstein hardly occupies centre-stage in contemporary philosophy. That the book is more than a commentary on Wittgenstein will not matter. It calls for a style of reflection at variance with mainstream philosophy.

Second, there is a likelihood of the wrong kind of reaction from some writers on Wittgenstein; a reaction of a purely defensive kind. Wittgenstein feared that all he would bequeath would be a certain jargon, and said that obstacles in philosophy are often obstacles of the will, rather than obstacles of the intellect, a refusal to give up certain ways of thinking. Over-familiarity with Wittgenstein's terminology: language games, family resemblance, a family of games, and so on, may lead to an uncritical acceptance which resists any attempt to explore the limitations of these analogies. Such a reaction is philosophically sad.

Third, I am sure that Rhees' book will provoke a great deal of discussion about the reading of Wittgenstein's work. Here, there can be genuine disagreement. On the one hand, it could be argued, Rhees' criticisms depend on concentrating on certain aspects of Wittgenstein's philosophy, while neglecting others. Rhees admits that Wittgenstein's analogy between language and games is meant, in the main, to combat his early views about the relation of logic to language, and to emphasize that 'saying something' does not always come to the same thing.

But, it will be asked, what of the developments in Wittgenstein's later philosophy which, Rhees admits, emphasizes the importance of 'agreement in form of life'? Do not Wittgenstein's discussions in Part Two of the *Investigations* show how he appreciates that this cannot be captured solely by emphasizing notions like 'following a rule' and 'going on in the same way'? People can be blind to certain aspects of life, and one person can be a complete enigma to another. His 'Remarks on Frazer's *The Golden Bough*' underline these conclusions. Rhees wants to say that we need to reject the question of how language is put together, and concentrate on how it hangs together. But is not that the central contention of *On Certainty*? In short, Rhees' main contentions bring him to a philosophical position very close to Wittgenstein's own.

On the other hand, Rhees can be seen, not as criticizing Wittgenstein's work, but as *extending* it with respect to certain issues, albeit central issues in philosophy, concerning the possibility and unity of discourse. Rhees is second to none in acknowledging the depth of Wittgenstein's investigations, and he never criticizes his analogies without also bringing out what they have to offer. Yet, Rhees does say that having turned from regarding language as a calculus, the analogy retained a hold in Wittgenstein's later philosophy. 'Speaking' remains a 'way of doing things': following the rules in a game, continuing a series, or performing a function in an institution. For Rhees, *that* is not what one learns when one learns to speak. Rhees thinks that, for the most part, Wittgenstein makes 'saying something' too external a matter. 'Saying something' is not saying *how* the language is used, but saying something *in* the language one speaks with other people. And that 'saying' is not a matter of applying rules. Saying something in a language one speaks with others is internally related to the possibility of growth of understanding, whereas saying how language is used is not. Rhees need not be committed to holding that what he emphasizes is never to be found in Wittgenstein, but simply that it is not the emphasis that predominates.[8] It is in the connexions he draws between 'speaking', 'growth of understanding' and 'dialogue' that Rhees can be seen to extend Wittgenstein's work, and to bring out important limitations in some of his central analogies.

I have made no attempt to resolve the two readings of Rhees' work in relation to Wittgenstein, interesting though that discussion could be. That is because it is possible in a fourth reaction to go beyond *that* dispute in responding to Rhees, and to discuss what he says about 'saying something' and 'the unity of discourse' on its own merit, irrespective of how similar or dissimilar to Wittgenstein's his conclusions may be.

Wittgenstein influenced Rhees more than any other philosopher, but, when Rhees discusses philosophy, there is no mistaking the independence of his own voice.[9]

---

[8] It might be argued that Wittgenstein's work has greatest affinity with Rhees' emphases in Part Two of the *Investigations*, the discussion of the terrible in rituals in the 'Remarks on Frazer's *The Golden Bough*', and *On Certainty*. For reasons for thinking that Rhees might not disagree see *There Like Our Life* (see f.n. 3).

[9] For further evidence of that independence see Rush Rhees, *On Religion and Philosophy*, ed. by D. Z. Phillips, assisted by Mario von der Ruhr (Cambridge University Press, 1997).

PART ONE

Philosophy and language

CHAPTER I

Plato, language and the growth of understanding
(26.5.57–7.6.57)

I

The people who argued with Socrates and Plato may have thought that language was just a collection of techniques, and that that was what understanding is: knowing the technique. So that if they know the lot, well, 'understanding' would be this or that, according to what you were doing. For them, the growth of understanding could only mean the growth of skill (efficiency, I suppose) or the multiplication of skills (so that there is nothing he does not know). A skill would have the sort of unity that a calculus does. The sort of unity that is fostered by motion study.

Is understanding just competence? Is language a skill? Whether speaking is a technique; whether thinking is a technique; whether living is. Again: whether life has the unity of a skill. The perfect life. (Thrasymachus and the despot.) You might even think of methods of producing it to order then. This is the question whether virtue can be taught. It is all a matter of the method. That is what it comes to. And that would be the same as solving problems of life by calculation. Reaching an understanding of life by calculation.

Solving philosophical problems by calculation. 'Philosophy is just a matter of sorting out various grammars that have got mixed up.' Helping you to see where things go so that you do not get into a snag. If understanding is a matter of competence – if the criterion is in results or achievement – then there is no such thing as a general competence. Compare also: 'If you talk about understanding language, in the sense, perhaps, of understanding what language is, well what can that be except understanding how to use or what to do with it? What is it except competence to use language effectively?'

And so with understanding life: understanding the business of living. Knowing how to live effectively. Being a success. Doing it better than anyone else. The question of what it is to understand life. Or simply: of what it is to understand.

Doubt or distrust of understanding – Was this what made Socrates wiser than other men? Then, you might ask, why were not the sophists wise by the same measure? Were they not also sceptical? The point was that they did not know they were; in the sense that they thought they had the answer – in their reliance on competence and results. What is the difference between speech that is intelligible and speech that is not? The sophists answered: it is the difference between speech that is effective and speech that is not. You speak intelligibly if you speak effectively. Does this mean: what you say is intelligible if people are likely to agree with it? Or that what you say has been understood if people do agree with it? Almost: that there is no difference between understanding something and assenting to it, or being prepared to say it yourself.

At any rate, that was a measure that could be used, and a measure that was fairly plain to see. And the sophists would argue: if you want to make your speech intelligible, you can know what you ought to do. Look to the way of speaking that gets results. 'How *else* will you distinguish between intelligible and unintelligible speech? What other criterion is there?'

If you say that a conversation has sense if living has sense – well what determines whether living has sense? Or rather: how does *that* help you to distinguish between sensible and meaningless discourse? It does not seem to be a measure that you can see, or to which you can appeal. (If we said, 'Understanding is possible if living has sense', that would amount to: 'Understanding is possible if understanding is possible.')

Does it matter *what* sense living has? And anyway, what determines the intelligibility of *that*? What determines the intelligibility of living? What is the difference between understanding that and failing to? If no one ever does really or fully understand life, then no one ever really or fully understands what is said; or sees fully what there is intelligible about it. And if people differ regarding what is intelligible and what is not, there is no final way of deciding between them. None can show that he is right, and none can show that the other is wrong. And if people did differ about that, they would be differing regarding what understanding is.

'Plato says that if we want to know what understanding is then we must look to see what it is to seek understanding; or to what the growth of understanding is. But is there any right or wrong here? Or may each have his opinion? You say that all this makes things clearer. But to me, it makes them more bizarre and meaningless than ever.'

This seems to be what is at issue when people asked whether there was any difference between knowledge and opinion. That was not the question whether there is any difference between calculating correctly and making a mistake, or between what can be shown to be right and what can be shown to be wrong in the practice of a science. The question would be whether there was any right or wrong about the sciences themselves; or about the criteria of correctness.

For Plato that was challenging the reality of discussion. And to say that there was no difference between knowledge and opinion in that way is equivalent to saying that nothing makes sense.

II

For Plato, the central question is that of growth of understanding. The whole conception of the growth of understanding is one which the sophists would have questioned. And if we ask how Plato's notion differs from the notion of growth as growth in skills or efficiency, I suppose it would be in the sort of unity there is *in* that growth.

If we talk about growing more skilful, or growing more efficient, well obviously there is a certain growth or increase in that (it is not just the multiplication or addition to what is there). But all the same, it is not like the growth of understanding. It is not so *essentially* a unity in time as that is.

I do not know that we could even show the different stages of progress by showing the different mistakes that had been corrected. That is the sort of thing you might do when considering the progress in the understanding of a calculus for instance. But when one is considering understanding in the sense we have in mind, then it is not so easy to say what a 'mistake' would consist in, or to say just wherein the correction of a mistake would lie. As if one could show, or trace, the departure from the correct procedure. No doubt this is all connected with difficulties in the notion of 'the correct' procedure, or the correct understanding, anyway. We do not have an apprehension of that with which we could compare what has been done.

Incidentally, we could hardly find the connexion between the growth of one skill and the growth of another, which would be anything like the growth of understanding in one field and another, as Plato thought of that. (This may be at the root of some of the disputes about 'transferred training'. The acquiring of competence or skill in one field, need not make you any better fitted to become competent in another.)

But if we talk about the growth of understanding, it is a different matter. Has this anything to do with what is meant by saying that philosophy is contemplative? I expect Plato thought it had. Anyway, it looks as though the two issues hang together: (1) whether understanding is just competence; (2) whether we can talk in a general way about understanding, or the growth of understanding. Certainly we must agree that there could be no sense in speaking of the growth of understanding as Plato might have wished to, if understanding is just a matter of competence. ·

Philosophy cannot simply be a matter of sorting out different grammars that have got mixed up. This is not the kind of understanding that is sought. This is not the kind of puzzlement it is. That kind of sorting out may be an important part of the work of philosophy. But that is not the problem. And you cannot in that way show what is meant by saying that you have reached understanding. (Like saying that when you have got things straightened out – then you understand life better, because that is what understanding life is.)

Seeing how language makes sense. This is not just a matter of keeping different grammars from getting mixed up. (The confusion of kinds of which Plato speaks in the *Sophist* is not the confusion of forms. It is a confusion about discourse. But it is not a confusion about how to speak, or even how to understand. It is a confusion around the question of how discourse – or understanding – is possible. If reorganizing the relations between the kinds – if this were a matter of being able to carry out definitions correctly, or give correct accounts of things – then philosophy *would* be the mastery of a number of skills. That is what Plato would be saying.)

Perhaps you could still speak of understanding the language, rather as you might say of someone that he was good at games. But Plato would have asked how there can be understanding in the exercise of the various techniques themselves. If there is, then there must be something more than skilful operation with words and sentences. It cannot be just a matter of knowing what to say next, or anything of that kind. You must understand the sort of technique it is, for one thing. You must see the difference between this and something that is not language at all. Which means that you must understand something of its relation to other rhetorical techniques as well. In Plato's view, at least, you might know the technique – you might know how to use the expressions – but would not understand it (or them) unless you could see how it was connected with the other ways of speaking: unless you could see what it is to be a technique of *speaking*.

If you understand anything in language, you must understand what dialogue is, and you must see how understanding grows as the dialogue grows. How understanding the *language* grows. For the language is discourse, is speaking. It is telling people things and trying to follow them. And that is what you try to understand.

You understand what is said when you learn *from* it, not otherwise – or not fully anyway. Or in other words, when you understand it in a discussion. (If the sentence itself were a 'meaningful' sentence, but you could not see what it was doing there, then you would not understand. You would get nothing from it. No more, probably, than you would from a meaningless rigmarole – though it would be more perplexing.) You understand when it adds to your understanding of the discussion. Or of what the discussion is about.

And what *is* the discussion about? Is there any general answer to that? Plato thought there was. I think he would have said that all discussion is concerned with reality or what is. And this would have been just another way of saying that in all discussion we are trying to understand. But it seems a queer way of putting it, and we might wonder why anyone should want to.

We might even wonder whether it says anything at all. We discuss different things: the guilt or innocence of someone who is under suspicion; the rights and wrongs of capital punishment; the chances of success of a particular business venture – and so on. And if anyone asks what the discussion is *about*, well you tell him – whatever the question happens to be. It does happen sometimes that two different discussions are on the same question, but more often it is something different.

But you are trying to understand something; that is the point here. There is all this offering of views, and criticizing and asking questions and raising further objections and wondering whether . . .

So that it is not simply what it would have been if I were asking you to answer a question for me. If we are discussing the rights and wrongs of capital punishment, then we want to reach some conclusion. But we do not *just* want the conclusion. We want to understand it, too. That is why we cannot do without discussion. And it is why discussion is not just a way of getting an answer. Not even when we are discussing whether the man is guilty or not. Here you might say you would give anything if you could only know definitely. But the question is disputed, and you cannot accept a simple answer to it just like that. You want to sort things out; that is the point of discussing it. And that, in a sense, is what the discussion is about, trying to see how it all stands: 'Well, what about this matter then? And what about what so and so said, and what was found there?' Trying to get things straight. It is in this sense that you may be wiser for it. And the final piece of information (even a confession), unless it does something like that for you – unless it helped you to see how things are – will not make you wiser. And it will not be something that you understand.

But is this a way of saying that all dialogues have something in common? Not in the most obvious sense, certainly. It is not as though we might say, 'This at the very least is what you should be able to learn from any dialogue, namely . . .' And if we say simply that in any dialogue we try to understand, that seems empty. Yet it is, or may be, a way of saying that one is connected with another, just as we said of the different rhetorical techniques that they must have some connexion with other parts of discourse by belonging to a discussion. And they have this in common with the rest of discourse, that we can learn something from them, that they bring something to the discussion, so that we can get something from them.

And similarly with the various sciences. What we understand in them is what they bring to the discourse in which they enter. (Say they have their meaning in some language then. But remember that language is discourse or discussion for Plato.) Perhaps it seems queer to think of geometry, for instance, as something that is put forward in the course of a discussion. It seems easier to think of geometry as fairly self-contained. But if it were really that, we should get nothing from it. It would be as unintelligible as one correct sentence in a jumble of others, where none makes sense because they do not come together in any kind of discourse or statement. We might see our way through all the proofs and sequences of proofs in geometry, and we should still have nothing we could understand, if it *brought* no understanding. We could not understand geometry unless we could understand the discourse *in* which geometry comes. For that is what geometry should help you understand – that discourse. Or in other words, if you do learn from geometry, then you are learning . . . we might say 'about life'. Or about understanding – that is probably how Plato would put it. For that is what geometry teaches you. You will not know what understanding is from geometry alone, but you will not know much without it, either.

What do the different sciences have in common, then? Just that. Just that you can learn from them. Not that you can do something, which may be unintelligible, but that they help you to understand what it is you are seeking. They help you to see things. They make it possible for you to think about things more clearly. Which we might put by: they help you to understand your own thinking. That was what we meant when we said that they may help you to understand the discourse in which they come.

What did you learn from the dialogue or conversation you have just had? Has it made any difference to the way you understand things? Do you see things at all differently? Or was the whole conversation just one more thing to add to the disconnected jumble? If it were, then you could not have understood the conversation itself. For a conversation or a discussion is not something you can simply go through, like a dance, or the movements of workers in a factory. Nor like a game either. You would not be discussing anything then.

When we are discussing we are trying to understand. Sometimes this concerns us more deeply, and at other times it does not matter so much. But if we are talking, if we are trying to understand at all, then we are more or less interested in the sense of the whole conversation. Otherwise nothing that is said makes sense or tells us anything.

And we cannot begin over again, just where we were, as we might replay a game. If you repeated a conversation, well then it would have no sense at all. It would not be a conversation. And yet if the conversation *were* something quite self-contained, then it would have just as much sense if you repeated it as it would the first time. It would be an absurd game anyway. The conversation comes in your life. And conversation makes sense if living makes sense; not otherwise.

If you understand, you learn. That is why it is not just performing the movements correctly; why you cannot go back. And *what* you understand – well, you might even say that what you understand is its connexions with the rest. But this is not the connexion of parts in a formal system. This is important. It is the connexion of parts in a dialogue.

We do speak in a general way about understanding the language. I can understand what someone is saying, whether he is calling for help or stating a geometrical proof, and it would be unnatural to say that I 'understand him in different senses'. What he said was intelligible each time, he made himself intelligible each time, and that was not in different senses either. But this does not mean that if, for instance, you were doubtful whether I really had understood, and wanted to find out, it would be the same thing you would be looking for in each case.

What you understand is not the *formal* connexions, simply. And for Plato the unity of discourse could not be a purely formal unity, like the unity of a calculus. It is not through that kind of connexion that our statements are intelligible; or not that alone, anyway. It is rather the unity which shows itself in growth of understanding. Which is why it must happen in time; and why our understanding is in time, and has to be. (This is the sense of the *Parmenides*, I think). It is a unity of dialogue; a unity of thinking or of life; not the unity of a form. And it is in this way that different dialogues are connected with one another too; not because there is some form that they all follow.

If we say that a man understands the language, we do not mean that he is proficient in various rhetorical techniques. That is Plato's view. We do not mean that he can use language effectively. If we say of a man who does use language effectively, that he understands what he is saying – and especially: that he understands the discourse in which he is engaged with other people – we are not just referring to his proficiency. If he understands anything that is said, this is not just a matter of knowing the usual reaction to these words; nor of knowing the correct reaction either. If Plato says you must know the *logos* of it, what that means is that you understand the discourse in which it comes. (It is in this way that you recognize that it is itself – a *logos* at all; that it says something.)

Understanding a discussion is not just a matter of knowing how to make a point in it. Not even of being able to take part in it. You

might have made your point there, and yet have got nothing out of
it. This may be like the question: If you must see the connexion
between what is said here and other things that have been or will be
– should you not be able to say *what* the connexion is? Certainly you
see the connexion if you do understand. But that is not to say it is
something you could set out, as though it were independent of the
time and place of the statement. It must be a connexion in time, just
as the unity of discourse must be a unity in time. It is the kind of
connexion we recognize when we speak of a growth in understanding. And there is no meaning – for Plato – in speaking of understanding unless one is speaking of the growth of understanding or of
learning. (No more than we can say that a man is speaking, unless
we mean that he is taking part in a discussion; in which he is trying
to understand.)

III

You can understand a discussion if it increases or deepens your
understanding. If you ask 'Understanding of what?', we might
answer 'understanding of life'; but that really adds nothing, and is no
more definite than 'understanding' by itself is. Or suppose someone
asks: 'What is it you seek, when you seek understanding? If it is not
understanding *anything*, then . . .' Or suppose someone objects:
'When someone has gained understanding, then what has he
gained? If he has understood something, then surely he can say what
it is.' Compare perhaps: if you can tell the difference between
intelligible discourse and nonsense, then surely you can say what the
difference is. If you raise that objection, then you have not seen what
discourse is. (You have not seen the difference between language and
a wallpaper pattern.) You have not seen that language should
actually be spoken and understood.

For Plato, the unity of language was bound up with his conception
of the growth of understanding. He thought you could not give any
account of understanding anything said, except by reference to that.
But the sophists could have made nothing of the notion of the
growth of understanding in this sense, if only because they would
probably have asked, 'understanding what?'

If Plato spoke of 'understanding life', this may have thrown a
certain light on what he meant; but it would not have been an
answer to the question of the sophists, because for him the concep-

tion of 'life' and the conception of 'growth of understanding' were so nearly identical. I mean, it is not as though you were coming to understand something that is there before you begin to study it. In fact, I suppose we should say that understanding life is not a matter of studying anything at all. (Unless it might be the studying of various forms of understanding. It is a matter of reflexion; and so of dialectic: of question and answer in an attempt to give an account. That is how it is an attempt to give an account of what you are doing, for instance.) The notion of the growth of understanding is connected with that of finding a (or the) meaning of life.

For Plato the point is that unless there is a meaning in life – unless there can be something which can be understood – and he might have added that it can also be misunderstood – then nothing else that is said can be understood. This is the point that you can understand what is said only if you can understand the discourse in which it enters. In other words, if you can talk of the meaning of things, or the sense of things, or the reality (point) of things. This helps to show why Plato should have used the analogy of dream and waking when he is speaking of the distinction between understanding and illusion. Compare the notion of a man who has lost his senses. The understanding that is contrasted with that is not something of which you can ask, 'understanding what?', I suppose.

Philosophy is concerned with the intelligibility of language, or the possibility of understanding. And in that way it is concerned with the possibility of discourse. (Not so much, perhaps, with the question of *what* can be said – the form which all intelligible utterances must have, perhaps – as rather the question of whether anything can be said at all. The question of the distinction, if there is one, between sense and nonsense.) But even there, it would be a mistake, I think, to imagine that the task was that of defining that distinction; with being able to say wherein it lies. This is what leads in the direction of the idea of the form of intelligible discourse. When philosophers have tried to find the form of intelligible discourse in that way; when they have tried to give the general form of the proposition; or when they have tried to answer the question of what it is to say something – to show wherein that differs from making a noise; to show how statements have meaning; or how they relate to reality, perhaps: how they refer to something; to show the difference between assertion and denial; the question of how words mean, and so the question of what understanding is and what thinking is; – in all this they have generally been concerned first of all with philosophical *difficulties*, and with scepticism.

Plato was concerned with the impasse in which Parmenides seemed to have landed himself. (And Parmenides himself was concerned with philosophical difficulties raised by the Pythagoreans and by the Ionians.) The question seemed to be how there could be anything like negative statements, or false statements; and so how there could be any discourse at all. It seemed as though any reflexion on the conditions of the possibility of discourse led one to deny the possibility of discourse altogether.

That is typical of a philosophical difficulty, of the sort which we should recognize at the present day as well. And it cannot be resolved except by attention to the considerations that have caused it. But we should say that what you do in all this is to make plain certain things about the way in which language is actually used. This can be done superficially and cheaply; and then one will be tempted to say that it is not philosophy at all. If it is taken more deeply, it will bring in a good deal of reflexion on what language is.

A dialogue has sense – or anything that is said has sense – if living has sense; not otherwise. Whether living has sense – this is rather like asking whether understanding is possible. Not only 'rather like'; it is the same question. To see this is the same as seeing how discourse is possible.

The despair of understanding: this is not a matter of wondering whether the machine can ever be made to work. For one thing, part of the trouble is that we cannot imagine what would be *meant* by its working. On the other hand, there is something of the notion of jamming in it. That is how the trouble comes about; or often. But – and this must be emphasized – what I am trying to see, when I am trying to see the possibility of understanding, is not just *how* it all works; how it all fits together. For I might have been puzzled about that, without even doubting the possibility of understanding. As I should be in the case of an actual machine, for instance. If the problem had really been of that kind, then it would have been a perfectly straightforward mechanical problem – or analogous to a mechanical problem – with a right and a wrong answer, capable of being empirically verified. It would suggest then that the philosophical puzzlement was just puzzlement about this particular matter. 'I can't see how this business here goes.' That would be comparable to coming on a snag in mathematics, for instance, or in any science.

And there need be nothing philosophical about that. In fact, that is the position of those who question whether there is any sense in asking about the possibility of understanding in general; and the doubt regarding the reality of seeking understanding – rather than an understanding of this or that subject – would go with that. In other words, the doubt of the reality or the sense of philosophy. So also the scepticism regarding the sense of asking about the nature of reality – rather than asking how one distinguishes between reality and illusion in this or that particular field.

Philosophical puzzlement: unless this does – or may – threaten the possibility of understanding altogether, then it is not the sort of thing that has worried philosophers. If you overlook that, then you do not see what the understanding is that is sought in philosophy; or what it is that may be reached. But the understanding that is sought, and the understanding that may be reached – the understanding that has been achieved if the philosophical difficulty has really been resolved – is not something one could formulate; as though one could now give an account of the structure of reality, and show how language corresponds to it; and to show the possibility or reality of discourse in that way.

Plato tried to do something like that, but he does it in the course of his attempt to resolve the difficulty of Parmenides. And what he does say in the course of his account of the interrelation of kinds, for instance, does go some considerable way towards clearing the difficulty. What I would emphasize is that what we are concerned with is the possibility of understanding; and that it may be very ambiguous to speak about the conditions on which the possibility of understanding depends. The possibility of understanding – it is not by being able to say, 'statements of such and such forms are ruled out, or cannot be said'; 'these are the laws of reason' or 'the laws of understanding', and so on. That is to mistake the kind of understanding that is sought; and possibly to mistake the kind of nonsense that is feared with the loss of it.

'The importance of the laws of reason or of thought, is not simply that you could not make yourself understood to other people except you follow them; it is rather that you could not have any understanding yourself. The possibility of understanding is not simply the possibility of communicating. It is the possibility of distinguishing waking from nightmare.' That is why philosophy has been in a way a matter of much more personal concern than science has. A matter of settling one's own difficulties; of coming from darkness into light – where this is a personal darkness and a personal light.

Not that philosophy simply clears the way to make understanding possible, though; removing obstacles, and so enabling you to have a kind of vision, perhaps. (Cf. Philosophy as purification.) Rather, understanding lies *in* being able to say the sorts of things that are (or should be) said in philosophy. There are two misconceptions there, then: The one that philosophy must give an account of the forms. The other that philosophy simply removes difficulties and misunderstandings and so enables you to apprehend what cannot be said – the latter being what is of real importance. Whereas what one is concerned with in philosophy is – *philosophy.* I think that should be emphasized. And I think it is in line with much that Plato was saying too. Once again, the understanding sought is the understanding that must be given *in* philosophy if it can be reached at all.

IV

Unless you can see the kind of unity that a dialogue has, you cannot see what it is for anything to have sense. This understanding is not just a matter of proficiency. That is why the sophists were sceptical of it. The sophists evidently thought that one should speak only of the growth and multiplication of competence. Plato was talking about growth in a different sense. I suppose about understanding in a different sense also. As regards growth: we have the question of what the difference is between that and addition to a collection. I suppose it should be growth of what was there: development of that, and alteration of that. Not simply addition to it, leaving it as it was. The importance of unity again. One man and not many ('Knowledge of many things does not bring understanding'). Rather of coming to see things differently, of becoming wiser, not of learning more things or skills. The kind of unity that there is *in* growth. That is what Plato is insisting on – in the *Parmenides* for instance. This was connected with the idea of understanding things or failing to understand them. And that was the kind of difference that Plato spoke of as the difference between waking and dream, of passing from illusion and twilight and darkness into light. And it is clear that this is something fundamentally different from what the sophists were concerned with. Nobody would speak of the passage from clumsiness to skill in those terms; or from inability to competence.

Plato was not the only one to find that simile natural. Heraclitus had used it, and many have since. Heraclitus had also emphasized, as Plato did, the way in which this makes it a personal matter; that it is important to the individual, in the way in which a public accomplishment or the perfection of a technique need not be. Socrates and Plato wanted to insist on the reality of this kind of understanding. Socrates did so by insisting that it is possible to be without that understanding; and by insisting that the skills and techniques – the sciences as the sophists taught them – did not give that understanding; did not make one wiser. Socrates and Plato insisted that there was a difference between understanding and illusion in that sense – not the difference that was defined within the sciences themselves.

There are certainly difficulties in connexion with the notion of the measure of this understanding. In other circumstances we can ask how one would find out whether he had understood or not; we can give a pretty straightforward account of what it would mean to say that he had *mis*understood; we can speak of criteria and so on. But in the present case it is by no means so clear what it would mean to say that someone had misunderstood. And Protagoras seemed to think that it would have no sense. But Plato would have said that in that case you could not talk about the growth of understanding at all. And you could make nothing of the intelligibility of discourse. It would be a jumble of absurd games. Or again: there would be no sense in *trying* to understand. There would be no way of distinguishing between a sensible discourse and what seemed to be one. You could not ask whether anything could be learned from it; you could only ask whether it works. The fact that it is possible to learn things; and especially, that one can *try* to learn things or try to understand; this seems to have been one of the chief points in the criticism of Socrates.

What we have to see is the connexion between this and philosophy. Philosophy is concerned with the possibility of understanding in a general way – at least often is. But there is in Plato's preoccupation something that is personal; and that lends support to the view that it is concerned with understanding life, or possibly with understanding one's existence. I suppose it is all of it the understanding that is carried out in the cave. It is the understanding of life as it is lived. And that of course includes the various forms of discourse that go to make up life as it is lived. And that is why the growth of understanding is the growth of virtue, I expect. Of understanding life. Of why virtue is understanding life: and there is something immensely profound in that.

The only question I have is whether Plato is taking the notion of understanding life to be too much a single track process. Whether it is quite as single as he would imagine. And that is where I would suggest that the various forms of 'non-conceptual understanding', which are analogous to discourse in many ways, although they are certainly not the same, are important. Because so much of growth of understanding goes with that; and in fact even the understanding of discourse goes with that too. The way in which we speak and think about things has been developed partly from what we learn from art, just as well as the other way round. There is probably a connexion between what you might call seeking understanding and what we sometimes call 'seriousness', especially in art, but also in science. And those are connected with what one might call seriousness in life, I suppose.

Plato's idea of the unity of reality is bound up with this, the idea of unity as *analogian* (proportion); *genesis eis ousian* (coming into being). (That is the source of a certain difficulty, because it does seem to suggest that there is some sort of paradigm of understanding; and that for instance art is a kind of reflexion of that. Perhaps this business of dream and waking, the idea of the dream being a more or less imperfect imitation of the waking life, is misleading in this kind of way.) At any rate, it is not the sort of unity that there is in a dialogue; not the ordinary sort of dialogue.

Socrates and Plato both thought you could think you understood the sense of things, when you did not; think you were awake, when you were dreaming. And the test of that, for Socrates, lay in whether you could give an account of the way you were living, and of the practices you were following. I think there was something wrong about that, though probably there was something right too. It is what seems to lead to the idea of 'philosophy as a science'. And that seems to ignore the kind of difficulty it is – the kind of difficulties that philosophical difficulties are. I do not think it would have any sense to try to show you that you *ought* to be puzzled in that way. And that is what Socrates and Plato seem sometimes to have been suggesting: show the prisoners that they are concerning themselves with only shadows, and so forth. I think there is something deeply mistaken about that. I suppose there would be no point in telling such a man that he did not understand the sense of things; or that he did not understand the nature of reality, either. Maybe the sophists were right, if they were insisting that there would be something empty and meaningless in that.

All the same, there was an importance in running counter to philistinism. Just as there is something important about revealing the character of art; something important about the shock it can give you. That should be emphasized, and there should be some way of asserting it in opposition to the sort of practicality and philistinism which the sophists were purveying. It is also true that issues concerning education, and the importance of education were connected with this. And so, I suppose, the whole idea of culture.

And yet – the fact does remain that there seems to be no sense in telling someone that he ought to feel the sort of scepticism with which philosophy is concerned. What is clear, is that scepticism is a real enough condition, and that it cannot be met by suggesting that it is all nonsense and that the only intelligent thing is to attend to the sciences – which give practical results. That is *part* of what Socrates and Plato were trying to do, and there can be no doubt that it is important. Philistinism. The want of seriousness. 'To lead a life of philistinism, is to be without understanding.' What is it that he is missing – the person who likes bad art and good art equally well, for instance?

The reality of the perplexity. Or of the despair, perhaps. If there is no point in philosophy (nothing to do), there is no point in art either. Nor in science, for that matter. But it is clearer in the case of art. I think this has to be taken together with the point that understanding that is reached in philosophy is *philosophy*.

v

It is not as though there were something else you could point to and say 'that is what philosophy teaches you' – something, almost, you could look at without doing philosophy. 'The value of its results' cannot be divorced from the value of philosophy itself. I have an idea this may have some connexion with the point that virtue is understanding – not that understanding leads you some place.

I think this is important when one is considering the relation of philosophy and religion. Those who have thought of philosophy as the *ancilla theologiae* seem to have been thinking along lines similar to those I have just been considering: the view of philosophy as a kind of propaedeutic, whose importance lies rather in what it enables you to achieve. I do not think it is strange or accidental that philosophy should be thought of in this way; and there would not be at all the same inclination to speak in the same way about science. But all the same, it *does* misconceive what philosophy is concerned with; and what philosophical difficulties are. I think it has a bearing, also, on the difference between the understanding of life that may be sought in philosophy and the view of life that is the concern of religion. I would question whether there is anything religious about the philosophical concern to show that life is not meaningless. For that reason, I do not think it can have a bearing on what the believer takes his life to be. And conversely, I do not think that religious belief can throw any light on the question whether there is any meaning in life, in the sense in which that is raised in philosophy.

Emphasize the ways in which the problems of philosophy are problems which leave you wondering where you are: thing and quality, for instance: taking all the reality out of things: and so with time, too. It is important to emphasize what the philosophical problems have in common if only because once we abandon the idea of searching for the general form of the proposition, it is easy to lay too much emphasis on the diversity not only of forms of discourse but of philosophical problems. And then one loses their philosophical character altogether.

On the other hand, it *is* important to insist on the way in which philosophical problems are personal – just as scepticism is. Otherwise you get into all sorts of difficulties about the 'subject matter' of philosophy – imagining that it is space-time, perhaps, or something comparable. And perhaps you think of philosophy as a kind of very general physics. And then you are getting away from the problems. And the danger is that you will produce something sham, as Hegel did. This is in a way just as evil as philistinism, because it helps to make one blind to the difficulties that are in question. *And I imagine this is what Plato has in mind*. It is *this* kind of lie in the soul that is particularly objectionable. That is why sophistry, or any kind of sham philosophy is particularly evil.

If you call a work on philosophy great, that is not like calling someone a great physician. And this is connected with the point that you can learn something from it; not simply learn how to cure people. That point about Hegel, for instance, shows that there is a sense in which one may distinguish between genuine philosophy and counterfeit philosophy; even admitting that there may be genuine philosophy in what Hegel wrote as well, even when the whole conception is wrong headed. The point is that one *can* say that this is all wrong. And that is what Socrates and Plato were emphasizing. On the other hand, it does not mean that we have to do here with theories, and that the objective is to discover the right one. It is still perverse to talk about philosophy as a science. That is why a great philosopher is as rare as a great artist is. If it were a matter of mastery of a technique, that would not be so. Or if it were a matter of intelligence, that would not be so. You need understanding of something different. And first and foremost, you need understanding of difficulties. That is where the situation is unlike that of any science. There the positive technique is the thing, and the difficulties are incidental. But in philosophy, it is the difficulties that are the whole matter. That is *why* Wittgenstein was inclined to compare it to psychoanalysis, and to refer to therapy. There is misunderstanding in that, but one sees where it comes from.

It does not mean that there is nothing positive in philosophy. That is one thing I would insist on. And that is what has to be pressed against those who think of philosophy as therapeutic. Something we may have to indulge in because some people are unfortunate. You could never understand why Wittgenstein (and others) have wanted to compare philosophy with poems, in that case. The man who finds life difficult. And the man who wants to 'put the difficulties right'. The artist who finds sense in it all, does not try to put anything right. But the difficulties one has in bearing life are not difficulties of how to do something. And certainly the difficulties in understanding life are not that.

The reality of philosophy. That is what Plato was urging against the sophists. One might almost want to say: Philosophy is no more essentially therapeutic than music or poetry or any form of art is. And against that view, I *would* say that. There would be no greatness in Plato's dialogues, for instance. Probably there would not be much sense in distinguishing a great work in philosophy from a mediocre one, anyway. It would all depend on whether it did the trick. And there we are back at the position of the practical sophists again.

CHAPTER 2

'What is language?'
(13.1.60 – 2.3.60)

I

The sense of the question, 'What language is'. The difficulty in knowing how to answer this; which is a difficulty in understanding the question. At the same time, the notion, persistent in philosophy, of misunderstanding what language is – where this does not mean giving a wrong answer to the question.

I may know what 'game' means although I am not able to *say* what it means. But this is a matter of understanding the word, of knowing what you *call* a game. Whereas it is not this in connexion with language: it is not that I am perplexed whether to call something language or not. Neither is it the question whether I can use the word 'language' correctly, or whether I could give a satisfactory explanation of the meaning of that word if someone asked me. More nearly: one is perplexed as to whether something *can* be said or not; or what one is trying to say shows one is confused about that. A confusion or uncertainty associated with being able to speak, with what it is one learns when one learns to speak. The difficulty in the whole idea of 'being able to speak'. Making yourself intelligible, seeing the sense of what is said. The distinction between learning what a game is and learning to play. But the misunderstanding of language would be much more like a confusion in learning to play – or in what is learned. Cf. a confusion about following a rule.

We cannot say that philosophical problems are children of the confusions of particular grammars – though this may well come into it. Appearance and reality, things and sensations, time, thought, things . . .: Puzzles connected with scepticism, and the way these go all through language (cf. laws of thought and the idea of understanding). When Wittgenstein treats learning to speak in terms of learning the meanings of particular expressions, does he make it harder to see this distinction between confusions about language and confusions of particular grammars? I want to say that philosophy brings a better understanding of what language is – not just that it unties knots.

How is this related to an understanding of what 'language' means? Once again: the relation between 'an account of language' and an 'account of "language"'. If it is the latter, then we might look at how we use the word or how we learn the word, as perhaps with most common words like 'game', 'singing', 'farming', 'multiplication'. The word 'thinking' might be different. We might hardly say 'If you want to know what it means, consider how you learned the word', although this might be relevant in bringing out some things about the way we use it – if someone wondered if we ought to be able to 'say what we are referring to', and so on. But although you have to learn the word 'thinking', you do not in any comparable way learn how to think. And with 'language' and 'speaking' it is different. And so we have the question 'How do you recognize a proposition?', 'How do you recognize that as a *language* game?', 'How can you tell that he is speaking to you, that he is trying to tell you something?', and so on. The questions about intelligibility, understanding, and so of how language hangs together.

(1) 'How do you recognize that as a proposition?'
(2) 'Why do you call these all propositions?' (or perhaps, 'What are you saying about them when you call them propositions?')

But putting (1) and (2) together as though they were the same may give trouble. As if the first question were asking for a *criterion* of a proposition: 'What have propositions in common?' Whereas this is hardly more to be expected here than it is in aesthetics.

This is connected with the question whether you are saying something about something, when you say it is a proposition. The point that when you say that this is brass you are saying something about it, and something different from what you would be saying if you said it was gold: there is a method of finding out whether it is brass or not, and so on. But what would you be saying about the 'nature' of anything if you said it was a proposition? At least it is not as though there were a method of finding out whether it is a proposition or not, comparable to the method of finding out whether this is brass. (Compare questions about intelligibility and interpretability.) Contrast also: (1) 'I can *tell* you what it is (the mowing machine); explain it to you.' (2) 'I can tell you what it is (when he is speaking).' Here the more natural thing would be 'I can tell you what he is saying.' (As though 'saying something' were meta-logical. As though we never *get* to telling you what saying something is.)

On the other hand, he does know when you are speaking to him. And if I suggest that if he knows this in one case he will know it in others; that makes it look as though we had a case where you could speak of 'recognizing it as . . .'. I suppose this is where the considering of 'seeing something as something' is relevant; the idea of seeing that as an 'F', and so on.

Wittgenstein wanted to compare speaking a language with a 'move in a game'. What are you saying about all those moves when you say they are all moves in a game? Are you saying that they have anything in common? This is one reason why it does not tell you anything about properties which language must always have; or what all language is like, or what all propositions are like. Although Wittgenstein might say that giving examples of 'moves in language games' *is* the only way of telling you what language is like: 'This, and this and other things of this sort. That is what we *mean* by the logic of language – the logic of colour, the logic of expressions of value, the logic of measurement, and so on. And it is in these that the understanding or misunderstanding of the logic of language is to be found. There can be no such thing as the logic of language in general: that would lead us back to the idea of principles of language, and the suggestion that somehow we should have decided already a good deal about the logic of any future development of language.'

I do not think it need imply that. Much of what Wittgenstein said about the logic of language was of a general kind when he said that what we call language is a family of language games, when he said that language had not the formal unity that he once supposed, when he suggested that one ought always to look on language as an instrument, and so on.

The logic of language, and the logic of 'description' – of which Wittgenstein says that it is *eine Familie von Fällen* (a family of cases). The suggestion then might be that what we call language is a *Familie von Fällen*, and the analogy with games would fall in with this. But is 'language' the same kind of word as 'description'? (Write me a description. I can refer you to several descriptions and you can read them. A description is given at a particular time, or it is to be found in a particular text, and so on. Nothing of any of these sorts could be said of language.) There might be something similar in connexion with 'proposition', and possibly 'word' or 'expression' or 'sign'.

The difference lies with the way in which language hangs together. Or with the fact that you have here something other than a conceptual unity or formal unity. Wittgenstein was trying to get away from the idea of a purely formal unity in language. I suppose this is the sort of thing that he would insist on in calling it a conceptual investigation. This is what would distinguish it from a philological or a psychological discussion of language.

With regard to 'description': you might raise the question of how a child learns to give a description of anything. And in this connexion you could bring in the various examples of descriptions which you might use in teaching him. But this is not applicable in connexion with 'language' – if here also you mean something like 'giving him some idea of how it is done'.

The point is: I could not assume that perhaps speaking was something strange to you, and wonder whether you understood it. And understanding speaking is not knowing 'what he is doing as he speaks'. To recognize it as an extraction of the square root – to understand what it is – is the same thing as to understand it. To understand the calculation is to understand what he is doing. Or, being able to follow what he is doing – to follow the calculation. Compare also: being able to follow the game. And contrast this with being able to follow the conversation (or even follow what he is saying). Recognize the game; recognize what they are playing; I can follow the play. If you do not follow it – if you do not know what they are doing – I might try to explain it to you. But I could not in the same way try to explain the conversation to you. ('If it is a game with which I am familiar – say football – I can follow what they are doing.' But not: 'If it is a conversation with which I am familiar . . .'. At most it would be: 'If it is a type of discourse or discussion with which I am familiar: if I have an idea of what they are talking about.') Cf. 'If I know the grammar – if I do not imagine that they are talking about physical objects when they talk about their feelings, I still may not follow it, because I have to understand the things they say. And for this I need more than "knowing what they are doing".' In the game it is not so.

'Do you understand the game? Do you understand football?' But not 'Do you understand discussions about paintings?' 'Do you understand love scenes? Then you will certainly be able to follow this play.' And you may not – perhaps because you do not understand the character of Hamlet.

And the remarks in the discussion are not related to one another like moves in a game. 'If you understand football, you will certainly be able to follow this match.' 'If you understand discussions of paintings, you will certainly be able to follow this one.' Why is this wrong? Why does is not follow here? For one thing: making a difficult point in the course of the discussion is not like making a clear or brilliant move in the game. The move has to be met as the game goes on. The point in the discussion may never be more than half understood by the other.

Following the discussion is not following the *course* of the discussion, as you might follow the course of a game or of a constructional operation or surgical operation – almost as if you were watching to see how it would go and what the outcome would be (once again: as if the things that were *said* in it were of no special consequence) or admiring the skill with which it was done.

If you are a surgeon, you may learn from watching the operation, and because you can follow it. But if you learn from discussion, because you have understood and followed it – this does not mean that you have learned how to conduct such a *discussion*. And understanding the discussion does not mean understanding the structure of it, or being able to follow it as an *operation*.

People could not carry on a conversation in signals, if they were like railway or traffic signals, or signals in football. (Was Wittgenstein over-impressed by Sraffa's example of the Neapolitan gesture of contempt?) Was he trying to give a more general account of language which would allow this also as 'speaking'? Cf. what he says of the situation where one builder calls for a stone that is not there, and the other shakes his head. 'Dies könnte eine Art Bedeutigung der Beiden sein.' ('Both could be a kind of signification.')

It seems to me that gestures of contempt, of ridicule, insulting gestures, and so on, are possible only among people who speak a language: because contempt, insult, ridicule cannot be imagined else, just as it makes no sense to speak of insult or ridicule in animals. For this reason I do not think people could communicate *only* with such gestures – without any language besides.

II

'The logic of language' does not mean the logical analysis of language, nor the construction of a calculus which would give the logical *foundation* of language. (Cf. 'The logic of language – is meta-logic. Foundations for logic.') Cf. the idea of whether language (or our language) is *correct* or not. 'Perhaps it is all just arbitrary. Perhaps it has nothing to do with things.' This does not mean 'Perhaps people could say something quite different, and it would still be just as good.' But rather: 'Perhaps people can understand the language – in the sense, for instance, of knowing the words and syntax – and yet it never tells them anything.' (Talking to one another and singing to one another. Talking to one another and doing a dance.) The question whether there may not be something *wrong* with our language.

'*Either* you must be saying that they may speak and answer one another and never say anything; in which case what they say – the language – has nothing to *do* with anything; or *else* you must show that language is not just a hubbub. You must guarantee that it makes sense. You must guarantee that it *has* something to do with things.'

'If you say there is no question of the *correctness* of language, then you might say *anything*.' And in a sense this is what Wittgenstein did hold. Here 'say anything' seems to mean 'any form of expression'. 'There is nothing about the way in which we *express* the negative that makes it negative.' And consider: 'There might be *any* sort of relation between the utterances that are made.'

But not in the sense that it makes no difference what you say. If what you *say* has something to do with things, this does not mean that *language* has something to do with things. ('Wo knupft die Sprache an der Wirklichkeit an?') ('Where does language attach to reality?') Unless perhaps you are going to hold that 'language' means 'die Gesamtheit der [sinnvoller] Sätze' (4.001) ('the totality of meaningful propositions'). When they speak of a 'foundation for language' they are thinking of language as a kind of *method*. Or even: that it is a kind of theory. ('Eine Notation annehmen heißt, eine Weltanschauung annehmen') ('To adopt a notation is to adopt a worldview.') The chief way in which language is *not* a theory, is that it is something that is *spoken* (that people carry on together). In this way it is not in the least like mathematics. Nor like a notation either. 'Eine Sprache verstehen heißt, eine Lebensform vorstellen.' ('To imagine a language is to imagine a form of life', *Philosophical Investigations*, §19.) And a *Lebensform* is not a theory, and is not correct.

'The language', of course, is not what they *say*. And it is not clear how it might or might not have 'something to do' with things. As though the language could be written down; like a system of geometry, perhaps. Confusing to think that the language is related to *what is said in the language* as pure mathematics is related to applied mathematics.

If the language is not everything that is said by those who speak it, it may be natural to think of it as a set of rules. 'What the foreigner learns when he learns the language.' 'What you are ignorant of when you are ignorant of the language.' (On the other hand, if you had never learned to speak at all, I would not say you were ignorant of anything. And if they told me you could speak now, I would not say you had learned the language.) Learning the language is not what enables you to speak. ('Before he can speak he must learn the language.')

'Belonging to the language' – 'The relation of language to what you say.' 'Unless it is in a language it is not intelligible.' Return to the question whether language – or our language – can be justified. (Whether in following the rules of language we can say what things are like.) Whether it has any relation to reality. Whether it is not 'responsible to' reality. Otherwise it would not be language at all. But in that case, the question is just 'whether it must not be a *language*'.

Almost as though language were a kind of grappling iron. (Or photographic apparatus?) This is a form of 'language as instrument' again. (1) 'We communicate with one another by using paper and ink.' (2) 'We talk about things by learning language.' But in (1) we can point to what we use and say how we use it. We know what we want to do, and we choose this way of doing it. But if we should talk about using (or choosing?) language *in order* to talk about things, this suggests that we had some idea of 'talking about things' before we decided to employ language to accomplish it. (Cf. the idea of 'inventing language'.)

There are certain analogies between learning a notation and learning the meanings of particular expressions. 'Showing you the game we play with them; showing you what we do with them; showing you how it goes.' If you speak of being trained in the correct reactions, I do not think it helps. (Again the idea of the reactions as part of a technique – an instrument.)

I suppose that when a child learns to speak, he *picks up* as much or more than he gets from any special instruction. And if this were not so – if you had to show him or train him in the game we play with *every* expression he learns, then I do not think he would ever speak at all.

I still think the chief reason and the chief need for talking about language in a general way is connected with the question of why it is that we call them all language games; and also with special features of learning to speak – for I do not think we can describe this as the learning of particular expressions.

III

It would be hard to know (imagine) what 'explaining what speaking is' would be. And yet we try to do this in philosophy. Plato thought the difference between philosophy and sophistry lay there – that the sophists were in darkness about what speaking is. They were 'estranged from that with which they have most constant intercourse' – without understanding of their own speech or thinking. And yet of course they did understand what is said to them, in ordinary matters anyway, as well as Plato did, and they could answer as clearly.

It is when Plato tries to explain what speaking is, or what discourse is, that his discussions grow most difficult. And, as he would own, the trouble is partly – largely – in seeing just what it is he would explain. The sophists themselves saw no problem where he saw the deepest one; as he would have said, they were unaware of their ignorance.

The difficulties of a general account of language. Are we looking for some general law or general principles (as if it were like a general account of heat or of digestion)? We need not be. We speak of a common language. And what is important here is nothing like a common form or a common way of moving or reacting; nor the presence of a common measure either, if this means anything like commensurability in mathematics.

Whoever says anything, says it in a language. And those who speak the language can understand him. If people speak together, they have a common language. And I can at least try to understand remarks if they are in the same language as I speak. If we think of a general account of language – it is not simply that they are all *language*, or that they are all speaking, as though the question were 'does *this* mean they must all have something in common?' (Then it would be like 'they are all games'.) The difficulty is rather in this idea of 'the same language' or 'a common language', and in the idea of what we may want to call 'a common intelligibility' in the remarks that are made in the language. (Whatever it is that makes it possible for people to say different things to one another and carry on a conversation.) It is probably the same difficulty if we say that the difficulty about 'explaining to someone what it is' does not arise with 'game'. And there is nothing strange there in explaining by illustrations and 'and so on'. Consider helping someone to a better clarity about what to call a game and what not. And then think how you might help one to know more surely what to call speaking. At any rate, when we think of what various remarks have in common (and all the various things people say) this is nothing we can reach by describing what speaking is – what people are doing when they speak – or by examples of it.

What they 'have in common'; the several meanings remarks have *whenever* there is speaking, and in any example of it. It is what makes the difference between a jumble of sounds, or it may be a jumble of sentences, on the one hand, and a sensible discourse or a conversation on the other. So I have felt like saying that the question of what speaking is, is just the question of how the remarks in the language hang together.

If someone learns to speak, he does not just learn to make sentences and utter them, nor to react to orders either. He learns to say something. He learns what can be said; he learns – however fumblingly – what it makes sense to say. This is an accomplishment over and above being able to work together. It is not just an addition to the technique, as you might learn to operate a new tool. And to do this, he must learn how remarks hang together, how they may bear on one another. This is something different from learning general rules or general principles – even though it does not go without that.

And because he learns to speak, and learns what can be said, he can go on speaking and go on learning. (Shall we call this the generality of what he has learned? At least it is not the generality of a rule.) And the being able to go on is not like being able to continue a series, say, or being able to do further multiplications. This is not the same as learning the meaning of particular expressions, although it is impossible *without* that.

IV

If you did try (outside philosophy) to explain what 'speaking' means, it would not be like explaining what 'game' means to one who has never played. You would not begin by describing how it goes, for you would never think he might be ignorant of that. More important: you would never think he could learn in this way what to call speaking or how to recognize it. He recognizes it when he understands what the other man is saying – or when he cannot understand it.

There need be no trouble if you start to explain to someone what playing a game is. You may wonder whether he has ever played a game at all. In any case, you may begin by describing one or two games to him. You describe what people do when they are playing football, or when they are playing dominos, and then you can see whether you think he has got the idea. Or it may be just that he is puzzled about what you would include in it. 'When people are dancing, are they playing a game then?' And then you may have to go into what guides you in saying that this is not a game and that something else is. (Maybe you can't cheat in dancing – I don't know – but is it never a game if you can't cheat?)

But if you were beginning to explain to someone what speaking is – what kind of ignorance or misunderstanding would you be trying to meet? With regard to playing a game, it is possible, though it would be a bit surprising, that he has never done it. But speaking?

Once again: If someone were playing a game or running a machine, I might ask 'Do you know what he is doing?' But if someone were speaking, I could not ask 'Do you know what he is doing?' – meaning *speaking*. I could not assume that perhaps speaking was something strange to you and wonder whether you understood it.

And *understanding* speaking is not knowing what he is doing as he speaks. It is understanding what he says. Or perhaps: understanding what makes sense – i.e. being able to speak. And this is not something you can explain to anyone or something he might learn from examples.

Suppose that 'describing what people do' will serve to explain 'how we use this or that expression'. Consider how you would *teach* him that expression. You will then be thinking of a primitive language game with that expression, or a primitive use of it. The latter phrase suggests that you will have a concrete example of how it is actually used. But I wonder if this holds for more than a limited variety of expressions. It will not explain what using the expression is. (That is what we try to do in explaining the *logic* of language.) In other words, it will be pointless for anyone who does not speak already.

We bring in the idea of *Abrichtung* (training) in order to show how it is possible to teach people to understand what is said: without explaining what it means: in order to get over the difficulty that we cannot teach them the meanings of words by explaining the meanings of words: or teach them how to use words, by explaining to them how words are used. The notion of 'a family of language games' does help one to see more clearly in the questions Wittgenstein was raising about the logic of language. But I wonder if it has not limited Wittgenstein in certain ways as well. (This would be something like what he himself recognized as the typical source of confusion in philosophy.)

Learning to speak is not learning the meanings of words. And a creature might learn to react correctly to a number of words without ever learning to speak with people – without ever trying to understand what you were saying to him.

Wittgenstein talks in this way because he is interested in the relations of words to things; and because he wants to say these lie in the various games we play with them. This went with the difference between the meaning of a name and the bearer of a name. Perhaps this is still the question of 'how words symbolize'. But I think that question is not the right one here; that for our purposes it is misleading. Certainly people may misunderstand or be confused about that – about how words symbolize. And Wittgenstein illustrates this in connexion with names 'standing for objects'.

But it takes us away from the question of what speaking is. And I suppose it tends towards the conception of some sort of mechanism. Almost as though we had to do with the *behaviours* of certain expressions. He had asked once 'Where does language connect with reality?' – which is another way of asking how language has sense, or how words have sense – and once again leaving out speaking or learning what can be said – and although he would not have asked just this later, we still have the conception of doing something with the words as though *this* were using them or perhaps understanding them.

It is this way of looking at it that allows the emphasis on particular expressions and their grammar. How words symbolize. How language can be meaningful. This is the question of meta-logic too. And that is open to the same objection. Notice the conception of 'nur in der Verbindung mit dem übrigen *Mechanismus*' ('only in connection with the rest of the mechanism') – as if this were what were important. And this *is* just the outlook of meta-logic. Almost: How language can be constructed. Cf. *Republic*: on how a society might be constructed from primitive beginnings, and so on.

Explaining how signs symbolize is not explaining what speaking is. (Not what you learn when you learn to speak.) It is concerned rather with the distinction between sense ('meaningful') and non-sense. And whereas you learn 'what can be said' when you learn to speak, what you learn is not how signs symbolize.

Does 'how signs symbolize' bring it near the question of interpretability again? Wittgenstein rejects this notion of 'interpretation' – 'we just *do* it that way'; 'that is what he does'. He would say also that you cannot formulate in a meta-language any rules in virtue of which signs have meanings or refer to things.

Wittgenstein thought there was *often* an analogy between speaking and playing a game, hence his readiness to use the analogy. Of course it is easy to misunderstand an analogy because you do not realize just how far it is supposed to go. The person who offers it expected you to use your nose. We may be puzzled because we find what seem evident absurdities as we try to work out the analogy; and the speaker may complain that we have simply missed the point of it: 'Can't you see how this does illuminate things? – even though it will of course not work in those ways about which you are objecting.'

But it is possible also that the writer himself will let the analogy carry him further than he should – if only because it was such a relief to him when he thought of it.

CHAPTER 3

The reality of language
(14.7.59–17.12.59)

I

The question of the relation of logic to reality is not the same as the question of the relation of language to reality. This latter is found in the idea of talking about something; and it has its clearest example in conversation. Whereas the matter of the relation of logic to reality would be different. Probably it lies chiefly in the question whether there is any reality in the difference between valid and invalid arguments and in the ruling out of contradictions. To believe in logic, or believe in the reality of logic, is to calculate.

To believe in language is to try to tell somebody something; to believe that it makes a difference what you say, and therefore that you can tell somebody something. Or we might say equally: to believe in the reality of language is to ask somebody a question. This may be important, because it would suggest that you do not get at the reality of language by studying the logic of the language, or through an analysis of language. (Cf. the idea of 'there is some reality corresponding to it'.) Wittgenstein had earlier held that it was a matter of logical analysis. In any case, you cannot get at the reality of language – which is perhaps synonymous with: you cannot see what understanding is – by looking at or studying the reality of logic.

On the other hand I do not want to deny, of course, that they are closely connected in some way; and I wish I could bring out how. *Without* the reality of language, there could be no reality in logic. This has to do with the point that the mere rearrangement of signs would not be drawing a conclusion, for instance, even if it were done according to strict rules. (Especially if they were rules which held only of this kind of arrangement of signs or marks.) The force of logic – and incidentally the whole idea of laws of thought – depends on certain uses. And this is getting on to the question of what a rule

53

of language is, or a rule of speaking. Anyway, the point would be that the expressions must be intelligible in some other way than in the sense of 'logically permissible', if the notion of 'logically permissible' is to have any reality at all. This would suggest that the idea of 'understanding correctly' and 'making yourself understood' may be primary here in some way.

When you have an *Abbildung* (representation) of one part of mathematics in another, or of a machine in a diagram, then you can point to the correspondence it is (what sort of projection it is, perhaps). With the *logische Abbildung* (logical representation) it is different. If you point to the correlation between names and objects, then you might show the *Abbildung* of that *spatial* configuration of objects. But the *logische Abbildung* is of a possible existence or non-existence of atomic facts. And the configuration – if you could point to it in any other way than by the enunciation of the proposition – would have to include the relations of existence and non-existence in some way.

The analogy with an ordinary picture may be confusing, especially if one neglects the idea of understanding the picture; or of what the picture 'says'. For I do not think Wittgenstein was always thinking of what the reconstruction of the accident in the law court says. (In a way that was presupposing the other sense of picturing and of intelligibility.) The reconstruction in the law court is something like a diagram to assist you in explaining. You look at the diagram in order to understand something *else*. Whereas, when you understand a genre picture, for instance, it is not like that.

'The picture says how things are.' This is different from: 'You hold up a picture and say "*This* is how things are".' That is not what the picture does. In the former case I understand the picture. In the second I understand you.

Metaphors and figurative language. If I cannot speak your language and try to get my point across by drawing something, this is often like using a metaphor. My drawing need have no close resemblance to what I want to mention. What is being pictured in a metaphor or a simile? In what sense could you speak of 'depicting' here? If the drawing is inaccurate, this does not mean there is anything inaccurate in what it says. Is there a literal use of language which is more fundamental than the metaphorical use?

If the application of a measuring rod tells you something, this is probably not like the way in which a picture tells you something. Wittgenstein probably had other reasons for wanting to speak of language as a measure. And it was confusion to suggest that this was the same as the idea of picturing. You do not use the measuring rod to say something: though you may use it in connexion with what you are saying. (I might trace a configuration quite accurately. And you might still say 'Well?')

To say that a proposition is an *Abbildung der Wirklichkeit* (representation of reality) means that a proposition can be understood. We do not mean that someone can understand what it is a picture of; we mean that he can understand what it says. He could not do this unless it were possible *die Wirklichkeit abgebilden* (to represent reality). If we talk of the difference between what can be expressed in propositions, and what cannot be expressed but merely shown – well then we should be able to give some idea of what propositions are. This is a problem which does not arise in Russell's logic. And it was in this direction especially that Wittgenstein was going beyond Russell.

The distinction between sense and nonsense. If you do certain things (with signs), then you have nothing to which any reality could correspond; nothing which could be an *Abbildung der Wirklichkeit*. The difference between what is 'out of the question' and what cannot say anything or cannot be a proposition. The study of logical form is the study of what can be said and what cannot, in this sense.

There is no sense in asking what the relation of propositions to reality is. (You cannot compare them with reality in that sense. What you get in verification is always the comparison of one proposition with one another.) You cannot compare them as you might compare a drawing with a machine or a map with a landscape. You do not tell what their relation to reality is when you have said what the names in them refer to.

How does the fact that a proposition is either true or false enter into 'its relation to reality'? How does it enter into what we mean by a proposition? To ask, 'What is the relation of propositions to reality?' (What kind of *Abbildung* is it?) would be like asking what makes propositions intelligible. Or asking how you can sensibly ask anything. (Or: asking how there can be an answer to a question.) Is this the kind of thing that Russell wanted to escape by his idea of a hierarchy of languages? You recognize that a proposition is an *Abbildung der Wirklichkeit* when you recognize that it really says something. This is the reality of language and the reality of logic too. And the application of logic. (These were questions which had to be answered, in Wittgenstein's view, if there was to be any sense in logic. He also thought that the possibility of science and the reality of knowledge – the difference between science and arbitrary play of words; perhaps mythology also – depended on that. Once again the application of logic depends on some account of propositions.)

The hierarchy of languages does not escape this problem; or not obviously, anyway. The different languages have to be intelligible, and presumably intelligible in the same sense. There will be certain things which it is possible to say in a language of one order, and which it is not possible to say in a language of another order. But the general question of what a proposition is, and the general question about the idea of being 'possible to say' altogether, will remain. And in this sense you are assuming what you ought to be explaining – and which apparently you are trying to explain. If you use language to *establish* the intelligibility of language, you seem to have done nothing at all. *Scheinesinns.* (The illusion of sense.)

It is possible to lay down the rules which are to hold in one 'language', and for this you may say that you are using language of a higher order. (What it in fact amounts to is that you are setting up a particular notation, and laying down the rules for that.) But this does not answer what it is to call either of them a language at all. What the hierarchy of languages amounts to is: you can avoid contradictions by laying it down that in certain kinds of calculation or investigation, you are not to go along such and such roads. And this is all right. Is it a way of saving 'the reality of logic' though?

Neither does it make sense to ask whether perhaps reality does *not* correspond to language (or: whether no reality corresponds to language); the kind of question Descartes put forward. Or Gorgias. You cannot talk about anything like a 'metaphysical faith' in connexion with what Wittgenstein was saying, anyway. (Hierarchy of languages. Conferre: 'Kein philosophisches Problem kann durch ein Kalkül gelöst werden.' ['No philosophical problem can be solved by a calculus.']) You can test a proposition; verify it. But you can do this *because* it is an *Abbildung der Wirklichkeit*; because it says something.

The idea of what makes it *possible* to construct logical systems (the general form of the proposition). Wittgenstein wanted to show (I think) that there can be only one logic, and so only one logical constant; there cannot be any irreducible differences between forms of inference – and nothing arbitrary about it. If there were anything arbitrary about logic, then *language* would be impossible; for we could not try to find out the sense of a proposition. There would be nothing to distinguish understanding correctly and taking it wrongly or misunderstanding it. 'Can we know the relation between language and reality?' ('Can we really know what we are saying?') This is how the question of solipsism becomes important.

We could never know whether we were really saying anything if it were necessary to look at language from without and observe its connection with reality. But there *is* a clear distinction between sense and nonsense; and this is all that is needed. You can check a map to see whether it is accurate by looking outside it. But you cannot check language to see whether it is accurate by looking outside it. And this means especially: you cannot find any such check to determine whether the method of logical analysis is the right one. The method of logical analysis tells you all you can ever know about the relation between language and reality, i.e. it tells you what saying something is.

The aim of the picture theory is to show that logic must take care of itself; that logic must look after its own application. The point is that you can say 'This is a proposition' as you may say 'This is a picture.' The picturing relation is not something outside – as it might be if you said 'This is like that.' The picturing relation is what makes it a picture. 'This says something.' Sometimes when you understand a picture you may say that it says something. Here there is not the difference between true and false. But there is an analogy between the way in which the elements make up a picture – something which may be understood – and the way in which the elements make a proposition.

Apparently a proposition has something in common both with a picture and with a diagram. It is when you think of a diagram that it is more natural to speak of an internal similarity of structure. And it is more natural to think in this connexion of a model, in the sense in which Euclidean geometry may be treated as a model for some non-Euclidean system. It fits in also with the idea that the actual or suggested happenings are what you think of when you understand the proposition. The difference is that you do not pass from the proposition to reality in the way in which you pass from the drawing to the machine, or from the score to the music. You can follow verbal instructions too, of course. But consider: I said to him 'Do it

like that', and handed him a drawing. And he did it like that. He
followed the drawing. He also followed my instructions. (Could you
point out *this* correspondence?)

Apparently part of the business of picturing is to make clear. ('Der
Zweck der Philosophie ist die logische Klärung der Gedanken')
('The goal of philosophy is the logical clarification of thought',
Tractatus Logico-Philosophicus, 4.112), or, we might say, to make intelligible. It is not simply some sort of correspondence with reality. It is
showing reality as it can be understood or talked about; as something
by reference to which we can understand one another.

'A proposition is a picture': remember that a proposition is a
symbol, and that the 'real symbol' is what all symbols which 'do the
same job' have in common. We might ask how we can discover this
real symbol, since we can never be sure we are familiar with all
symbols which 'do the same job'. (Could we go further and ask how
we should ever recognize these symbols? how we tell that they do the
same job?) The point is that we can carry out the logical analysis.
The *complete* analysis will be the same, no matter from which of the
symbols we start.

'How can we be sure our method of analysis is the right one?' Is
this one of Wittgenstein's chief concerns in the *Tractatus*? It is the
right one if it makes clear the thought expressed in the proposition.
The general criteria are to be found in the consideration of what the
expression of a thought is or what a proposition is. The idea of
'doing the same job' would be misleading if it suggested that you
look to some sort of external criteria to discover what the job is. The
job is the job of picturing: of expressing a sense. The job is what the
analysis shows.

The very possibility of logical analysis is the assumption that the
physical symbol as we have it in colloquial speech, say, is not 'the
picture'. At least, if we speak of an internal connexion between
picture and reality – if we think of picturing *as* such an internal
connexion ('. . . in jener abbildenden internen Beziehung zu
einander, die zwischen Sprache und Welt besteht') ('. . . all stand to
one another in the same internal relation of depicting that holds
between language and the world', *Tractatus*, 4.014) – then it is not
anything we can check by comparing the physical characteristics of
the physical symbol with the reality. For these might be very
different, and the picturing would be the same. On the other hand,
the primary datum is the propositions or sentences with which we

speak to one another. When we understand these, it is like understanding a picture. To call it a picture is to call it something that can be understood.

The notion of the *innere Ähnlichkeit* (internal similarity) is what makes possible the inclusion of such different conceptions as that of a painting and what the painting 'says', or of a metaphor and of a diagram or a musical score or a map. I do not think you can see what the 'inner similarity' is unless you see why it is that Wittgenstein wanted to call a proposition a picture at all: what sort of problem in connexion with language and logic this was thought to meet. *Abbilden ist kein metalogischer Begriff.* (Representation is not a meta-logical concept.) You cannot show what makes this a picture. Or should we say: you cannot show what makes this a picture of so and so?

In the case of the musical score, you might mention the general rule. But if you say '*This* is the score of *that*', you are saying this is how the general rule appears here. Can you explain what it means to be a musical score? You can play the music from it. And you can write the music down in it (or: write the score from the music). And we say 'can'. There is a distinction between correctly and incorrectly, and this is why we speak of a rule. But I do not suppose we can do anything further to explain the 'can'. I do not suppose we can show what makes it possible to write a musical score at all; even though you might show how *this* particular notation works: you might show how with these symbols you can write down that particular run. 'And the symbols are so related that if you do this and that you have got it down perfectly.' But this is all *assuming* that the symbols are being used in a musical score. It is assuming the inner similarity which they are going to fulfil. The idea of writing music at all.

I think Wittgenstein would say it is similar when you are describing a state of affairs. I am guided by what I see before me, and I want my description to be an accurate account of that. I might almost say: to be a *copy* of that. If I have mastered the language or am fluent in the language, this will help me. I shall be able to see how by using these and these words I can put it more clearly. But this does not show what is meant by copying in words or describing even though it may show something of the difference between the right description and a wrong one.

The picture theory is also supposed to show the justification or necessity of logical analysis. What should we mean by 'a logically perfect language' in which what is written needs no further explana-

tion, and you can tell from the way it is written what each symbol is
doing there?

II

Wittgenstein wanted to avoid the assumption of *einer Logik des luftleeren
Raumes* (a logic for a vacuum). This was a consequence of his view
that we must give up any idea of a general form of proposition; and
that we cannot hold that the principles of logic can be derived from
the general form of proposition. They are not principles of intelligibility in that sense.

It probably went along with a change in his view about symbolism
too. I am thinking of what he said to the effect that the whole
philosophy of logic lies in the fact that we can see the truth of logical
formulae simply from their symbolic expression (*Tractatus*, 6.112,
6.113; also 6.124, 6.126). 'Wenn wir die logische syntax irgend einer
Zeichensprache kennen, dann sind bereits alle Sätze der Logik
gegeben . . . Ob ein Satz der Logik angehört, kann man berechnen,
indem man die logischen Eigenschaften des *Symbols* berechnet.' ('If
we know the logical syntax of any sign language then we have
already been given all the propositions of logic . . . One can
calculate whether a proposition belongs to logic by calculating the
logical properties of the symbol', 6.124; 6.126.)

The idea seemed to be that if we had signs with clearly defined
rules, then we could *see* what combinations or 'structures' of signs
were possible, and what were impossible. The phrase 'die Natur der
naturnotwendigen Zeichen' is a curious one; and in his later writings
he would not have used it. He would not have thought that we could
understand what logic is, and what the differences between the
various logical principles are, simply by understanding a symbolism.
(Apparently on the older view it was important to be able to
recognize what sort of symbolism might 'work' and what would not.
Logical insight might have lain chiefly in the recognition of difficulties or unclarities in the symbolism, and of what should be done to
rectify them. And this notion of 'rectification' would be one that in
his later view he would have criticized.)

'Die Logik muß für sich selber sorgen.' (Logic must take care of
itself.) The difference between logic and a wallpaper pattern.
Granted that we have 'rules for the transformation of signs', what is
there logical about this? It does not help you to understand the

difference between what is logic and what is not. I suppose this might be part of the objection to the *Logik des luftleeren Raumes.*

If you simply say that you can *see* certain combinations of signs to be impossible, this still leaves it arbitrary. Or: it just expresses our refusal to admit any such combination of symbols; or that 'we' will not admit them. It does nothing to explain *why* we do not admit them; nor to show that no people *could* have admitted them.

The move away from the view that we can give an account of what the rules of logic are if we consider the structural rules of the symbolism – this is one to which I am sympathetic. But there is a survival of these views in the idea that we have to start with the game which we play with the various expressions of the language.

Wittgenstein is emphasizing, 'Do not look at the sentence, but at what we can do with it.' (Perhaps the 'rules for the use of signs' were 'what to do with them' too.) And he takes this to mean, 'what we use it for, and how we react to it'. In so far as he is assuming that it would not make any difference whether the person were 'bedeu-tungsblind' (meaning-blind) or not. The point is that the signs *have* a use, which does not depend on the kind of signs they are. And the possible combination of signs is to be found in the way they are used – not in the way in which they *could* or *could not* be used.

This use is something which we teach people, or in which we *train* people. And this is very important; otherwise there would be nothing to teach; otherwise there would be nothing to learn. It means, apparently, that the use – what we do with the sign – is something which could be learned – in which the pupil could be trained – without his knowing or understanding the uses of any other signs at all. Signs have their uses. And when we have been trained to use them, we can speak.

Speaking is the exercise of a family of acquired capacities. And so far it seems hardly different from the exercise of acquired accomplishments in building techniques. Or more particularly, it is hardly different from learning to work together with other workers in a team: when to swing one's hammer, when to push, when to give, and so on.

I think this shows there is something wrong in the notion of *Abrichtung* (training) in an account of what speaking and understanding are. This goes with the point that learning to speak is not learning to do something, in that sense. In many ways it is hardly comparable with learning to walk, for instance.

Wittgenstein wanted to avoid the suggestion that when we are teaching someone to speak, we teach him the *meanings* of various expressions, as we might teach them to someone that could speak already. A foreigner learns a language in *addition* to his own. And if you say what he learns now – what this addition is, what the special words and rules are – you have not said what it was like when he learned to speak. But he still clung to the idea that we teach him particular expressions. And I think that the kind of teaching he describes would be helpful only to someone who could speak already: that in this respect the substitution of 'training' for 'explaining' is not much help.

Teaching him what to do with an expression; teaching him what to do with an instrument. Understanding what he is telling you. Understanding what he is doing. 'You must teach people the *use* of expressions, if ever you are to be able to speak.' 'You must teach them what to do.' 'And what they learn is a technique or a *rule*.' 'They cannot speak if they do not know what to do. They will never know the difference between one sound and another. They will never see the point of making one sound rather than another.' 'They will never see what you are getting at – or rather they will have no idea that you are getting at anything at all – in the sounds which you make to them.'

I agree that they have to learn the difference between one sound and another, in this sense. But I do not agree that this is an account of what learning to speak is. As though it might be compared to learning the difference between one piece and another in chess. As though understanding what he is saying were like understanding what he is doing when he moves that piece; perhaps also, understanding the difference which it makes to the situation in which he and I are engaged.

When he makes the move in chess he is not telling me anything. And if I understand what he is telling me, it is not just like understanding the sort of moves he is making: knowing the rules or the uses of the expressions he is 'moving'. There is much more of a background of common understanding than that. This is what enters into our trying to understand one another at all. In understanding one another, there are other standards than simply those of what is grammatically correct; standards such as good faith, and so on, come in here as well. And more is taken for granted than is held in grammar books and dictionaries. *You have to learn the way people speak.*

You have to learn to understand and make yourself understood. This is not learning a rule or rules. Making a blunder here is not the same as using language incorrectly. But unless you can tell the difference when you have blundered and when you have not, you cannot speak with people. Cf. the difference between 'having a certain sort of intelligence', 'being able to cotton on to what you are telling him' – and showing competence in a certain technique (cf. the conception of 'fluency' in a foreign language).

But the main point is in connexion with 'going on speaking'. And this is not like being able to go on playing the game with these pieces. *It is not going on with anything that anyone has shown you, in that sense.*

Whether logic can be restricted to a particular technique. You learn logic when you learn to speak. Laws of thought. Generality. How language hangs together; the relation between this and 'what it is that he can go on with, when he has learned to speak'. The idea that you can give an *external* account of what he goes on with, or what he learns.

Compare the idea of telling someone what pain is, or what feeling is. When you have described these movements and noises and facial expressions, you have described someone in pain. 'Does this mean that pain is the movement or the facial expression?' No. And someone might say that it is similar with the description of speaking or of understanding. Or of thinking. 'When he draws on the board, is that thinking? When he places the measuring rod on the frame and makes marks on a pad, is that thinking?' 'You can perfectly well say he is thinking when he is doing this; and you do not mean that when he is doing this there is a special sort of process going on in his head.'

Now will this sort of explanation serve when we are giving an account of language? Is it all right to give an external account of language, or of speaking, in the same way? My difficulty centres on the idea of how language hangs together. And perhaps on the range which understanding is supposed to cover. If I insist that it is not just external when two people are speaking together – and that in this way it is different from playing chess – it is this question of how the remarks hang together which interests me. It is not so much the question of the relation between thought and its expression, although I guess that does come in here too.

How is it that if you understand one part of language you understand others; if you understand when I ask you certain things, you will understand when I ask you other things; if you can say something now, you can say something on other occasions? This is not like saying that if you understand one part of a technique you will be able to understand others, or you will be able to understand the rest.

'If you have learned this amount of arithmetic, you will be able to go on and work out the rest for yourself.' The trouble is that in speaking with people, it is not a matter of being able to work anything out, in that way; nor of being able to apply what you have learned. 'You will be able to do it alone, now, because you know how it is done.' 'Do you think you will be able to go on yourself, now?' This is a question you would never ask, in connexion with learning to speak. This is one reason why we should not call it the mastery of any skill. But also why it is unnatural to say that speaking to people is a kind of performance (which you may do well or ill). This is where the difference between being able to speak with people and being able to do exercises correctly comes in.

Objection: in describing what it is that he has learned we may describe various sorts of conversation, and say 'he has learned to do that sort of thing' or 'he has learned that sort of thing'. To an extent, I think this is all right. One might add that of course we do not mean that he has learned to go through the motions, only. The difference between going through the motions and really speaking is like the difference between going through the motions of suffering and really suffering. And this difference would be presupposed whenever you said 'and that sort of thing'.

The difficulty is that we do not speak of his *learning* pain, or of his learning suffering, though we may speak of his learning the meaning of those words. 'What is it you teach him when you teach him the meaning of the word "pain"?' is not like 'What is it you teach him when you teach him to speak?' The use of examples, or of ostensive definition – you do not teach someone to speak by examples. Partly this is the difficulty about teaching it to someone who already can speak, and teaching someone to speak.

Why is it that Wittgenstein begins the *Investigations* with a discussion of how a child *learns* to speak? Or how a child learns words? He is wanting to show the connexion of logic with reality. He had earlier – in the *Tractatus* – said that this lay in the fact that names have meaning and that elementary propositions have sense. He is now in the position that there are no elementary propositions in the sense in which he had used to speak of them. This means that we cannot use logical analysis to show the relation of logic to reality, for instance. For this reason he is examining the ideas of naming, pointing, referring, and so on. And in general, the notion of talking about things. Above all, perhaps, of understanding, or of what it is that we understand when we understand language. The relation of thought and reality. What he had previously spoken about in terms of picturing. The idea of meta-logic. The idea of formal concepts. Formal series. The idea that there are certain laws of understanding. What you must understand if you can understand anything at all. This seems to have been something which he has come to give up.

But we cannot say that learning to speak is a matter of going through training or *Abrichtung* in certain techniques and certain reactions. It is not like knowing what is permissable and what is not permissable in the movements of certain pieces. It is not that describing a game is merely external. It is that describing a conversation is not like describing a game. Cf. the suggestion that when we say how we would teach anyone the meaning of a particular expression, we have given a primitive language game, or a game with that expression. Can one say the same thing about teaching someone – not the sense of a particular expression – but speaking altogether? Can we say that we are explaining what speaking is, in this way? I have an idea that there is some sort of confusion here.

III

The idea of the generality of language. This is partly the question of giving a general account of language, or of being able to say what language is. One of Wittgenstein's points in the later works would be that this question does have some sort of sense. Cf. Austin *per contra*.

But then the difficulty is that one thinks of giving an account of language as though it were something like giving an account of a particular sort of activity or practice; and the idea of language as an institution would be similar. I think there is something fundamentally misleading in that idea. I almost want to say that is just what language is not.

If you do put it like that, then the discussion might be a discussion of what kind of institution it is. And it might seem as though the generality of your account will be of the same sort as the general account you might give of carpentry or of banking. How does language differ from such practices and such institutions? Why do you call *them* language? This is one of the forms of what the relation is between our speech and what we are doing (whether our speech is part of what we are doing; whether we are doing something when we speak, and so on).

I think it is wrong to say that speaking is engaging in an activity – at least if you take building or marketing as examples of activities. No less wrong than it would be to say that thinking is. This is connected with the difficulty about treating the understanding of language as the understanding of particular expressions, or the game that we play with particular expressions. And this leads to the question of whether there are certain fundamental principles of language; certain principles, or perhaps certain formal properties by which all language or all intelligible expressions are connected. And in this way it may lead on to the question about the relation between logic and language.

Logic comes into the account of language because of the idea of intelligibility; and because of the idea that it is when a man has lost his understanding that he is no longer able to consider reasons that may be offered for or against what is being said, and so is not able to learn. And of such a one we should say that you cannot converse with him – or 'not in the normal way'. But although he does not use language intelligibly, in one sense, it is interesting that he may use it in a way that is grammatically correct. This idea that being able to understand goes with being able to learn, was one of the ideas which Plato emphasized.

The ideas of intelligibility and the laws of thought. If you said that all language must be in conformity with the laws of logic, you would not have gone far towards explaining how language hangs together. Nor would you have gone far to make clear the notion of intelligibility; or the idea of speaking or of saying something. When we speak of how language hangs together, or of the connexions between whatever it is we are calling parts of language we do not mean logical connexions. Think of the relations between the remarks in a conversation. It is here that you find how language hangs together much more clearly; and this sort of relation is not the relation between parts of a logical system. I suppose this is the reason why no idea of a general principle of language would be much help in bringing out the general notion of intelligibility. Or the general notion of language, for that matter. This is part of what Wittgenstein did see in his later work.

That is one point. The other is the way in which intelligibility is connected with the ability to go on speaking. If he can say these things, he can say other things. (This is what I had first of all in mind in connexion with the example of Wittgenstein's builders.) Part of my point is that this is certainly not like continuing a series; neither is it like continuing a technique. It is not just a matter of being able to follow a rule, any more than it is a matter of being able to follow the principle of language. When a child learns to speak, this is not much like learning a rule.

All of this has to do with the matter of the unity of language and belonging to language and the generality of language, and in fact with this question of what it is to give an account of language. And this is necessary for an account of understanding.

In what I took to be important in the ideas of learning or trying to understand, there is much that is related to questions about style, and the sense in which intelligibility depends upon style. And this is connected again with the question of how our speech is related to the activities in which we are engaged, or to what we are doing. For those considerations – trying to understand, trying to make yourself understood – are emphasizing the ways in which understanding depends on familiarity with the sorts of things that people say, the ways in which the intelligibility of what is said is connected with the ways in which they happen to live, the characters of the individuals and the general character of the culture of the age.

The idea of his saying something that interests me. This *may* be because of its connexion with the building job on which we are engaged. But it may interest me for other reasons as well. This is particularly obvious when someone stops me in the street to tell me something or just to have a chat, about various unconnected things. I do not see quite how this is to be described by analogy with a game: in particular, I do not see how you can give an account of the connexion the remarks have with one another in that way. If we were just cracking jokes with one another or saying witty things in banter, it might be something like that. This would be something like just kicking the ball about anyhow or throwing it at one another for the hell of it. But not if he just stops to chat. The main point is that it does interest me. And it is for this reason that its intelligibility may be connected with the job.

For Wittgenstein this kind of question was connected also with the question of how it is that the principles of logic hang together – the idea of centres of variation, for instance – and of whether there is any single principle of logic. Whether logical necessity and logical connexion must always be the same thing. I imagine that this question about the unity of logic was always prominent for Wittgenstein when he was considering questions about the unity of language. This would be connected with questions about the truth of logic, and about the relation of logic and reality. The whole matter of contradictions and of logical necessity; the difference between logic and a wallpaper pattern; the apparent need for a close connexion with 'what you do with it'.

This probably had much to do with the emphasis on language games, and with the idea that the intelligibility of language – the difference between *language* and a wallpaper pattern – lies in its connexion with the activities in which one is using it.

But Wittgenstein seems to have taken the questions about the sense or truth of logic and of mathematics, and the sense of language, as too closely parallel. When he said that the propositions of mathematics and of logic say nothing, he meant to *distinguish* them from empirical statements. And in some important way the account of empirical statements must be different. You cannot talk of the application of empirical statements in the same way in which you would talk about the application of propositions of mathematics or of logic.

He might say that the different principles of logic were connected together, not by some common principle, but by similarities in their uses. 'The important thing is not their connexions in a system' – and perhaps he could add 'any more than the important thing about the parts of language is their connexions in a system'. But it is here that I think the analogy fails and is misleading.

The question whether the expressions we use can be counted as parts or moves in the carrying out of a particular job, for instance. This is connected with the question of how we think of the particular expressions as related to one another. Whether the idea of a family resemblance among the games we play with them is much help here. (This seems to be modelled on the notion of the family resemblance between the games we play with the principles of logic.)

It is hard to see the relation between whatever it is that leads one to talk in terms of chess and formal relations, and whatever it is that leads one to talk in terms of style, familiarity with the sorts of things that people say.

IV

In teaching children to speak, we may teach them games; but we are not teaching them to go on with that. (We are not teaching them the mastery of the game, so that they may play *that* on their own.) Any more than we are teaching them to carry out the kind of tasks and solve the problems with which they are presented in grammar exercises. If someone asked what we teach them (when *would* one ask this?) we could not point at these and say 'That, and things of that sort'. In this way teaching him to speak is not like teaching him 'right' and 'left' – where it *is* a question of being able to go on doing what he does in the games and exercises. This is an example of teaching him the meanings of particular expressions. And it would be similar with teaching many expressions (though not with all).

It is often thought that there must be some sort of commensurability of things that are said; or perhaps: that they have some common intelligibility. (These notions of 'commensurability' and of 'common intelligibility' are sometimes taken to be the same.)

Connexions among remarks in a common language. ('What is it that makes you say they *are* in a common language, since this remark may never have been made before?' 'Do you mean that it is hard to tell whether a speaker on the wireless is speaking English or not? Surely you may tell in the first instance by noticing that he uses nothing but English words.') 'English words' is not equivalent to 'words I am familiar with'. I might be more familiar with Welsh.

If the language is what you speak, why is it not the remarks that you make? 'If the language is what you speak' – but this tells you what *language* is, more than it tells you what speaking *is*. You might say, '*What* you speak is what you learn when you learn to speak.' Cf. Wittgenstein's reference to 'our musical language'. He did not mean the diatonic scale or the rules of harmony.

The important points are: 'If they are to understand one another they must speak a common language.' 'If they are to take part in any "language game" together, they must speak a common language.' Intelligibility – making yourself understood – depends on familiarity with the sorts of things people say; i.e. people speaking this language. (Contrast: intelligibility – having the *form* of an intelligible expression.)

'Understanding correctly' depends not just on formal relations between 'propositions' – 'whether this really follows from that, whether this can really be substituted for that', and so on. It emphasizes rather the understanding between *people*. 'Being intelligible to one another.' How remarks hang together. 'Speaking a common language' is necessary but not sufficient. 'Understanding correctly' is something you learn *as* you learn to make yourself intelligible, or as you learn 'what it makes sense to say'.

When he can speak he can go on. But this is not like saying that he can go on playing the game, or that he can carry on with a technique as a trained worker now; neither is it like being able to go on doing multiplications; nor like being able to go on and work out the rest (or go on and work out).

If we asked what he has learned when he has learned to speak, we could not answer that he has learned how to use these and these expressions. All of this is connected with the point that if he can speak on the present job, he will be able to speak in other connexions as well. Being able to go on speaking is not like being able to go on using this word or this phrase.

We could ask in this connexion about the generality of what he has learned. If we said (what would be unhappy and misleading) that he has learned how remarks hang together: that this is learning what speaking is – this could not mean: he has learned how the parts of a technique hang together. Learning to speak is not learning 'how people do it': as though one might be guided through the motions of a drill until one was able to go on with it alone.

One of the points about learning to speak is that it is *not* something that you learn to do alone. But I would not call it learning to *do* anything anyway. Understanding what you are saying is not like understanding what you are doing (and in this way not like understanding a move you make in a game). I imagine these two are connected. And they may be connected with the point that learning to speak is not learning to *use* language, in the sense of learning to do something with it. When Wittgenstein speaks of learning the rules of various expressions, like those of the builders, for instance, he does make it seem like learning to use a tool or to operate part of a machine. As though understanding it were understanding its function in a way comparable with understanding the function of moving the stones this way or that. Wittgenstein seems to speak of the role of language in what we are doing (would he call this the application of language?) as though it could be described in this way.

If there is a confusion here, it would appear in the idea of having a language which they used only for this or that purpose, or only in connexion with this or that job or activity. I find something unnatural in speaking of a language which they used for this or that. Especially since it suggests that they might have another language which they used for something else. Which seems to be what Wittgenstein does say. Would it follow that if some members of the community learned one job and not the other, they could never speak with one another since they would have no common language?

I do not think it makes sense at all to speak of using language – although it would make sense to speak of using a calculus or using a particular development of mathematics. I suppose this is where the notion of the application of language comes in as well. Anyway, it is connected (a) with the idea that the meaning of the expressions, or what it is that you understand when you understand them, is 'what you do with them'; and also (b) with the idea that the builders may be speaking a common language, even though these expressions are never used elsewhere than in these connexions. So that the connexions of the expressions with one another is no different from different connexions of different parts of the technique with one another. To understand their bearing on one another would be to understand the parts they play in the technique.

I have been suggesting that the language that we use is in a way distinct from what we are doing; and that unless you recognize this, you could not see what speaking to one another is: the builders could not say anything to one another, since they could not ask one another for an explanation of what has been said.

When Wittgenstein suggests that 'to be able to speak with people is to be able to play a game with them' he is making the very important point that understanding one another depends on more than a knowledge of formal grammatical differences and of vocabulary. Yet, learning to play a game is not learning what makes sense. And for this reason being able to play a game is not being able to go on speaking or to speak on other occasions. (Neither is taking part in a game like taking part in a conversation. This brings in also the relation of language or of speaking to our lives, which is so different from the relation of a game to our lives.) And the interrelations between various games could not give you anything like the way in which language hangs together.

You would not talk with people if you *never* thought you could believe them (unless you thought you might draw inferences from what they did say). (I almost want to say speaking depends on friendship, which is absurd.)

Speaking and 'understanding' – in the sense of people among whom there is understanding. This sometimes means they have certain common beliefs. More often, that their ways of doing things and talking about things – the kinds of question they ask – are similar. The connexion of a language and a way of living (form of life). Wittgenstein did not make very explicit or very detailed what might be included in this idea. And sometimes – as in the builders case – he was speaking rather of a way of *working*. In fact, his examples are generally of the way people *do* things: an institution like money, an institution like buying and selling wood. And of the relation of language to that. I think this is confusing. In the first place, the discussion of how the remarks are related to what they are doing, gives a wrong idea of the relation of the 'way of living' or 'common understanding' to language, I think. There are other difficulties, analogous to the confusion between the meaning of a name and the bearer of a name.

But in the second place, a form of life or way of living is not a way of working, and it is not an institution. A way of doing certain things – marriage customs, for instance or manners of taking meals – may be taken as characteristic of the lives of people; some more, some less. (Danger of thinking you could construct the way of living from these.)

Once more the question 'What life is' – the meaning of life – and of what a common life is. *The importance of literature*: finding the sense in, and giving sense to, the life that is lived. The difficulty and limitation there would be in trying to speak with Frenchmen if you know nothing of French literature, or of the other side of French life – theatre, politics and art. Why is it that a writer (and also a composer) always writes in the same or in characteristic style: so that you may recognize the authorship of a page by the style it is written in? Why should he not write differently each time? (Why should you feel almost that he was hardly worth serious consideration if he did? And similarly with a composer.) This seems to be connected with the notion of *having something to say*. And also with the point that you try not merely to understand the sentences he utters; you try to understand him. 'Le stil, c'est l'homme.' But why? The immensely important idea of relations of people to one another; including their problems and difficulties.

Once more: Wittgenstein seems to have taken it too much in the formal – and impersonal – relations of individuals, or 'players' in an institution.

'The breakdown of communication.' 'Only one currency – money.' Doris and Sweeny – further in that direction and they will have nothing to talk about – there will be nothing to say. Of course, if it were just a question of operating a mechanism this would not matter. Or going through a drill. But that is the trouble with standing external to it in this way.

If the child is too young to speak yet, this is not – or not simply – because the techniques are too complicated or too difficult. (Any more than the reason why a dog does not learn to speak is because he cannot learn such complicated tricks.) The connexion between understanding life and understanding one another. The difference between understanding one another and understanding what is shown on the indicators of a machine.

'Talent has a face, and is always debatable.' The idea of a remark that is debatable (and therefore *interesting*: conferre: having something to say). A move in a game is not *debatable* in that way. And neither are the utterances of the builders. This is why they never *discuss*. (Or if they do, then the rules and reactions which belong to the building techniques are not the whole of their language.) 'Volkommen idiotisch.' ('Completely idiotic.')

I think this is more important than I have made clear. Important for the whole idea of speaking together and understanding; and what it is when someone learns to speak. 'Intelligent enough to cotton on to what I am telling him.' Not just reacting properly, but seeing what it means. Some understanding of the sort of person I am, perhaps. (Is this what is excluded from certain forms of insanity, where we speak of delusions which are not just mistaken views?)

The differences between one form of life and another, are not like the differences between one form of some institution (say marriage customs, or property or financial institutions) and another. That would be like saying that a language is a game, like chess. Whereas a language is something that can have a literature. This is where it is so different from chess. It must be a language of people; and *in* which people develop; in which people develop their own lives, their own ideas and their own literature. (Which it is possible to speak 'with a face of one's own'.) Something consisting 'solely of orders and reports in battle' would not be a language at all. This has to do with what we may call 'the form of language' or with the idea of learning 'what makes sense' – the difference between this and learning what can be done in connexion with a building technique.

I suspect that Wittgenstein thought of 'giving an account of language' too much an analogy with 'giving an account of pain' or 'giving an account of feeling' or 'giving an account of intending'. Cf. giving an account of thinking.

In these cases it seemed all right to give an account of how we use the *word* 'pain', etc. Or, '*when* would you say he was in pain'.

If someone is puzzled about what 'pain' means, or what 'justice' means, or what 'duty' means, we may begin by asking him to consider how we should teach anyone – or how you learn – what any of these expressions mean. 'In doing this, you will have given a simple language game with that expression.' So the pupil can see how the word is used in practice. In the course of this, you may refer to actual examples of pain or of pictures or of duty. ('How does anyone get the idea of duty? How do you learn what "duty" means?' 'How do you tell if he *understands* what duty means?')

'What is the objection to saying that the learning of these various expressions *is* learning to speak? There is not any *single* thing which is learning to speak, comparable to learning the use of any of these expressions. But knowing the use of various such expressions – being able to use them on the occasions in which they arise in connexion with other people – that is speaking.' My answer is that if he can speak, he can go on to say and ask other things. And if this answer is cogent, there is something wrong with that way of explaining what speaking is – *although* it would seem as though we might offer examples like this and add 'and other things of the sort', and we might seem to have given a general account of language.

The language game, or the way we learn the expression, is supposed to show the relations of words to things; or to show how it is that words have meaning. (Cf. 'What it is that makes it possible for language to have meaning.' Earlier 'the world': now 'the way of living' – which seems almost to come to 'the games we play with one another'. Answer to the question of Gorgias.) What it is for people to talk about things.

But *do* the language games with the particular expressions show you the relation of words to things? 'Nur in der Verbindung mit dem übrigen Mechanismus.' ('Only in connexion with the rest of the mechanism.') Only on the assumption that they are *language* games. (Only on *some* sort of assumption of what the adult is teaching you – or teaching him.)

Only because in this way you can learn to *talk* about things. Which is not the same as learning to go on with this game. If it stayed at that, you would not have learned to speak. (Cf. doing exercises.)

I do not at all want to question the importance of distinguishing different games or different grammars, when we are talking about sensations, and when we are talking about physical things. (Different conception of 'talking about something'.) Nor the importance of avoiding the confusion of such questions as 'What *is* a question?' as though there were one simple grammar in all we do. Perhaps the question is concerning the relation of grammar and understanding. The futility of thinking that *all* discourse must be truth functions of 'elementary propositions'. Different ways of talking about something; different ways of having meaning. (Confusion of grammar, like 'sensations are private'.)

The idea that when you learn to speak, you learn what can be said. This is learning the rules. Is this the sense in which you learn logic also? Or learn thinking?

Only in the sense of learning – coming to understand – how one might go on: or coming to understand this. But understanding is not learning the rules, as if one knew what a rule was. Neither is it simply doing what you have been trained to. Learn what can be said. Learn to recognize what is intelligible; what can be understood. Learn to understand. I think this depends on more than 'rules' – in the sense of rules of grammar and vocabulary. This is one of the reasons for insisting on the difference between 'being able to speak' and 'knowing a language'. Still more, the difference between being able to speak and having a facility in or mastery of a notation – which would leave out entirely such considerations as familiarity with the sorts of things people say.

If you leave that out, you leave out what is 'internal'. You leave out really understanding one another. You have only the external relations between moves in a game which are never debatable as a remark may be. You may debate whether that is the move he ought to have made – whether it was clever or a blunder perhaps; or you may debate as to whether it was in accordance with the rules, whether it was a permissable move. But this is not like considering something debatable that has been said; an interesting remark. The idea of an interesting remark is very important. One that really says something; gives you something to think about. The question of its relation to the rules of the grammar does not seem to enter.

If my life is changed – in lesser and in greater ways, by things people have said to me – this is not like a difference in the course of the game. And if we considered only the difference it makes to the course of the conversation, this would be treating the conversation as too self contained (as though I were external to it as I am to a game), and it leaves out the way in which I *learn* from a conversation and from what is said in it. The fact that I am taking part in the conversation is connected with *having something to say*. And so it is connected with the fact that I speak in other connexions as well.

This is one reason *why* there has to be a common understanding for this; whereas there does not, in that way, for playing a game together. Here we need only agree on what the rules are and how they may be interpreted.

Once again: What is the difference between rules of logic and rules of the building technique? 'No, you can't even *try* to do it that way.' There is a difference between a logical absurdity and a meaningless sound.

We learn logic when we learn to speak – not a logic of airless space. The dance with rules in which 'and', 'or', 'not', 'if . . . then' appear. But the rules by which the organization carried on its work would not have been laws of thought either, if they were rules only of that technique. A technique may be the same in two languages, as engineering is, or as mathematics is. The difference of language (French and English) is not like a difference of technique in the sense in which Wittgenstein is speaking of it. We might say rather that when he learns to speak then *incidentally* – perhaps inevitably – he learns a technique. But if you were *teaching* him a technique, and if this were what he was trying to learn, it would be different.

We do speak in connexion with what we are doing, and we use the language of the workshop, we make the remarks that belong to the job, and we discuss the job; we are discussing a question of law, and we talk in that way, or we may be telling another how we feel. There are different ways of speaking (and it is a different use of language) that belong to what we are doing, to the discussion we are engaged in, to how it is that one comes to be talking to one another at all. But if in some sense we understand the differences – in the sense of having enough sense to talk the way we are talking now and not in the other way – should we say that this is the sort of thing the foreigner who learns the language does not have to learn? What I have in mind is the conception of what it makes sense to say. And the sense in which I may *mis*understand what you say – not just fail to understand it. He learns to speak when he is able to do *this*. And this is not like learning a technique.

Wittgenstein seems to think you could learn to *understand* by *Abrichtung*; and understand in a way that does not yet allow for misunderstanding. In that case, I do not think it is understanding what is said. The rhetorician also spoke of a technique.

The connexion of language and thinking. When I speak of an internal connexion between the remarks that are made in the language, I mean partly that it is a connexion you can see only when you understand them. Perhaps, that they have something in common which enables you to pass from one to the other. They do not bear upon one another simply because of their functions in this situation – as moves in a game might. Rather, it is *because* of what they say and what they are, that they bear upon one another here. This is why they have to be *understood* in a way the moves in a game do not; and this understanding cannot generally be reduced to an appreciation of the role in the game or in the conversation (does a profound or an interesting remark have a different role from a commonplace one?) even though it cannot be *separated* from that either.

'Almost as though the remarks do not simply meet externally, but that they interpenetrate, or meet quasi in another medium.' This would be the point of speaking of the connexions as internal, in some such sense as that in which one speaks of thoughts as internal.

'Relations of meaning.' 'But the meaning does not happen at a particular time as the remark does.' If this means anything, I do not see that it means much. The remark which is made here and now *has* the meaning; and this is why it has the bearing and relation to the other remarks which it has. (If you thought of the meaning as a kind of aura which each remark carries, and that this aura interpenetrates – this would be just as external, in our sense, as anything else.) They hang together because they are understood, not just by one person (as one might understand different statements in an argument) but because the people who make them understand one another. 'In describing language, or in describing the connexions of the remarks in the conversation – the personal experiences of the people concerned do not come into it. It does not matter what goes on in their minds.' (Cf. Bedeutungblindheit.) (Meaning blindness.)

v

Wittgenstein used to say that we learn logic as we learn the language, or learn to speak. And somehow I feel that it would not be speaking unless we did. But there is a difference between rejecting something as absurd, and rejecting it because it would have no place in what we do. There is a difference between what is nonsense and what we cannot understand because we have never met it. But would anyone learn this if learning to speak were merely learning to do what those builders do? This is not *merely* a matter of learning logic, but I think something we should call logic would belong to it.

Wittgenstein considered at one time how one might imagine a language game which would show what drawing a logical conclusion is. He mentioned certain primitive sorts of language games in which, he said, it is doubtful whether we should speak of drawing conclusions. But then he considered a case in which there is an organization. There are men having three different functions. There are stones marked with the letters 'A', 'B', 'C', etc. And one man gives the orders. 'Put the A's in that pile', and so on. Another man receives these orders, and asks the third what stone it is he has found. The third person tells him, 'It is an A', and the second one says 'Then that goes in that pile.' Here we have the drawing of a conclusion. And an important factor is that there are various people involved. If someone asked, 'How do they *learn* to draw conclusions?', Wittgenstein would answer, 'They learn when they learn the language; when they learn the meaning of "all".' There would also be the question of how contradiction comes in: of how these people regard contradictions, or how contradictions function. Suppose there were a series of orders, beginning perhaps 'Take that stone from here', and later in the course of this series of orders 'Don't take that stone from here.' Here Wittgenstein said that one cannot predict exactly what the effect of this would be.

In discussing this case he did not suggest that the people involved spoke *only* on this job. And it is not quite clear to me whether he meant that learning to draw a conclusion was something like learning to work in that organization. But I think he did mean that; or at least he was wondering. But if they learned to use the expression 'all' only in connexion with this job, then I wonder whether they would draw a conclusion. Would they not have to be taught what to shout each time, as they are taught the other rules of the job? Drawing a conclusion would just be part of the technique, and would have nothing to do with what makes sense and what does not.

In that case, it would not be a logical conclusion, anyway, and Wittgenstein would agree. For instance, in the *Remarks on the Foundations of Mathematics* he says 'It is the use outside mathematics, and so the *meaning* of the signs, that makes the sign game into mathematics. Just as it is not a logical inference if I change one configuration into another (say one arrangement of chairs into another) unless these arrangements have a use in language that is not confined to these transformations' (p. 133). Of course it need not be a logical conclusion, and most of the conclusions people draw are not. But I am doubtful if we should call it a conclusion of any kind; it is just part of the routine.

In any case, Wittgenstein's point about a logical conclusion is one of the reasons why I would say that they do not distinguish between sense and nonsense, and they are not speaking, if their utterances are confined entirely to these situations in this job.

You might ask why this should make such a difference – the fact that the same expressions are used elsewhere. And one reason, I think, is that the expressions are not part of one particular routine. Their uses elsewhere have to do with the point or the bearing of them here; and in particular, with the way in which they make sense together here: on whether one can be substituted for another here, on whether they may be combined or are incompatible, and so forth. For example, any expression which is used in a mathematical proof, is used in the same sense in the application of mathematics; any sentence which forms part of a formal argument is a sentence that is also used outside that argument, and so on. What the expressions mean, even in this game, is not to be seen in what we do with them or how we react to them in this game. (Whereas the expressions the builders use are something like empty demonstratives; as though we were back at something analogous to the confusion between the meaning of a name and the bearer of a name.)

Wittgenstein was constantly thinking about logical necessity, about the 'force' of a logical conclusion, and about the difference between a calculation and any other transformation of signs according to rules, which might be a wallpaper pattern. It is in this connexion that he used to discuss so often what the impossibility of a contradiction is, and whether it would matter much if there were a contradiction in logic. His point was that there is nothing in the forms of the expressions we use, and there is nothing in the ordinary uses of 'and' and 'not' which would make it impossible for a contradiction to work or to have sense – as though there were certain combinations of signs which could not be given meaning; or as though two meanings (e.g. of a proposition and its negative) could conflict. The conflict comes from the usual uses which we make of them, and it is in this connexion that we rule out contradictions. The 'impossibility' comes not from any characteristics of the propositions or the symbols themselves.

Perhaps a short reference like this is worse than none. For the discussion would be concerned with logical necessity and with logical principles altogether: with the question whether logical principles, like the law of non-contradiction or the law of excluded middle, for instance, *themselves* were necessary; and if we said they were, what account should be given of this. In this way Wittgenstein was giving attention to the 'office' of logic, or to the question of what there is that is logical about such principles. And I doubt if anyone has gone into this as deeply.

He no longer held that all logical principles could be deduced from a common principle; and in any case, he would not have said that this would show what there was logical about them. When he wrote the *Tractatus* he was able to do this, because he connected logical principles with the idea of logical form, and he connected this with the notion of an intelligible expression or a proposition. So there was no question of the sense in which they were principles, and there was no question of the position they held in relation to what could be said or thought. But in the *Investigations* it is different. His position is still that if you want to see what kind of principles they are, you have to look to their applications, or to the special uses which such principles have. But their uses or applications are not always the same; and there is often considerable difference between principles which 'formally' seem to be alike. If you consider any actual use of the law of excluded middle, for instance, you will find that it is generally unlike any use of the law of non-contradiction, however close the symbolic expressions of them may be.

This seems to be extremely important. But it led Wittgenstein, sometimes at least, to views about the unity of logic which make me wonder. He no longer thought that the validity of logic depended on the possibility of a consistent and complete logical system. This went with the point that the 'validity' of the various principles lay in the ways in which they were actually used: or, as he would sometimes put it, in their roles in those and those language games. To say that their logical character does not depend on belonging to a consistent system, means that if someone should discover a formal contradiction between two of them, this need not impugn the 'validity' of either of them. Once again, if you want to see in what way a contradiction shows that something is wrong, you must look to what we do in our actual investigations and inferences. And you will not find there anything which will show that there is something wrong about a contradiction in logic. There is something wrong when there is a contradiction in an argument of course, or in a calculation, but the various principles of argument themselves do not form an argument. And neither need logic be 'complete'.

One consequence, of course, was that you cannot say that 'logical connexion' must always be the same. In fact it looks as though Wittgenstein were saying that logical principles form a 'family of cases' (although I do not ever remember his putting it just so); just as he used to say that proof or inference 'belongs to the language game'. But the difficulty is in seeing just what *that* means. For instance, when Wittgenstein wanted to show that the character of the law of excluded middle was to be found in its application, he might illustrate by the way in which it would be brought in by counsel in a logical argument in court. And then it might almost seem as though the logical principle were tied to or were part of, or even that it had its meaning in, the conduct of court cases. He would *not* have said that, of course; any more than he would have said that the validity of the principle – or its character as a logical principle – was limited to its character as a rule of this game. But I did think sometimes that his exposition half suggested that. And I think the trouble once again was in the tendency to think of the 'language game' as the activity in *connexion* with which people are using language; as though the meaning of what they say, and the sense or absurdity of it, had no other source than the rules and requirements of the work in which they are engaged. If it were like that, then I wonder how we should maintain any clear distinction between what is a logical principle or what is not; or perhaps: between what is a logical conclusion and what is not.

VI

It was because you play a game with other people that Wittgenstein took it as an analogy with speaking. It is not easy to see how far one is meant to take the analogy. It does emphasize important matters such as the way in which a *rule* – its authority and office – depends on playing with other people. But it still leaves out the idea of telling one another things.

A sham conversation that you may carry on when you are learning a foreign language, where it is a question of being able to construct 'appropriate' sentences and give 'appropriate' replies. The difference between this sort of exercise in speaking and really speaking. That there *is* this distinction between the games we teach him, and what he tumbles to when he begins really to speak, is very important. Conversation is not like playing a game together, because the point of the moves and the countermoves in the game is within the game. Whereas we may learn from a conversation and from what is said in it. In any case, what corresponds to asking someone something, in a game? Unless there were the distinction between genuine speaking and sham or pretence, speaking *would* be much more like playing the game correctly. You do not learn from a sham conversation; nor from one in which you think someone is shamming: at least you do not learn from what he *says*. This is one way in which the relation of these remarks to other things that are said, is different from the relation of the expressions in a calculation to other uses of those expressions.

As regards *understanding correctly*, what is important is the relation to the sorts of things which people *actually* say: what people say to one another and how they understand one another.

The difference between (a) the external relation of moves in a game, and (b) the internal relations of remarks made to one another. 'Connexions of meaning' cannot be reduced to connexions in the game. (In so far it is analogous to connexions in a logical inference – although it is not an 'internal connexion' in the logical sense.) This goes with the fact that we learn from a conversation: that its point is not contained just in what happens there.

The difference between talking together and acting a play, where the actor does not tell the other anything. This goes with the fact that he does not decide to say anything (he reacts in the way he has been taught). Connected with the idea of having something to say. (Almost: 'bringing something to the game' – without which you could not make a move. The point about chess is that the pieces are furnished for you – you do not have to find them, nor decide what they shall be. They belong only to the game and are, so to speak, determined by the game. Answer: 'This means that the sphere of possible reactions is limited in this way. You make your reaction from among those possible in this game and with these pieces.') But that is not how it is when I have something to tell you – which is what brings me to the game in the first place. Analogy with mathematics, where you have limited operations with specific expressions. (Note that in each case you can calculate the possible moves. Cf. 'possible forms of intelligible expression'. Wittgenstein hoped to avoid this by the multiplicity of language games.) In mathematics you do not say anything. And this has to do with the fact that you can calculate what can be said. Or: that no one brings anything *to* the game: there is nothing like an interesting remark, although there may be problems. An interesting remark in a conversation is not an interesting remark about what it is possible to say.

All this has to do with the distinction of sense and nonsense: which, if it were a game, would be empty. 'The authority of the prior definition of a rule depends on the fact that you are playing with other people. The importance of agreement as to what you call following a rule.' But I think it leaves it difficult to distinguish between a rule of language and a rule of building. ('What is it that makes them all *language* games?') This does have an importance for the conceptions of sense and nonsense, and of understanding and of saying something.

PART TWO

Games and language

CHAPTER 4

Discussion and discourse
(29.6.67–11.7.67)

I

Wittgenstein used to insist that 'that is how we do it', especially
when he was arguing that there is no necessity about doing it –
mathematics, for instance – in that way. Any more than there is any
necessity that we should speak of 'going on in the same way' when
we do, rather than in connexion with some very different procedure.
It is not because that corresponds to something in the nature of
reality, for instance. And probably such considerations could be
brought in criticism of what Plato says about the inter-connexion of
kinds, which is supposed to make discourse possible. This is connected with understanding the language, too, and Wittgenstein used
to emphasize that. You know how words are used because you have
been taught; or perhaps it is something you have picked up. And in
fact most people agree in what they regard as 'going on in the same
way they have been taught'. This might be otherwise. But if it were,
it would have considerable consequences for what we should
understand by 'understanding the language' or 'understanding what
is said'. In fact, unless there were some such agreement, there could
not be anything like what we call 'teaching someone the language'.
Nor should we mean anything like what we do when we say that
someone now understands it.

It is important to emphasize that when one is asking 'what the
possibility of discourse depends on', for instance. It is important to
point out that it would be nonsense to say that it is the meanings of
terms that determine how we use them. And this is important also
when one is considering what it is that is meant by 'rules of
grammar', and whether one must assume anything like Plato's forms.
'Agreement in reactions' – something like that is really prior to
anything like judgements. This is important for considering any such

question as 'What is it that you know, when you know what is meant?'
Or: 'What is meant by the meaning of an expression?' Or: 'What is it
that you teach anyone, when you teach him what it means?'

But this has most clearly to do with the meanings of words or
expressions, rather than with the understanding of sentences, or with
the understanding of what is said. I suppose that if you tried to tell
someone what a given sentence means (he might have remarked that
that is a curious thing to say) you might try to tell him how it is used.
In other words, you tell him the circumstances in which it might be
said – you give him examples – and you may try to explain the
difference it would have made if he had said something else: perhaps
in terms of the conclusions that his listeners would have drawn from
it; and so on.

Here again we seem just to be emphasizing how the language is
spoken, but all this may seem to make 'knowing the language' a
matter largely of knowing how to do the job. Compare the conception of members of an organization performing their various
functions. 'When he does that, I have to do this; but if he did so and
so, I should have to do something else.' That conception is important
for understanding what we mean by drawing a conclusion, I
suppose; and for understanding what we mean by 'the laws of
thought'. And there is something like drawing a conclusion in a
great deal of discourse and discussion.

But I have tried to emphasize also that the laws of thought or rules
of logic are not typical of the connexions between the various
statements and utterances of the greater part of discourse. The
question of the way in which language hangs together cannot be
answered simply by reference to the performance of various functions in an organization. That gives you no conception of discussion.
It supposes that there is some agreed way of doing the job, and men
simply give the right reactions according to the variations in the
orders or reports they receive. There is no suggestion of trying to
find out something, or trying to learn.

'Whether you can understand what is said, does depend on
whether you know how the language is spoken. (And that is what it is
that you can teach someone: you can give a pretty definite answer if
someone asks you what it is that you do teach him, and so on.) Also,
I suppose it were inconceivable that anyone should know how the
language is spoken, and yet be unable to understand anything that
was said.'

Is our question something like asking whether the ability to understand what is said is subsequent to knowing how the language is spoken or prior to it?

The trouble with placing all the emphasis on 'how the language is spoken' is that it seems it is a matter of mastery of various techniques ('being able to use the expressions correctly'). This would give you no conception of what it is for the language to be spoken at all. Knowing how to produce one expression out of another. Knowing what expression follows on what: this will not be an account of speaking and understanding what is said. (It is more like knowing how to operate a machine. Supposing a number of operators are working together on a complex machine, for instance.) The 'performance' of the language is not speaking it. Any more than the operation of a calculating machine is calculation. Granted that you have mastered the use of these and these particular expressions, and supposing someone makes a statement employing them, then if you understand him, that is not simply a matter of recognizing how he is using the expressions in question. So that you know what to expect, or so that you will be able to judge if he has gone on correctly from there, for instance.

'Eine Sprache vorstellen heißt, eine Lebensform vorstellen.' Yes; but *understanding* the language, or speaking it, is not simply understanding the *way* of life. (Or should we say that you have to understand what a way of life is? Understanding men's actions and understanding their lives.)

There is a difference between the question of what it is to understand the language, i.e. to be able to speak it (and this would go with the kind of tests we should use to discover whether a person does understand the language or not); and the question of what it is to understand something that has been said. If you want to tell whether someone knows the language, you would use various familiar criteria. And it might be something not too dissimilar, if you wanted to find out whether he had followed the discussion. Suppose it were a discussion of capital punishment, for instance, or a discussion of a proposed logical calculus, or of yesterday afternoon's football game. But the question of *what* you are trying to find out is different here, all the same.

If you are testing his capacity – if you want to know whether he is able to follow discussions of that *kind* – then it is more like trying to find whether he knows the language. (Here we have the matter of general and particular coming in.) If the discussion was a test as far as he was concerned, then he might begin by answering, 'Yes, I could follow it. What about it?' As far as he is concerned the discussion might just as well never have taken place; but if that is what you want him to try, well all right, he can follow it.

This is widely different from taking *part* in the discussion. If he does that, then it is not *simply* a question of finding out whether he can – whatever your interest in his performance may be. Our question is what it means to understand a discussion in *that* way. And that is why I put it in the form of: what it means to learn something from it. And the same goes for understanding anything that is said in the course of the discussion. I suppose you would not understand the remark in this sense unless you *were* taking part in the discussion. At any rate, it is the question of what it means to take part in a discussion that we are concerned with.

If you do not see how the remark bears on anything else, then you have not understood it. But to say that is not sufficient. For you might do that if you were simply watching a discussion as you were watching a performance – a performance which seemed to you pretty pointless.

I have suggested that if you could not see the bearing of the discussion on anything else at all – however trivial – then it would be absolutely pointless for you, and would not be able to see the point or bearing of any remark that was made in it either. And I think that is true. Could anyone follow a philosophical or a logical discussion perfectly, if he could see no possible point in it? 'I don't know, he said this and the other man said that, and that is how it went on, though God knows why.' Perhaps adding, 'As far as I was concerned, any one of them might just as well have made a remark about the weather.' 'One man says truth is one thing, and the other says no, truth is something else. But what difference does it make?'

If you cannot see what difference it makes, then you cannot see what the discussion is about, I suppose. But then you cannot understand what is being said, either. And that is not because you do not know the language. I want to say: understanding what is said in a discussion is not a matter of capacities: not in the sense in which knowing Welsh or knowing arithmetic is a capacity; or being able to read.

This goes with the question whether being able to take part in a conversation is a capacity that one has learned; or whether it is something you could teach anyone.

If you want to know what is meant by the intelligibility of some remark or some discourse; if you want to know what is meant by understanding it; or by knowing what it means – then it may be important to ask how we distinguish between what is intelligible and what is not; how you would try to find out whether someone had understood it or not; and how you would teach someone what it means. Here we seem to be saying that whether you can understand it or not depends on whether you know how the language is spoken. And also: what you understand is something you have been taught or have picked up (and could teach to someone else): i.e., the way in which such expressions are used.

I agree that all that is necessary. I agree that you cannot understand what is said, unless you know how the language is used. I agree also that if you wanted to know whether someone could understand you, you would take steps of the sort that we mention in this connexion: steps similar to those which you would take if you wanted to know whether he could speak the language or not.

But I think that if you try to make this the whole account of it – the whole account of what it is to understand what is said, or, for that matter, the whole account of what it is to speak the language – then you may well be (probably are) describing something which would not be either speaking or understanding. This may appear in the use that is made of certain analogies; when speaking the language is compared to carrying on the work of an organization, for instance, or even to playing a game. This is a distortion of what speaking the language is; since playing a game is not like carrying on a conversation, and carrying on in an organization is not like taking part in a discussion.

II

Speaking the language is not always discussion, of course; in fact generally it is not. But there is something about most of what we call speaking the language, which can be seen by considering its similarity (approximation to or deviation from) discussion – by taking discussion as the centre of variation for various forms of discourse.

Plato said that discourse must be *about* something. Understanding what is said in a discussion is not the same as understanding what is said in a charade. That is the sort of thing I want to emphasize. And yet in one sense you might say that you were using the same language with the same meanings in both cases; that you are speaking the same language, if you like. And if you know how to play charades and I do not, we might not say that you know the language any better than I do on that account. That would already be a certain distinction between knowing the language and being able to understand what is said.

Suppose someone said, then: 'There is no one thing which you can call "knowing how the language is spoken"; and there is no one thing you can call "understanding what is said".' All that is important particularly inasmuch as it emphasizes the role that the language (i.e. the game on which one happens to be engaged) plays in the lives of the people that are speaking it. And that is bringing it closer to what I have in mind in emphasizing discussion. (Those who catalogue various 'uses' of a phrase without considering what is done with them are on the wrong track.)

The notion of 'the role that it plays' may still be a bit confusing though. In any case, I think we may still ask what makes us call it a *language* game. There is no general or all-embracing language game. I think we are agreed about that. Nor are there any general or universal rules of grammar which must be followed if we are to say something or if what we say is to be intelligible at all. And so I question whether we can speak of any general method of determining whether anyone has understood what is said. But I do not think it follows that we can say nothing generally about it – about understanding and about the intelligibility of discourse.

You can see what is meant by understanding discourse if you can recognize the reality of discussion; not otherwise. The same goes for seeing what is meant by the growth of understanding.

We have noted what seems to be a difficulty here: if you can speak of the growth of understanding, can you not say what it is that you are coming to understand? Or: does that not mean that you understand something better – that you are learning more about it, perhaps, or that you are avoiding misconceptions? What is it that you understand now better than you did?

That objection is rather like saying that in education you must be teaching the pupil something. And the aim of education must be to teach him more and more about it, until he has attained the complete mastery of it. If he is a pupil he must be studying something – studying medicine, say. And in the happiest cases he may eventually be able to go far beyond his teachers in the knowledge and the competence that he shows there. (He makes discoveries. That is important: that seems to be what we mean here by adding to our understanding, or adding to our knowledge.) This goes with the idea that the successful pupil is the one that is talented in the field he is studying.

But if the aim of education is the development of understanding – or we might say 'intellectual growth' or 'wisdom' – then it is not so clear that we can say in that sense that we must be teaching the pupil something. That seems to have been Socrates' point. (And if someone can add to our understanding here, it will not be by making discoveries; though it will be by helping him to see things.)

If someone says that you cannot talk in a general way about the growth of understanding, but only about the development of special capacities, this amounts to denying the reality of discussion. It amounts to saying that understanding discourse (or being able to understand it) is a matter of knowing how the language is spoken.

How are we to read my suggestion that 'A conversation makes sense if living makes sense'? You understand what is said if you can learn from it. I have taken that to mean: if you can see what it brings to the discussion, or if it helps you to understand the discussion. So far there is no reference to the question of how the discussion fits together with other things in my life. And we might say that unless the different people taking part could understand the discussion in pretty much the same way, there would be no discussion at all.

'Understanding grows as discussion grows.' I want to hang on to that. Unless people had something like a common background, they could not discuss. It is not enough simply that they should be masters of the same vocabulary and the same syntax. They might still not be able to understand one another. Cf. English and Americans; or English and Welsh. What we might call the importance of *ideas*, I suppose. It seems as though there must be some sort of community of ideas before you can even say that people differ or that they disagree. We develop and clarify our ideas in discussion. But also: this sort of community of ideas sets the limit within which communication is possible, I suppose. (This is the sort of thing the Marxists used to emphasize in what they said about ideology.) The conditions of the possibility of discourse.

The difference between taking part in a discussion and seeing whether you can follow a discussion: in the latter case, the question of whether you had understood might be the question whether you are able to answer pertinent questions about it; whether you could make an intelligent answer if I asked you why you supposed this person made that remark at that juncture of the discussion. You might answer, 'Well, he wanted to show . . .' or '. . . he wanted to bring out'. But in this case you might follow the discussion without the sort of growth of understanding of which I have been speaking.

If you are taking part in a discussion, you are trying to find out. Or more important: you are trying to get clearer. And here the question of whether you have understood it is the question whether you have got something out of it. And there are not such clear tests to apply. Compare the case where you are trying to estimate someone's appreciation of art. Or when you are trying to estimate his seriousness in science, for instance.

There are ways, often, in which one can come to some conclusion about this. His attitude towards pseudo-science and dilettantism, for instance. His attitude about 'being scientific' here, there and everywhere. And there are similar or analogous matters which show something about a man's seriousness concerning art (the difference between appreciation and aestheticism). And similarly with participation in discussion. Where there is no seriousness, there is not much understanding either. But for the other question of whether you can follow the discussion, it does not matter so much.

And suppose someone asked, 'Well what is the difference? What does the person who is seriously taking part in the discussion "get", which the other person misses? Is it something more, which the other man has overlooked?' What kind of question about the possibility of discourse have we here? Is it simply a question of participation in common ideas, now? If it were, there would not be that kind of difference between the participant and the onlooker. On the other hand, there could not be discourse without that, any more than there could be art without that. (Art and audience.) Or life of human beings with one another.

Well, I suppose if you were to ask *what* it is that he has missed, the only way to answer is to mention the ways in which it shows itself. The difference is not like the difference between having a skill and being without it. It is not a capacity in any such sense at all.

This is the question about the relation of discourse to reality. What is it we are seeking? What is it all about? The question of what is important and what is trivial. This is not quite the same as the question concerning the relation of words and things. ('Talking about something.') Understanding it: seeing the point of it. And sometimes: seeing how it is important. That seems to come in when you say that you can get something out of it, or that it is something from which you can learn something.

Somehow this seems to be connected with the idea of the reality of what is said. ('He really said something there.') Cf. the idea of the reality of discourse. (Whether it makes any difference what you say.) The difference that it makes is not simply the difference in the operation of a mechanism; or in the operation of a calculus either. If that were all that you knew – if all that you knew were the respective consequences that could be drawn according to the rules – then I want to say that you have not understood the difference that it makes whether you say one thing or the other; or perhaps even that you have not recognized any real difference at all. If the rules were simply rules for filling out the design in a wallpaper, for instance . . .

The difference between taking part in a discussion, and simply trying to make a point there. This difference is hard to bring out; and it is what Socrates pressed against the sophists.

There is a sense in which we may speak of 'seeking to understand', or perhaps 'to understand things', in which we do not mean trying to have a perfect familiarity with all the ins and outs of a technique; and in which we do not mean trying to give a causal explanation of what is happening either.

It is in this sense that we often speak of the growth of understanding. And we sometimes mean by that what we might also call intellectual development. When we use it in that way – when we consider the growth of understanding in an individual, for instance, – then it has no clear sense to ask 'understanding *what?*' Perhaps this is another reason why we should not think of the search for understanding as an attempt to find a theory which will explain something, or as an attempt to understand how something works. That is why we may speak of it as something like 'maturity of outlook'; or as wisdom. Anyway, it is a way of viewing things. A way of viewing them without perplexity, if you like. 'Understanding things' does not mean especially 'knowing more about them'.

What is not clear at first, is the way in which this is connected with understanding what is said, or with trying to understand what is said. But understanding what is said does not always mean being able to translate what is said, or being able to give the sense of it in other words, or to explain what it means to someone who may ask you. You might be able to do that, even if the remark meant little or nothing to you. Whereas if someone is trying to make something clear, perhaps in the course of a discussion, you may say, 'Yes, I understand that', or 'Yes, I see now; I didn't see what you were trying to say before'; and here you do not mean that you would be able to put the same thing in other terms for instance.

No doubt it were perverse to say that you understand something only when it is a remark you can get something out of, or when it is a remark that furthers your understanding in some way (as a remark may further your understanding of a discussion). For I can understand my neighbour's interminable babble about her daughter's housekeeping, although it neither interests nor instructs me. If she were speaking a foreign tongue which I could not understand at all, it would not bore me as this does.

The matter of its boring one has something interesting about it. The noise of a machine might get on one's nerves, or the incessant chirping of a bird might; but not in that way, and we should not say that it was insufferably boring.

Somehow, it is boring because it ought to be interesting. At least this is so of a boring conversation (though it might be rather different if you spoke of the boring parts of a subject, in which, say, you had to wade through masses of statistics. Or even the boring work of reading examination papers.) It is partly that I feel I am expected to attend to it (as though it were something from which I *might* learn something); and it only makes me wish she would stop, as I wish in fact that she had never begun.

It would not be boring if I could not understand it. That is true. Although there are qualifications even there. We may think that a man who finds a particular discussion boring – perhaps a philosophical discussion – that he would not be bored by it if he could understand it. If I were to listen to a highly technical discussion of some question in nuclear physics, I should hardly be able to follow a single step; and probably I should stop trying. I might eventually be bored at having to sit here when I could be doing something else. But that is not the same as finding the discussion boring. And I should hardly say the discussion was boring unless I thought I could understand what was being said. Someone may feel that about a discussion in philosophy, just because the questions here are not 'highly technical' in the way that questions in nuclear physics are. In this case, where we say of the man that he does not understand it, and that he might not find it so boring if he did, we mean rather that he does not understand what it is all about, or why it is that people do want to discuss that sort of thing. It is not that he must have a considerable technical equipment before he can know what processes are being referred to. So what about the proposition that he would not find it boring unless he understood it? But it does not rule out the other consideration. Perhaps even my neighbour's babbling would not bore everybody (though I wonder).

This may even be connected with the point that if people are living together, that means that they are able to carry on conversations. The idea of 'having something to say'. As opposed to 'just babbling', I suppose. If he has something to say, then it is worth listening to him. That is not a capacity which you can teach a person when you teach him how to speak.

'Could you understand what he was saying?'

'I couldn't see that he was saying anything.'

There is something important in the connexion between the use of language and ideas: that it is not only needful that there should be a common vocabulary and a common syntax, but that there should be common ideas. Unless there were that, then in one important sense, you could not understand what people were saying. You could not understand the point of their remarks.

Certainly the notion of 'ideas' is a vague one. I mean partly ideas of what is important. Ideas of what is the normal way for life to be carried on. I mean what is developed through discussion. Even the discussion of a football match, I suppose. But especially, ideas that make it possible to carry on a discussion. Ideas which the different people engaged in the discussion have, and through which the discussion makes sense. (These are also the ideas that are developed by discussion.) Perhaps we could even say that otherwise there would be nothing to discuss.

We have the point (1) that if you are to understand the discussion, and so understand what is said in it, then it must have some possible connexion with other things in which you are interested. This is what I expressed at first by 'some connexion with other things in your life'; and that was suggested by the point that you get something from a discussion when you participate in it – and not, in this sense, otherwise – or in other words when your understanding grows in the course of it, and I did not think that was possible unless you say that it contributes to the growth of understanding, in the sense of the intellectual growth of the person in question. On the other hand, (2) unless the different people taking part could understand the discussion in pretty much the same way, there would be no discussion at all.

This is part of what is meant by saying that to imagine a language is to imagine a way of living. The point is that a way of living is not simply operating with a language. Compare what was said earlier about sharing a common life. Which goes with sharing a common history, for instance. But also common educational institutions and ways of carrying on business. The importance of science in a society, for instance. Or, in different circumstances, the importance of religion. Perhaps even things like the importance of 'fair shares'.

Language is obviously part of what there is in sharing a common society or way of life. Perhaps it is the most important thing. But it is not self-sufficient: you could not understand what was meant by carrying on the language if you did not take account of these other things and of the ideas that are connected with them. Ideas about education, for instance. Or ideas about science. Science as enlightenment, and science as engineering. Ideas about marriage and about life. Ideas about the importance of 'naturalness', or of manners and of style. Again I say, 'ideas about'. It is not simply a matter of knowing how it is done. That is why there is discussion in connexion with all the things I have been mentioning. It may be natural sometimes to sum these up as 'ideas about life'. As if all these attempts to understand could be thought of as attempts to understand life. But the point is that they are generally ideas which both (1) have developed through discussion, and also (2) can be discussed. Different ways of judging it. Even a football game.

When two doctors discuss the proper diagnosis of the patient's ailment, this is not a discussion of what is important here – whether you can see any point in discussing that at all, which depends on ideas (including ideas of what is important) which the doctors do not discuss. But in any case, is that the kind of discussion in which you would say that they were trying to understand? They are trying to find the right answer, and time will probably show which answer was right. You may have got something out of the discussion in the sense that you are surer and more competent in your dealing with ailments in the future. But this does not mean simply that you may have learned more, in the sense that you can learn more from an experiment or when you make a discovery. You may have come to a better understanding of what is important in the judgement of diseases, for instance. Whether it is wise to depend so much on laboratory and clinical examination; whether it is wise to be quite so off-hand in dismissing old-fashioned remedies; and so on. A discussion is not an experiment. An experiment can be repeated, and the question whether other experimenters get the same result will be important. It is not like that with discussion. But a discussion is not like a calculation either; and perhaps for somewhat the same reasons. The doctor may not have learned more about the disease, as he might if he watched the course of its development. And yet he may have got something out of the discussion, not simply the conclusion agreed to. If medicine were simply a matter of routine to him, there would hardly be occasion for discussion.

The idea of judgement. Where it is simply a matter of routine, of carrying out a routine which is laid down and prescribed by others, then little or nothing is left to the judgement of the operator. (Cf. the desire for mechanical methods in mathematics and in logic.)

III

Knowing how to read. 'I can understand what is written there.' A great deal of what is called 'using the language' consists in this. (Though there is a difference between carrying on a correspondence, and studying documents.) What is important is 'the relation to reality'. Suggestion that (for this anyway) these other ways of using language must have some connection, direct or indirect, with discussion.

'But why need they have any? Why should not those other practices exist as 'games', without any relation to discussion at all? Can you not imagine a people who only did that?' I want to say: 'Because it would not be understanding what is said.' Somewhat analogous to the way in which a formal game or formal pattern – a transformation of signs – would not be mathematics.

Application: what we do with it. ('Well, that is the use we make of these papers in conducting the business.') What is written there must be something that could be *said*, or has been said. Otherwise it would be nothing you could understand; and it would not be what we call reading it. (The difference between a meeting and the minutes of the meeting. You can go through the minutes: this is not like taking part in the meeting. The minutes cannot make any difference to what has happened. They are just a record of what has happened; and of course you can follow the record. But what about the notion of 'what has happened'? A record of what has been said. What was said at the meeting made some difference there. The record does not. The record still gets its sense and importance from what you may do with it, no doubt. Otherwise it might be just a piece of decoration. Without any other point than that people like the look of it. Like bowing when you leave a room.) 'If it says anything, if it is a statement, then it must make a difference to the way the discussion goes on.'

Compare the difference between what people were doing, and a picture of what they were doing. 'I wasn't there, but I have seen a picture of it.' What is the point of the picture, if it has no relation to what actually happened? Certainly the photograph may be important in various ways and we may have various uses for it. But all these assume that it *is* a photograph.

Of course, there is much that we have to read which is not a record of anything that has been said. I do not mean simply works of fiction. I am thinking of written statements (as well, of course, as letters, reports of what has happened, inventories, and so on). But then the written statements themselves play a role analogous to that of something said in a discussion. If you understand them, then they 'make a difference', rather in the way in which something said makes a difference to the meeting. Otherwise they would have no sense.

Being able to understand, and being able to read. Unless you can understand what is said – unless you can understand the language, in the sense of being able to take part in a conversation – you would not be able to read; you could never learn to read. And the criteria which you would employ to discover whether a person could read or not – do not quite give you what is meant by understanding what is said.

You may be able to read a foreign language without being able to speak it. But not, I think, without being able to speak any language at all; without being able to speak at all. Otherwise, would you ever have any conception of saying something? Would you be able to follow what other people were saying? Would it not be just a meaningless jumble?

It may be important to emphasize the difference between being able to read a language and being able to speak (or write) it; the difference between being able to understand what is said in a foreign language, and being able to speak it yourself. Is this just the difference between being able to translate, and being able to do proses? Doing proses is just translating from English into French, or whatever the language is. Admittedly this is more difficult than translating from the foreign language into English, and it is not so hard to see why (you have not the vocabulary at your command, in the same way; and whereas you may be able to follow a syntax construction, when you see it, this is not the same as being able to decide correctly between various possible constructions; and so on). But being able to speak French is not simply a matter of being able to translate from English into French. It is a matter of, as we say, being able to think in French. To move by taking those kinds of steps, so to speak. It is a matter of being able to *say* something in French. (This often means the mastery of a certain style, as well as of vocabulary and syntax rules.) Why is there more difficulty in being able to *appreciate* differences of style, for instance?

You have to be able to join in conversation with others. That is different from being able simply to render into French a piece that has been set you.

IV

You can speak of the application of mathematics, because what you have in mathematics *is* a rule. And similarly the application of a principle. But 'the application of language' would be queer. The connexion between the different statements in a conversation or in discourse is not the connexion of a rule. That is important. Certainly there must be a difference between a discourse or any kind of conversation, and a jumble of sentences which have nothing to do with one another. Nothing that is said is intelligible unless it does 'bear on' the conversation in the discussion in that kind of way. That does not mean that you could state in a general formula what that connection is. Or that knowing what the connexion is is knowing a rule. And yet of course you are using the recognized vocabulary and the recognized grammar and syntax. In that sense you are certainly 'using' the language in what you are saying. It still does not follow that *saying* something is the exercise of a technique. That is what I want to emphasize.

When you talk about using the accepted syntax and vocabulary, you think of this as opposed to some *other* syntax or vocabulary. (This 'using' is not very similar to using mathematics – where you have a particular technique for a particular purpose. It might be nearer to that if you spoke of using a technical terminology, because, perhaps, you could put things more precisely in that way. But using the vocabulary of ordinary English as opposed to the vocabulary of French, would not be a parallel case.) Anyway, this does not yet explain what a syntax or a vocabulary is. And I doubt how fairly you can do this in terms of *reactions*, especially obeying orders, or in terms of operating an organization.

You could also talk about using words as opposed to using gestures or facial expressions, for instance. If you ask, 'Using them for what?' – this might suggest that they are instruments for expressing thought, or something of that kind. Or perhaps using them for communication – almost as one might speak of using postal services or telephone. The idea of words and gestures as vehicles.

'It still does not follow that saying something is the exercise of a technique.' Being able to compose sentences in that vocabulary and syntax is a technique: the sort of thing that one does when one writes 'proses' in learning a foreign language. And in this the teacher can tell you whether you have got it right or have made a mistake. Perhaps this is a question of 'How you would say so and so'; and you might call that a technique, which can be more or less perfectly mastered.

The question is what that has to do with understanding something that is said. You must be able to understand the connexion of this sentence with others. And that is not something that you learn in the way you learn 'how you would say so and so'. That all goes with the point that you may be able to learn something from what is said.

If you are going to speak the language it is not enough to know how you would say so and so. (We might say: you have to know when you would *want* to say so and so.) You have to be able to do more than execute proses correctly. You have to be able to join in conversation with others. And this means, for instance, that you would have to be able to understand the conversation in which you would want to say that. This 'understanding the conversation' is not like being able to say how you would say so and so; nor like being able to translate. And for that reason, it cannot be spoken of as the application of a technique. We can hardly say that it is the *mastery* of anything that enables you to understand the conversation. And if you show an understanding of it, it is not natural to speak of that as following a rule. And yet the difference between making a mistake here (mistaking the point of the remark, for instance), and making a mistake about a matter of fact, is similar to the difference between making a mistake regarding what an expression means (the rules for its use) and making mistakes about a matter of fact. In both cases, the question of how you would find out that it was a mistake would have a different kind of answer than it would when you were concerned with a mistake about a matter of fact – whether the pipe really did run under the pavement or not, for instance.

Understanding what is said is not quite the same as knowing what it means. Could we put it like that? Probably that would be so ambiguous as to be misleading. If I do not understand the remark, I say that I do not see what you mean. What I want to avoid is the business that knowing what it means is knowing a rule: which is true, but which will not cover the notion of understanding what is said.

CHAPTER 5

Games, calculations, discussions and conversations
(21.6.57–16.7.57)

I

Wittgenstein was insisting that there is no *one* use of language (which would make it a mistake to say that the function of language is to communicate thoughts, 'words and gestures as vehicles', for instance, – although the criticism of that would be also that it says almost nothing). If you talk about the use of language, we can always ask *how* it is used. And this means generally, I suppose: how that expression is used. But for Wittgenstein this meant: give an account of the 'game' in which it enters. And it still seems to me that this does not reach the distinction between an imaginary conversation and a real one. And more especially, it ignores the way in which you can *learn* through discourse. Which is something that has no parallel in games. (By taking part in games you might learn something like greater skill, or how to avoid falling into the errors you committed that time, and so on. The difference between one game of football and another – or between one game of chess and another – is in the aptitude with which you play it. This is not like the difference between one conversation or discussion and another.) Incidentally, if it is a discussion, and not just a battle of wits, then the idea of success does not play the role here which it does in games. This is one of the points which Socrates was emphasizing. One would not naturally speak of one's participation in a discussion as a performance – to be applauded, perhaps. Or if one did, it would be a perversion of the discussion.

Well, but if that is the account you give of 'using' language – if the question of how it is used is the question of its role in the game, perhaps – then I think you have left out what it is that makes it language at all. *And understanding the conversation is not like understanding the game.* In the latter case, it is a matter of *knowing how.* But not in the former.

Playing the game is a matter of applying the skill you have acquired. Speaking a foreign language may be that too. But talking to people is not; understanding them and carrying on a conversation with them is not. You have to know how to say what you want to say; and that is a matter of skill. You could not understand them without that either. But that alone will not enable you to recognize the sense of their remarks, or to reply sensibly to them. (That is not a matter of knowing how the language is used. It is not even a matter of knowing that 'such a remark would generally be made if someone wanted to . . .'. It is a matter of understanding the conversation in which you are actually engaged now.)

'What is saying something?' 'What is making a move in chess?' (Will that do?) If you say that language is a family of games, does this mean that you cannot ask in a general way what 'saying something' is? Cf. 'What is a proposition?' Yet I think that was in some way different – and that the general question about speaking might have sense even where the question about 'the nature of the proposition' did not.

The question of how words refer to reality. The difference that it makes. Not simply that it may lead you to the house or away from it, like the difference between a wrongly marked map and a true one. Cf. 'The difference it makes whether you say one thing or another, is like the difference it makes whether you use one map or another.' That would not be what we meant by the difference it makes to the discussion. And if we are thinking of 'the reality of the discussion' – the difference between taking part in a discussion and imagining one, or even passively following one, for instance – the notion of really saying something: the notion of understanding what is said as seeing the reality of what is said – then the relation of discourse to reality, or the relation of what is said to reality, does not seem to be a matter of 'accordance with fact'.

Perhaps there are two questions: (a) Whether it makes any difference whether you say one thing or another? (b) Whether it makes any difference whether you say anything at all? Whether it makes any difference what you say? Whether anything has any sense anyway? These are not independent of one another. And maybe they even amount to much the same.

We had asked how saying something is different from making a noise. And we had said that when you use words in their meanings – when there is a way in which they are correctly understood – then there is a difference between making one statement and another: between using one expression and another. We sometimes said that this difference is to be found in the way it is taken. A difference in what it means: a difference in the way it is understood. The difference it makes to people; or even the different ways in which they react – in the one case and in the other. (Though there is something inadequate in that, since it is not the actual reaction but the correct one that is in question.)

Once again, this is bringing it close to the question of what difference it makes whether you move one piece or another in chess. And of course you could explain that to someone by explaining the game to him. You might even consider a particular match, and try to explain why that move was brilliant, whereas another would be less so. No doubt this would always come in if you were considering the 'reactions' of the other player. But what makes *that* difference between the one move and the other is not *simply* the different rules governing the use of the pieces.

Whether you ought to be able to set forth the results of every conversation (or dialogue) in a formal or systematic way. As though, perhaps, the discussion were only the rough and spade work. And you ought to be able to sum it all up in a precise fashion. But I wonder. Was this Plato's criticism of Socrates? 'Otherwise it is not science.' The question of the sort of understanding that is sought in philosophy. ('You cannot solve a philosophical problem by any calculus.') Why does one feel so often that much would be *lost* in any such formal statement?

Le style, c'est l'homme.

Hitting the nail on the head.

This is all very important in what you do understand. 'If it is badly expressed, it will not illuminate all. You cannot learn anything from it.'

'Philosophy cannot be just discussion' (with the suggestion that in that case it would be a waste of time). 'There ought to be definite results. *You ought to be able to say what you learn.*'

II

The connexion between the various things that are said in a conversation is not like the connexion between the various moves in a game. And this is important when we are considering the general question of what 'saying something' is. In carrying on a conversation, you do not demonstrate your skill, or mastery of the game. 'Shall we have another game?' 'Shall we have another conversation?' '. . . another discussion?'

The conversation need not always have a point, any more than the game need have a point – in the sense that one would have an answer to the question 'Why are you playing?' Often or commonly a conversation *is* about something, though. It is so whenever we should call it a discussion. And this is what makes the question 'Shall we have another conversation?' nonsense. We might answer, 'Why, we have just gone over that. Have you anything more to say?' And of course in the game there would not be the question, 'Have you anything more to say?' This bears on the way the conversation is connected with other conversations or with things said in other connexions. There is nothing parallel to this in games. The different games have something in common in the sense that it is the application of the same rules and the same sort of skill. If they decide anything, they decide who is the better player; there is nothing else to decide. Nothing 'emerges' in the course of the game – unless it is the skill or ineptitude of the players. And there is no question of having anything to say there. Especially, there is no question of having anything *more* to say. You would not vitiate the game by repeating yourself – that is why we can ask 'Shall we have another game?'

This is why you cannot learn from the game as you learn from a discussion. *And it is also why following the game is nothing like following a discussion.* But that would mean also that taking *part* in a game is not like taking part in a discussion. And this bears again on the question of what saying something is. 'It must bear on something else in the conversation.' That does not mean simply: 'It must be recognizable as a move in the game.' For this latter question, the question whether it was in accordance with the rules would be much more important. Whereas there are not rules of a conversation in a comparable sense.

What makes it 'saying something' – is connected with the sense of asking 'Have you anything more to say?' And it is also connected with the sense of asking you to explain what you mean: of saying, 'I don't understand; please explain.' There is nothing parallel to this in connexion with the move in a game. *Belonging* to the conversation is not like belonging to the game. That I must insist on, and I think it is important. (Cf. 'The unity of the discourse depends on the unity of the understanding, rather than vice versa.' It is a unity of dialogue; a unity of thinking or of life; not the unity of a form. And that is how the different dialogues are connected with one another, too. That is what they have in common; not some form or rule which they all follow.)

We are not always taking part in a discussion when we speak, of course; generally not. When I say 'Excuse me', or when I ask a waitress for a cup of coffee, or when I write out an inventory, I am not even carrying on a conversation. And yet in a way you might almost say that it is something 'like' conversation. Or rather, that if you consider conversation you may see something about these other ways of speaking that would be hard to bring out otherwise. I do not know whether Plato meant that all speech 'tries to be dialogue'. I think that would be a confusing way of putting it. But if we think of discussion as a centre of variation, with other sorts of speech differing in one direction or another, it may help us to see what it amounts to when one calls them all *speech*.

Suppose we thought of language as a 'family' of techniques or a family of 'games'. We need not suppose there is anything – any form or function – that is common to them all. But all the same there is a difference between a game in which we say something and games in which we do not. (Mathematics is a family of techniques too, but we can still ask what there is *mathematical* about any given proposition or procedure.) If you are speaking at all, it is something different from dancing, for instance. It is different even from proper language games, like charades or round games, for that matter. Well, if you are really speaking, and not just playing a game – what is that?

I do not think you can put it by saying that when you really speak you are applying the language differently than you are in a round game. It would be queer to speak of applying language anyway. But I suppose the idea would be that speaking the language is a technique, or a family of techniques, which has been developed for certain characteristic uses, and which may also be given uses that are fairly different from these. But I cannot see how you would bring out what we might call the reality of language in that way. And especially the reality of discussion.

I do not mean that there is nothing of that sort in it – that there is nothing you could call skill or the application of a technique in speaking a language. For it is plain enough, especially in learning a foreign language. You have to learn the vocabulary, and the grammar and the syntax, and you have to learn to construct sentences to say what you want to say, and so on. It is often a question of 'How you would say so and so'; and you might call that a technique which may be more or less perfectly mastered; some show greater skill in this than others.

But if you are going to speak the language, it will not depend just on that. You must be able to talk with other people. You must be able to understand the conversation in which you *want* to say this or that. That is what it would be to *make* that remark. To make that remark is not quite a matter of knowing how to make it. It is rather a question of whether that has any point or sense. That is not something you know by anything like a rule of translation or knowing what the words mean. You must be able to *make* remarks. You have to see how it bears on what is being said. If this remark had no connexion at all with the rest, it would make no sense. But this does not mean that you could give the connexion in a general formula; or that when you see the connexion you see the rule that holds here.

Admittedly there are different kinds of conversations, and I have said earlier that you might be able to follow one and make nothing of another. But this is part of my general point that being able to carry on a conversation is not a matter of knowing how to, in the way that playing a game is. It is not something that you generally teach anyone as you would teach him a game.

(There is something like an 'art of conversation', perhaps. And a person may become more skilled in discussion in the sense that he is better able to hit the nail on the head and keep to the point. This is something like the perfection of style or the perfection of clarity in writing. That is comparable to becoming more and more skilful in playing a game. But you have to learn the game. You have to be told the rules and how to play. That is not the way in which you learn to talk to people.

What is more important is that the connexion between the move you make and the rest of the game – what makes it a move with the knight or stealing second base – is not the kind of thing that we mean when we speak of the connexion of your remark with what is being said; or what it is that makes it a remark, or makes it a sensible remark at all. Belonging to the conversation is not like belonging to a game.)

When Wittgenstein spoke of speaking as *using* language (he some-

times urged us to look on language as an instrument, too) he did not
mean so much using the vocabulary and the rules of syntax you have
been taught, but rather using it in one way rather than another, or
playing one sort of game rather than another. There is nothing
which you could call *the* function of language – to express our
thoughts, or how it might be called – and there would be no sense in
trying to reform the language to make it a more perfect instrument.
But you can always ask what the game is that is being played here,
or how language is being used. If you say something with the
sentence – if it is not a senseless utterance – this is because when you
utter it you make a move in a game.

Would this imply that you cannot ask in a *general* way what 'saying
something' is, because the answer would be different according to
the game you were considering? Wittgenstein's criticisms of the
attempt to give any general account of 'the proposition' would seem
to suggest that. And yet I think the question is not quite the same.
Or should I say that they are both forms of the question of how
words refer to reality? or the question regarding the reality of
discourse? This is what Plato was concerned with, and I think it
might have a bearing on almost all uses of language even if we agree
that there is no general way of stating what the relation of language
to reality is; or even if we agree that it is misleading to ask, for
instance, what it is that language and reality have in common.

If saying something is something like playing a game, then it is
hard to see how we should distinguish between an imaginary
conversation and a real one.

III

Understanding what is said does not simply mean knowing the rule
for the use of the expression. If you thought it did, you would not
have understood what was meant by speaking of a rule for the use of
an expression at all, or by a rule of language.

Perhaps it would be as though you were following rules in reading
music: when you see the sign, you strike this key, and so on. The
mastery of that is the mastery of a skill, of course; and when you
show your mastery, you show your skill. But if you described this by
saying that you understand the notation this would not be the sense
we have in mind when we speak of trying to understand what he
said. Compare also knowing the rule in connexion with the carrying

out of a calculation. Or perhaps generally: knowing what conclusion to draw. Knowing what follows. We can also speak of knowing how to use an expression in mathematics. Knowing what to do with it. As opposed to coming upon a meaningless sign. And knowing how to use a word, especially when we think of colour words, may be something similar.

At a certain point you say that he has understood what you have taught him, and that he understands what the expression means. This is not the same as saying that he can understand what has been said. Or perhaps we should put it: when he has understood what you have to teach him, then he *can* understand what is said. But if he does – that does not mean simply that he has learned what you have to teach him, or even that he can apply that. In a calculus, I suppose you might say that if he knows how to use all the expressions involved, and that if he is familiar with all the procedures, then he ought to be able to follow the calculation. He ought to be able to follow a mathematical argument. But in connexion with ordinary discourse or discussion it is not just like that.

I do not know quite how to make clear the difference here, but I think it was what Plato was insisting on, and I think it is important. It has something to do with the point that you have to understand life if you are to understand discourse.

There is some difficulty in seeing clearly the relation between the general rule and the particular circumstances. I have been suggesting now that you might know the rules for the use of various expressions, and still not understand the statement when it was made. I have suggested that if you are to understand it, you have to see what it brings to that conversation. And if it is true that you must be able to learn from that conversation, then what you learn from a statement on any one occasion is never quite the same as what you learn from an earlier or later statement. And if what you understand is what you learn from it, that would suggest that you can never understand the same thing twice. And there is something absurd about that.

On the other hand, if one places emphasis on the general rule, and if the suggestion is that anything you say here is always something you might have said in other circumstances – then that seems to make it something that is not discourse or is not language at all. That makes speaking the application of a technique. And then there is no reality in discussion. That is Plato's point.

This is important when one is considering the relation of philosophy and language, I suppose. If language really were a technique, then the problems of philosophy might seem to be confusions between different parts of the technique. And it is plain that it is not that. If it were, there would be no connexion between philosophy and scepticism. You should not understand what was meant by the notion of the distrust of understanding. And certainly we could not understand why philosophy should have been thought as important as it has; or why the problems of philosophy should have distressed people in the measure that they have.

Of course there are plenty of circumstances in which a statement may be repeated. 'Will you tell the court what you said to the officer at the time.' 'Will you tell Mr Jones what you told me.' And if I hear you repeat the statement, I do not understand something different from it each time. Otherwise they would never ask you to repeat it. There is the further point that what I understand is something you have *said*, and that if I can understand it, so can someone else. If what I understood were always simply its bearing on the sense of my own life, that would not be so. Well, in that case, can we say at all that what I understand is what I learn from it?

This may have some analogy to the point that if your action is one that can be understood, then it is one that might have been performed by someone else. (Or it is one of that *sort*. We are up against the particular and the general business here again.)

There is a difference between understanding men's actions and understanding their lives. This is clear enough in any writing of novels or dramas. Cf. also the conception of the course of one's life. But we also speak of learning something about life; and this may be what we expect from a considerable novel or play. And this is not just a matter of skilful portrayal, as though the novelist were a specially gifted reporter (or biographer either, for that matter). What we learn from the novel is not simply what the author is able to point out because of his greater psychological insight (though that is important too).

Well now, does that bear on what we mean by understanding men's actions, or by asking whether they are intelligible? Should we say, for instance, that it bears on what we mean by speaking of them as men's actions at all? We might say that unless one was seeking the kind of understanding that we gain from the novelist, then trying to understand the man's actions would be no different from trying to give an account of his movements, as we do those of an animal.

Understanding a man's actions does not mean simply knowing what he is up to, as it does in the case of the cat or other animal. Being able to predict what he is going to do next, perhaps. All this has to do with the fact that men live in societies, whereas animals do not; and with the fact that the actions of men belong to that. Cf. perhaps the idea of belonging to a discussion. Where there is no discussion, there is no society – at least not in our sense. That is why it means something so very different if you talk of societies of animals. Compare the idea of a society and the idea of a conversation. And contrast the associations of animals – for mating and rearing of young, for instance, or for hunting in packs. I do not mean that a human society *is* something like a conversation in which everyone is participating; any more than it is the conduct of one grand enterprise. It would be better to talk of a hubbub of different conversations all going on at once and getting in each other's way. But unless there were the *possibility* of their carrying on conversations, there would not be the relations among human beings that we call belonging to a society (with or without the article) or living in society. Or if you like: unless they sometimes *did* enter into conversation with one another. This potentially is like 'knowing the language'. Being able to speak and understand.

And it would seem as though there must be that kind of understanding among men who live together: as though they must be people who understand the language, even when they are not speaking it. My point is that that is what makes the difference between the sense in which men live together and the sense in which animals do. And it is for this reason that you can try to understand the lives of human beings, in a way in which you do not try to understand the lives of animals. Now the point is that if you can understand their actions at all, you must be able to understand the 'conversation' in which they come or might come. And such an understanding of the conversation is different from understanding the course of an animal's life; or understanding the pattern of it. Actions in the life of 'the' otter. Any otters. (We are not particularly interested in which it is.) This is not what we mean by human actions and lives. If it were, then you might know what they are without understanding them. You can understand the other's actions, in the same way that, if you are an experienced observer of such animals, you can understand the noises that he makes. But you do not understand what he is saying, because he is not saying anything. This is because there is nothing here like carrying on a conversation. There is no intercourse, in that sense. And neither is there anything like trying to understand the conversation. And in particular, there is nothing like taking part in a conversation. There is nothing like discussion. That is the clearest point, perhaps. Actions have not the same kind of generality that speech has. (Cf. understanding what is said, and understanding a happening – including actions of an animal.) Certainly what is said may be repeated. And certainly Mrs Davies may have said the same thing. And what different people understand may be the same. But the 'repetition' is not just like the repetition of a movement or the repetition of a noise. Nor is understanding the same thing, like hearing the same noise. Any more than it is just 'making the same reaction'.

The kind of unity that there is in understanding. As though it were not because they understand the same thing that people are able to understand one another; but rather that if we say them understand the same thing, this means that they are able to understand one another, or carry on a conversation or discuss. This leaves us still with the generality to be accounted for. But it is important to emphasize that the possibility of discourse does not depend upon what we might call apprehension of a common object: as though it were somehow derived from that. This may have something to do with the question whether using 'is' in the same way – following a common logic, if you like – means exhibiting a 'conceptual unity' in what one says, or in the form of what one says.

Our problem is how the unity of understanding – understanding the same thing – fits together with the growth of understanding. For Plato they are inseparable. And yet in a way they seem incompatible. The unity of discourse is not the unity of a technique. Its parts do not hang together in that way. The reality of the discussion and the reality of the calculus – each depends on the way in which it hangs together with the other things in the lives of those who speak the language; but all the same, being able to see how a statement brings something to a discussion is different from seeing how a proposition is in accordance with a calculus. We should not talk about the application of a discussion, as we do of the application of a calculus. With the calculus, I suppose the point is that you do not calculate unless you have some reason for doing so. All this is connected with the idea of *application*. A calculus has no sense except in connexion with some application. The force of any steps that are taken within the calculus derives from the use of the terms outside the calculus.

We cannot say that a discussion has no sense except in connexion with some application. No doubt one can and does talk about using language: 'He got his point across without using language at all' (perhaps by gestures or by facial expressions). There is also the idea of using a particular phrase or expression; and also of using a particular style. But that is rather different from anything like the general notion of using language.

Achieving more perfect understanding is not just like achieving more perfect unity in a calculus. If we say that that makes the calculus more intelligible, then we are presupposing intelligibility and understanding in that other sense – in the sense of intelligibility of a dialogue. The unity of understanding is found in dialogue. This is what makes growth possible – in the dialogue of the soul with itself, for instance, though that is not the whole story. It is also the unity that there is when we have different people participating in discussion or in discourse.

I have spoken of the way understanding grows as the discussion grows. Perhaps we might also say that the unity grows as well. That that is what the growth of understanding consists in. Responsibility comes in here too. Responsibility and making mistakes, and learning. (If we say that an animal makes mistakes, or that he misunderstands, that is something different.) Responsibility when we are considering whether actions can be understood or not. And this is not the question of whether they can be understood from the medical point of view – as any other happenings might be understood. They belong to his life. ('The business of living.') Probably you would not talk of holding him responsible when making mistakes and learning are not possible.

Understanding men's actions, and being able to follow what they are doing. Comparable with being able to follow a discussion. Somehow, the 'way the language is spoken' is subsequent to that. Unless there were rules, and unless there was generality there would be nothing to understand. But understanding is not just knowing the rule. I want to say: it is not that kind of rule. It is not a game that can be repeated. In a way the game is not the same. There is a game which you decide to play. It is played on the same field or board, under the same conditions, and so on. And there is something almost more like an experiment. In a discussion it is not like that.

The nearest that would come to it would be a debate, where the aim is not to find out or to understand, but simply to win. And of course there are rules of debating, and we have skilful debates, and so on. But following the rules of language is not like following the rules of debating. 'Understanding grows as the discussion grows.' There is nothing comparable to this in playing a game. But what about the business of rules, then? Following the rules of the language, and following the rules of the game. The 'point' of the rules is quite different, for one thing.

How the game is played.

How the piece of music is played.

How life is lived.

The point, of course, is that the language might have been spoken differently; and likely has been and will be. But if you do not know how it is spoken, you will not be able to speak, or understand either.

'If you can tell the difference between intelligible discourse and nonsense, then surely you can say what the difference is.'

In a way you can, yes. You can give examples, and explain that if you said this or that sort of thing it would be an intelligible statement, whereas if you tried to say anything in that other form it would be nonsense. You might even formulate certain general rules.

But if by 'discourse' you mean not just a sentence or statement, but something longer, like an argument or an exposition or an account of what happened, then it is not as simple, and it is not so easy to think of formulating general rules. No doubt something can be done in that way even here, and I suppose that is what the rhetoricians did. Rules of composition, and so on.

I think that still would not give quite what one means by the difference between a coherent discourse – one that could be understood – and an incoherent jumble, in which you could find no sense at all. You might be able to go fairly far in explaining why this way of speaking was clearer than that, for instance; or why this is just a plausible appearance of a discourse, which is really waffle, and will not stand examination. I do not think Plato would have questioned that this is important; just as I suppose he might have agreed that the teaching of rhetoric was important, although he would have said that it ought to be controlled through its connexion with other considerations. I dare say he might have admitted that convention has a good deal to do with this too: what is clear and coherent, and what is jumbled; what is easily intelligible and what is not. The point would still be that you understand the statement if you can see what it brings to the conversation or the discussion; if you can see what it is doing there. If we say, 'In these circumstances you can, and in those circumstances you cannot' – that does not seem to explain what the difference is.

What it brings to the conversation. What you can learn from it. Even if someone could say (which I doubt), 'That would be a kind of remark which would be stimulating to make at such a juncture; or the sort of remark that would be pregnant in such circumstances' – I still do not think that would show what it is to be able to learn something from it. And that seems to be what is in question. (This has to do with the question of the reality of discussion, again.)

The mechanics of effective speaking. The mechanics of intelligibility. That does not tell you what the difference is between being intelligible and not being so. This is the question about furthering understanding. Or about understanding altogether. I might know all the tricks of intelligible discourse and still get nothing out of it. I might see why that remark was put in there, for instance. (I might think I can hear the machinery creak. Admirably constructed.) And it might still not help me to understand the discussion. I see why it is there; but that is not the same as saying that I see what it brings to the discussion. There is no growth of understanding. (This is another way of saying that there is no reality in the discussion.) Once again, this is the difference between a wallpaper pattern or a formal game, on the one hand, and speaking the language and understanding it, on the other.

Whether you are able to learn anything from it depends upon the discussion. And whether you are able to learn anything from the discussion – whether that means anything to you – that is the question whether the discussion brings anything to you. (Whether it is something more than an absurd game.) It depends on whether the rest of your life hangs together; whether it forms some sort of discourse. Whether things come together in your life as in some sort of discourse.

'It depends on whether you can understand anything at all.' There is something confusing about that, because it seems to suggest that 'the capacity to understand something' is prior to learning the language – almost as though one would know what was *meant* by understanding something, independently of the way in which discourse and language happen to be carried on. But I do not think that the latter turn is one that we need take.

In fact this is the sort of thing that is studied in philosophy – this 'whether you can understand at all'. It is in this sense that philosophy has been said to be concerned with understanding. (Perhaps also: the sense in which philosophy is the search for understanding.) Once again: the question whether you teach someone anything when you teach him philosophy.

'You ought to be able to say what the difference is between understanding and the want of it.' This is like saying: 'You ought to be able to say what it is that you learn in philosophy.'

'You ought to be able to say what makes language intelligible.'

PART THREE

Beyond Wittgenstein's builders

CHAPTER 6

Signals and saying something
(16.7.57–28.7.57)

I

If you describe a primitive use of language – describe what Wittgenstein's builders do, for instance – you may call this describing a primitive language game. And what seems to be important here is the rules or the agreements – the *understandings* – in accordance with which they carry on this language. They can carry on as they do because they can understand one another.

And yet I would say that when they are really speaking here, it is not like a game, and it is not like the operation of an organization, simply; though I agree that it comes pretty close to that. I want to say that if they are really speaking there, then we ought to consider it in relation to the idea of carrying on a conversation or discussion.

What they say seem almost like signals here. And that is why it seems natural to speak of their understanding in terms of reactions. Their understanding belongs to what they are doing: to the way in which they carry on their building. That is why it is not natural to speak of it as a discussion or as a conversation either.

If one gives orders, and the other carries them out – this is not like the behaviour of a trained animal: because we are assuming, I think, that the roles could be reversed: that this is essential in some way to what we should mean by saying that the subordinate does understand. He does not just react correctly, but knows what is meant.

Suppose we say that either of them *knows* this language. Does that mean just that he knows how to perform certain operations? Just that he can make the correct reactions – as one might who knew a dance? Well obviously it is not like a dance, if only because there is hardly any inclination at all to speak of the application of a dance. When we say that he knows the language, we mean that he can speak it. That is important. When he says something, even in this primitive language, he is in a way making a point. If there is no sense in his saying that there, the other man will not understand. There is a difference between really saying it – 'Beam!' for instance – and just going through the thing for the purposes of classroom illustration. (Cf. learning how to give orders and obey them in the army. Exercises; imagine the enemy is there, etc.) I suppose it would always make sense to say 'I know what you mean,' just as it would make sense to say 'I don't know what you mean.' If you are just acting it out, and not really building something, the idea would be 'that *would* mean so and so'; 'and of course he would then have to hand him the beam'.

If you were playing a game, there would not be that distinction. Of course there may be a difference between a game which decided the championship, and one which is just a kind of demonstration. But there is no difference between what a move means in the championship one. The one is just as real a game as the other. *And this affects what we mean by the significance of the move.* I mean, the significance of the move in the game does not give us all there is in the notion of what he meant when he said that; or indeed in the notion of his saying that at all.

If it is a question of applying a skill, or applying what you know, then that is the same in the demonstration game and in the championship one. But if it is a question of saying something, it is not. That is why I say that 'saying something' is not just a matter of applying a technique, even in this sort of primitive game.

Well, what about saying that the distinction lies in the purpose for which the utterance is made? That you really do want the beam, that you really are building, and so on. No doubt that is important, and there is no more reason to say that in their speaking they are playing a game than there is for saying that in their building they are. But I think that the notion of 'understanding the conversation' has to come in here, somehow. This example is difficult, because here the speech does seem to be just the carrying out of a routine. It seems to be just on a level with the motions that they go through in their building; something that might be perfected by motion study. Once again, like giving orders in the army.

And yet I want to say that you have to understand the point of it here and now if you are to understand it at all. And that is something different from knowing what move follows on that one, or reacting correctly with the move that follows on that one. If it were simply the latter, he would not need to give orders at all. And I think that is important. Cf. 'Give a shout when it is full.' 'Give a shout when you are ready.' And when he does, that is what you were waiting for, and you at once make the move you had to make – turning off the cock, say. But would you call that understanding what he said? Would you say that he had said anything at all? Certainly this sort of thing is on a level with just raising one's hand. And there is no sharp line dividing cases in which we should say that he was saying something from others in which he was not.

But if I know how this sort of construction work goes, I may know that when he has stood that plank up there, I have to place this one against it. And this belongs to understanding the operation of building. (If I am buying things in a shop, it is very similar.) We can call this knowing what comes next. And where it is a question of understanding shouts and signals, there is something different; that is why I think that it is misleading to place the emphasis on the operation of an organization, especially when that is made similar to the operation of a machine, or perhaps to the carrying out of a complex building operation; or the performance of a dance. You can call the latter the mastery of a technique, but the other is not so in the same way. The noises do not just fit into a construction or a pattern, in that way. Nor the signals either. The moves which I follow and with which I coordinate my own movements in the construction are *not* signals. That is important.

I know what follows or what to do because of a rule, or because I understand what is meant; not because I understand the construction, or because I know how the construction goes. It is pretty similar, oftentimes, I know. Perhaps especially in connexion with army orders. As though the noises were just as much part of a construction or a pattern as the steps in a dance are. And yet it is not that. Otherwise an army could never function, could never be manoeuvred about, and so on. The orders here are not even like parts of a ritual. That is important. But the orders of the builders are not like the responses in a ritual, either. And why not? What is the difference?

'How shall I know what to do?' 'I'll tell you when I'm ready.' 'Well what did you give that signal for, if you didn't want us to . . .?' You would not raise that sort of objection in the course of a dance. *There would not be that sort of understanding or misunderstanding of the steps in the dance.* I do not know what signal he is going to give; I do not know just what will follow on the moves he has made up to now. That depends on what he finds. The signal is related to what he finds, it is related to what is going on, it is related to what he is doing. The steps of a dance are not. This is one of the reasons why it can be understood or misunderstood. It is also a reason why the use of them is not simply like the operation of an organization. It is also a reason why we can talk about application here as we cannot of a dance.

But making the *signal* – as opposed to illustrating it for a definition – is not simply the exercise of a technique. You must have learned the technique before you can make the signal or before you can understand it. But making or understanding it is not just exercising the technique. *It is telling you something here and now.* That is what I am trying to emphasize. With the signal he can tell you something. He does not tell you anything by making a move in a game. Telling you something does not mean simply: giving you something you can react to. ('It depends on what he finds.') 'I know what he means.' 'Now I know what he wants.' This as opposed to that. He might have meant something else. There are not such alternative possibilities – not in this kind of way – in connexion with the steps of a dance. It does not belong to the *sense* of the steps of a dance – to be this 'as opposed to that'.

Where you can talk of meaning, you can talk of other things that might be meant or might be said. And this belongs to understanding, somehow. Not that you need think of any alternatives; generally you do not. But understanding what is meant, or knowing what is meant: if you are said to 'know something' then it is 'something' which allows for such alternatives. This is obscured if you speak simply of 'knowing what to do' when you hear it.

It is a sound or a gesture which 'has a use', as we say. And when I say that, I do not mean that when he makes that sound or gesture, *I* have to do so and so. (In any case, I might know what the signal means even when I disobey it, or decide to ignore it.) The idea of something that he tells me. Something the signal means. The signal is not a move in the work of building. It tells me what move to make.

Because it is something that means this as opposed to that – in some way this is joined with the point that it has its sense in connexion with other things that are said: by belonging to a conversation, we might say. Or with things that are being done? Somehow I do not think it is simply that, or not generally. The sense of the signal has to do with what I am waiting for, for instance. In all this the whole work of building – taking the signal together with the actual handling of materials, I mean – is something rather like a conversation. (But without the idea of learning something in the course of it.)

I want to emphasize that knowing what is meant is not just knowing what to do next. That understanding what is meant is not just understanding a technique. The question of what makes it a signal, or in what way it says anything.

II

If I say that saying something, or speaking, is not like playing a game or applying a technique, what am I to say about the primitive language (or language game) of the builders whom Wittgenstein describes? Something of that sort might happen; and then the speaking would seem to be part of the building operation; almost, to be as much a technique as anything else in the building. At least the connexion between this use of language and what we should ordinarily call discussion seems rather thin.

What they say is part of a routine; it belongs to the general operation of an organization. It might be guided by rules which are drawn up and followed. Almost: knowing how to speak is part of knowing how to build. Maybe. But speaking is different from other moves in the work of building, all the same. Each of them has to know his job. Each of them has to know the language too. And that is a different sort of knowledge. If either of them knows this primitive language, this does not mean simply that he makes the correct reactions when he gets the orders. When we say that he knows the language, we mean that he can speak it. That he can *speak*, anyway. He would not understand it otherwise. That means that when the occasion arises he can say something. And then he is making a point. If what he says has no sense in that particular connexion, the other man will not understand. The sense or significance of what he says is not the significance (or sense) of a move in a game.

When we say that the signal tells you something, the point is partly (or often) that there might have been a different signal. That is why you wait to see what signal he is going to give. But also, it tells you something about what is happening generally. And this is the more important difference. For the moves that the different players make in a hockey team might have been different, for instance. And the particular player takes his own course by seeing what the other players are doing. And yet, if I am watching the man with the puck and trying to get into place, his movements do not *tell* me anything, as a signal would. There are signals in connexion with the manning of a gun, for instance. The signals vary as the situation does: they vary with the movements of the enemy planes, for instance. And at first this might seem something like the varying movements of the other hockey players, in view of what the other side is doing. But suppose someone on the gun team gives the wrong signal. 'What did you give that signal for, if you didn't want us to . . .?' You would not raise that sort of objection to what the member of the hockey team did, even if it was clear that he had blundered. It would not be that kind of blunder. Or I may misunderstand the signal. I may misunderstand the situation in the hockey game, too; but that is different. 'What's the matter? Don't you know how to play?' Whereas if I do not understand the signal – well, I do not understand the gun drill, certainly, but learning what the signal means is something different from learning other parts of the drill. It is not simply a matter of learning what has to be done in the drill; it is learning the difference between one signal and another.

Suppose a squad is on reconnaissance. I do not know what signal the leader is going to give. That will depend on what he finds. The signal is related to that; it is related to what is going on. That is connected with the point that the signal tells you something. I do not mean that it tells you what is going on. But the signal is not something you can react to; and this hangs together with its 'relation to what is going on'. I know what the signal means. And that is not *simply*: I know what to do when I hear it.

When he gives the signal, he says something. It is not just like, 'He's moving over there now; we'll have to move up.' When he gives the signal, I know what he wants. This as opposed to that. There are not such alternative possibilities – not in that kind of way – in connexion with the movements which he makes. He might have moved there rather than where he has gone. But 'being this as opposed to that' does not belong to the *sense* of the movement he has made, as it does to the signal. That is what *makes* it a signal. And the signal is not a move that he has made. That is important. The signal may be a particular movement, of course, like raising his arm. But that is not a move that he is making in the manoeuvre, like his crawling to the top of the rise. (I may have had earlier orders to follow him in whatever moves he makes. But when he does make a movement now, that is not giving an order. If it were, he would not have had to give the detailed orders at the beginning.) When I come up after he has moved, I am simply following instructions. But when I follow the signal I am not simply following instructions. The signal *is* the instruction. It is the instruction I am waiting for. When I am waiting to see what he is going to do, I am not waiting for instructions. Perhaps in some cases it would be hard to say whether he was just making a move – just taking up a position – or whether he was giving a signal. But in general there is a difference between learning what the signal means and learning what to do in that sort of operation.

The connexion of the signal with the other things that are done is not that. And this hangs together with the fact that you have to know what it means, and that this is not the same as understanding the construction or understanding the operation. It is the kind of connexion that there is in conversation. Or it is analogous to that. And this goes together with the fact that it means something and that it can be understood.

Understanding what people are doing – that does not mean simply understanding the moves they are making. That is important. It means also 'understanding the conversation on which they are engaged'.

How is this different from being able to follow a game? (Both are different from being able to understand what is happening, in the course of a disease, for instance.) It is partly that the game has no essential connection with the lives of the players. Perhaps this is a part of the reality of what is said. (You might say that the ordinary casual conversation has no essential connexion with the lives of the speakers, either. But in a way it has. The importance of the person who is speaking. And this is not simply because he is more distinguished or more skilful – as a player might be important in a game.) Even if one says that there are other 'language games', those are not about something in the sense in which a discussion is, they do have a reality in some way that is analogous; and this is one of the important distinctions between them and a game. The fact that people are really speaking. Really saying something – even if it be only 'How nice your hat is.'

Doing something or carrying on your life, could never be wholly and entirely taking part in the work of an organization. Just as little as speaking could be the participation in a ritual. The taking part *itself* cannot be described as a move in the work of an organization. Otherwise it would not be something that this person is doing. 'The work of the organization is *about* something.' That has more sense than it would have to say that the game is about something. The work of an organization is connected with other things that people are doing. That is important.

The question is why we say that something is said, that somebody is speaking, in all these various uses of language. And in most of them there is a certain analogy to conversation or discussion. The phrase 'uses of language', and for that matter 'ways of speaking' – these are perhaps misleading here. If we talk of different ways of speaking, in this connexion, it is not a matter of different *façons de parler*, different turns of phrase, or different ways of saying the same thing. (And if we talked about different uses of language, someone might start thinking about what it is that is used. And one might then think of using language or saying something as an application of the vocabulary and the syntax which one learns when one learns the language.)

Never mind the phrases 'uses of language' or 'ways of speaking'. What we are concerned with here is the way in which discussion or conversation is important for understanding language; my point being that if you want to see what language is, then you have to consider what discussion or conversation is. Saying something and understanding what is said go together. And it is in order to understand what saying something is that I think it is important to look at other ways of speaking in their relation to or analogy with discussion.

III

Wittgenstein's builders have a primitive language. And in this language they say things and understand what is said. This language is part of the building operation on which they are engaged. Wittgenstein's suggestion – and this is not quite clear – is that the language is used *only* in connexion with that building. About this I feel doubtful. I am wondering if we should call it language, or even signals, if it were like that. This has to do with the fact that language games are connected with one another. And they would not be language games otherwise. That is important. Compare what has been said about laws of thought: if they were laws that held only of a particular dance – we should hardly call them laws of thought. This is something more important than just the question of whether 'we should call them' that or not.

Building would not be the only thing they would be doing in their lives. Why do I think there would be something absurd in imagining that, if they used such a language in connexion with their building, they would not use a language in connexion with anything else that they were doing? I do not think they could live like that. But my main point is that I do not think it would be a language in connexion with the building. Neither would be understanding what the other was saying. (Incidentally, we might say that they would not be carrying on the organization in building, if that were the only thing in their lives, either.) Taking part in the work of an organization is part of the business of living. But that is not really a 'business' at all. There is no total or all-embracing work within which these others fall. Just as little as there is any all-embracing discussion to which all these are contributions. And I think it would be absurd to suppose that there were. Just *because* taking part in the work of such an organization or business would have no meaning then, I suppose. Just as little as it would have any meaning to speak of taking part in an all-embracing discussion. But this is not to deny that the connexion of language or the unity of language is important. The way it hangs together. And in some way it seems to belong to 'the business of living'.

Wittgenstein once suggested that there might be a language which consisted only of reports and orders in battle. But I wonder if that is so. I do not really believe there could.

Wittgenstein's builders have to live, and they are not always building. If they do use a language in their building, they will use it in other things they do. That is what I suggest, anyway; and I do not mean just that it is highly likely they would. I mean that it would not be a language they were using in their building unless they did.

The skills they use in building may be connected with techniques they use elsewhere too. But there is not the same necessity in that. The different moves in the building form an operation which is much more self-contained. They are connected with one another as the parts of a mechanism might be; they could be the subject of motion study. But the words or signals are not connected with the moves of building as these are with one another. You understand the building operation as you might understand a mechanism. If you understand the words, it is not like that. I want to say that the connexion between the words and the rest is rather like the connexions between the different parts of a conversation. The signal must have a connexion with other things that are said. It is obvious that it must have a connexion with other things that *might* be said: this as opposed to that. Otherwise there would be no point in giving the signal at all; he would not be telling you what he wants.

If they do use a language in their building, they will use language in other things they do. This is because of what we mean by 'using language', or by 'saying something'. Contrast: 'There is one stage in the building operation in which the builder A makes the noise "beam", and the other then hands him a beam. At certain intervals, or at certain junctures, the builder A says "Beam", and B, if he has heard accurately, hands him a beam.' If he *says* 'Beam' – well, for one thing, he might have said something else. He is telling B what he wants. I think this is important: it is the difference between telling B something, and making a noise which is, shall we say, a signal for B to do so and so. If it were that, it would be like a signal which you might give to a dog.

I suppose a dog might learn to obey certain signals or commands only when he was bringing in the sheep, say: and perhaps at no other time obey such signals at all. That is not very likely, but perhaps it is conceivable. Or a horse might learn to obey certain commands only when he was ploughing – perhaps because the horse was used for ploughing and for nothing else. We might say that the horse and the dog know what to do, but not that they know what the signal means. And the point of that is that neither of them could use either that signal or any other himself. I mean, neither of them could use this signal as opposed to that: use this signal when he wanted one thing, and that when he wanted another. And I think that is essential to knowing what the signal means.

I think the builders in Wittgenstein's example *would* be able to do that.

When I give the dog a signal, I do not tell him anything. When the builder says 'Beam', he does tell the other something. I do not mean that he tells him that something or other is the case; certainly not that he is stating a matter of fact. But he is *saying* something. Something which the other understands. We do not say that the dog understands what you mean, because the dog cannot speak himself.

That is why you do not speak to the dog – or not in the sense in which you speak to a man. The dog learns to do this or that when he gets the signal. But he does not learn the language. He does not learn any language. Neither would you say that you were playing a language game with the dog when you give him the various signals. It is not like playing a game, because it is not making a move in accordance with the rules. (That is also why I say that you are not speaking a language – not *saying* anything – when you do that.)

If you say 'Basket!' the dog will go there. But he does not know he is going to his basket; he does not know what a basket is. (There would be something absurd in the notion of a language consisting only of logically proper names.) He might be trained to go to his basket when I clap my hands. (The runners may be trained to start when they hear the gun.) But I am not *saying* anything by clapping my hands in that case. (Could you call it – or would anyone want to call it – a 'private language'?)

For supposing that he does something else and I scold him. Then, even if he could speak, he could not try to justify himself by saying, 'You told me to . . . and that is what I am doing.' He may have given the right reaction, when I clapped my hands. He has done what he was trained to do, and he has done what I wanted him to do. But he has not done what I told him to do because I did not tell him anything.

Whereas the worker who gets the order 'Beam' does know what is wanted and does know what a beam is; and he can justify what he has done by reference to what you told him. It is this business of 'knowing what a beam is', 'knowing what a door is', and so forth, that is important. It goes with: knowing what you have told him to do. And unless he does know that, he has not understood what you have said.

But I do not think they could use even that primitive language there, unless it were connected with the use of language outside the building operation. (The language is not a technique which they apply here.) It is a language in which one of them says something to the other, and the other understands what has been said.

It is not like the orders or signals which might be given to a horse. If it were, there would be no difficulty in imagining that it were used only for this particular job; it need not have been connected with a language which the men use elsewhere in their lives, apart from the work of building.

The ploughman shouts signals to the horse while ploughing. One could imagine that the horse was not used for any other work, and that for some reason no signals were given – it was never called or told to start or stop – in any other circumstances. Even this becomes a little hard to imagine, in the normal course the horse would have to do with human beings in connexion with feeding, stalling, and so on. But it does not seem inconceivable that he should be trained to respond to those orders while ploughing, and that he should not be trained to respond to any other orders in any connexion whatever.

This is because he can be taught to respond to those orders, without learning to understand them (without being taught what they mean). 'He knows what you mean when you say "whoa"; he knows the difference between that and "gee-up"; and he knows you are shouting orders to him. Otherwise you would never bother to shout.'

If you say that he knows the difference between 'whoa' and 'gee-up', the point is that he will respond as you want him to when you say the one and the other. If he started to gallop when you said 'whoa', instead of stopping, then you would say he had never been trained and that there was no use shouting at him because he did not understand what you meant. He does not know what 'going' is, or what 'stopping' is. To know that, he would have to be able to use the language himself. ('The horse has no anxiety over its future, and it is not proud of its past.') We might also say: to know what is meant, he would have to be able to use the language himself.

Here it is important to avoid arbitrary fixing of terminology. It would be natural enough to say that the horse does know what is meant – since otherwise there would be no point in your shouting the order to him. What I am trying to emphasize is that if you say that the builder understands what it means when the other builder shouts 'Beam' to him, that is something different.

I say that the horse does not know what 'going' is – even if he does go when you shout 'go' (or similarly with stopping). If he knows what going is, then he should know what you are talking about, even when you are not shouting the order to him. (This hangs together with the point that the builders must have used language in other connexions.) He should know what an order was even if it were not shouted at him. He should be able to tell you whether the other horse is going to stop or should understand a question in that sense; not simply to stop or go himself when you shout. This is rather important. He should be able to know that *that* is going or stopping. Otherwise he does not know whether he is going or stopping himself, even though he does go when you say 'go' and stops when you say 'stop'. That is why I say that he does what you want him to, but he does not know what he is doing. And in that sense he does not know what you want him to do either. 'He knows what you want him to do' does not mean simply 'He will do it when you tell him to.'

If we say that the builders have a language or that they speak a language, then I suppose B would know whether a third person was carrying out the orders in that language when they were given to him. In particular, B would know what the orders were: perhaps: that he should understand the order, 'Stop when you see the other horse stop'; he would know what was being commanded or asked.

To 'know whether a horse has stopped or not': you have to know the language in order to know that. And I want to say that you have to be able to *speak* the language. But the horse cannot speak.

The main point is, then, that neither of the builders is simply carrying out orders as the horse does. When he learns to speak it, he does not simply learn to do as he is told. He learns to understand what he is told; and that means that he might tell someone else the same thing.

If they are going to say things in connexion with their building, they must be able to speak. If they learn a technique in laying stones or morticing timber, this might be confined to this kind of operation; they might never use it elsewhere. If they learn to speak and understand what is said, this is not like learning something which you apply for this particular sort of operation. May we say perhaps: you learn to talk about something? Even to talk about a beam. I do not mean that you must have learned various sorts of things that might be said about beams. But you do know what a beam is; and you know what the word means, even in other connexions than that of this particular order.

I am assuming that if these people speak the language, then they *both* speak it. Either of them could say what the other says. I think we imply that when we say that either of them knows what the word means. I think it is implied in saying that they have a language – even a primitive one. It is part of what we should mean by saying that the words have a use (and that is something that is different in fundamental ways from saying that the skill in masonry has a use). We mean that this is the way the word is used; and each of them knows that this is the way the word is used. Each of them would know if the word was used wrongly. (So far, this looks like knowing a game. And in this it is not like knowing masonry.)

If you know what is meant, and if you can say things, you can talk. The builder is talking about the beam when he gives the orders. The other understands what he is saying. He understands the order: he knows what the order is. He could give it himself. He does not simply know what to do when he hears it. He knows the difference between giving an order and receiving one. He knows how to talk. (Contrast: he knows how to keep the stones plumb.) This affects his relation to other people altogether. It affects how he lives with them. But conversely: it is because of the way he lives with other people, that he is able to talk here. (That is what I must bring out.)

You could not teach an animal this language. No doubt you could not teach the animal masonry either; and that is important. It is a special kind of teaching; which goes with the relation which men have with one another. You can train the animal to do so and so when you give the command. You can also train the dog to bring in the sheep. But you cannot teach him to lay bricks. You cannot teach him to go on as you have taught him, like that. That is what I mean by saying that it is a different kind of teaching.

('What about nest building? What about beavers?')

IV
(3.5.58–9.5.58)

I may be building a dam across a brook, just as beavers may; and I may run into difficulties – as beavers may too. I may talk about these difficulties. I may talk with myself, or I may talk it over with someone else. If I discuss it with you, you understand what I am saying. If you do not understand what I am saying, you must be able to discuss it, or to discuss questions of that sort. Now is this because you understand how people carry on their lives with one another?

My difficulty with the dam is not a difficulty in understanding *people*, although it may be a difficulty in understanding what is happening there. ('I don't see what to do to keep the water from working round there and undermining the whole thing.') I use language in connexion with it. I point this and that out to you. And you offer suggestions. This is speaking with one another. And the question is how learning – coming to understand what is being talked about – is a matter of learning to join in the life that people live. Is not the use of words here very like the use of instruments? (We might ask: how is finding the answer in words so very different from finding the way to do it by manipulation?)

A shepherd may get into difficulties in herding his sheep. The sheep dog obeys the orders, but he does not understand the order – or not in the sense in which a human being would; because he does not know the language. In other words, because he cannot carry on a conversation. I am trying to see what is involved in being able to carry on a conversation. If the shepherd can talk to me about the difficulties he is having (either talk to me at the time, or afterwards) then I think he must be able to say other things and talk about other things as well. Part of the trouble there is with the question 'Well *what* things?' And I think that the matter of knowing the use of language in personal relations may come in there.

You must be able to speak with people. You must know what it is to speak with people. 'All right, but the builders *are* speaking with one another in their operation with the building stones. Why need they speak in any *other* connexions?' There my point is that they must be able to speak in connexion with their personal relations with one another.

'But why? Why *could* they not learn to speak in that way, just in connexion with the building operation they were carrying out?' Partly because animals could not be trained to do it in that way. Animals could not be trained to give the right order in connexion with the type of stone that might happen to be there. Any more than a dog can make different noises according to whether he wants food or drink. That is not because using the language is something so particularly difficult. Certainly not that making sounds is, for a parrot would be even further from it than a dog. It is rather that using the language is part of a way of living together which is entirely foreign to animals. Or rather, animals do not live together in that sense at all.

What has this to do with the matter of knowing what word to use when you see this or that stone? (Or perhaps with being able to ask what stone is wanted? Cf. the dog's look of 'What now?') Simply that you have to be able to say it in the language; you have to understand the language if you are to do that. Why is that so different from being able to tell the difference between one order and another when it is given to you? This is connected with the matter of *wanting* to speak with people – as a child does, and as an animal evidently does not. And that is wanting to enter into the way in which they live; wanting to join with them – and this means wanting to join with them in speaking. Learning to *do* one thing or another with the stones is like learning to carry out orders. Learning to *say* something is different from that. And for this you need to be able to talk with people. An older sheep-dog may help to train up a younger one. It can show disapproval, it can encourage and prevent. This is something much more *like* the conversation of human beings. But this is the sort of thing the younger dog would understand in other connexions as well – not *just* in connexion with sheepherding. And we could hardly imagine his understanding it there unless that were so. That is about the nearest that the dog gets to *saying* anything. And it had to do with taking that kind of interest in what others are doing and joining in. (The difference between Wittgenstein's idiotic person who could 'follow' the steps of a Russellian proof, in the sense of nodding or shaking his head in the appropriate places, but who could not perform any calculations or *use* any calculations.) Wanting to make yourself understood. This seems to be what is important for the *using* of language. It is not simply a question of knowing which sound will do the trick. That would be a consequence of the former, I imagine.

The question of *identifying* one sort of stone rather than another. The dog may 'identify' something he wants to eat by its smell. But that simply means that when he smells that, he goes for it. It does not mean that when he smells that he knows what it is. And I suppose this is important.

The idea was that the builder who was taught the 'game' was supposed to know one sort of stone from another – and to know that in a *different* sense from that in which the dog does. He has to know which stone it is. And I think this is different from being trained to make a particular noise when presented with it. I think it has to do with 'knowing the role which the stone plays in the life of people'. All that seems to belong with 'knowing what it is'. Or if it is simply a question of 'the red one' and 'the white one' – well there again, he must know which colour it is. And that once again has to do with knowing how those colours, and the difference between the one colour and the other, enter into the lives of people with whom one speaks.

That is why I say that I do not think he could make any such identification unless he did carry on conversations with people. Unless he had come to share in the life of people who did talk about such things. (Cf. Wittgenstein's point about 'being able to ask what that is called'. His point is that this is something that comes late, and that it is something which could be done only by someone who already had a language.) That is true and important, but something of the same holds of anyone who could be taught the sort of game that he imagines his builders to perform. In fact we might even wonder whether the sort of *training* of which he speaks is something which anyone could be given if he could *not* ask the name of such and such. The person would have at any rate to understand the difference between one sort of stone and another. Just as he would have to understand the difference between the other man's doing one thing or another. In other words, what the child learns first of all, when it learns to speak, is to speak *with* people. And this is different both from learning to carry out orders, and also from learning to make noises or movements of the hand or head in the presence of certain objects. It may learn to speak in the course of learning games. We may use games in teaching it. But the main point is that it learns from the people who are teaching it.

This is not to say that the reference to primitive language games is of no help in clearing up confusion regarding language. Especially questions regarding the essential form of the proposition, and so forth.

Certainly this notion of 'the way in which such an object enters into the lives of people', or of the 'different roles which those stones play in the lives of people' is vague, and needs further discussion. It brings in the matter of memory, and also of generalization. And once again there is the difficulty that these seem to presuppose language, and so hardly explain it. But I doubt if that need worry us at the moment. Anyway 'knowing the role which the object plays' is not simply a matter of past association, nor of correct reactions either.

(a) Why do I say that the builders could not be speaking in their special job, if they never said anything in other connexions?

(b) What you say now has some connexion with other things that are said (said in a language). It would not be intelligible otherwise; and would not be saying anything. But what sort of dependence – what sort of connexion – is that?

These two questions are related. The second seems more general. How does the possibility of saying something depend on its being said in a language? ('You cannot say anything unless you say it in a language' – does not really tell you anything. For 'saying something in a language' does not mean anything other than 'saying something'. Just as 'asking something in a language' – or take an order: 'ask me something in a language' – would not mean anything other than 'asking something'. I suppose the point is that a language is something that you speak with other people; and if you say something that is connected – and internally connected – with the intercourse which you and other people have with one another. It is that idea of 'internally connected' that is so often confusing.) In order to see what is meant by 'its being in a language', I had examined the question of what it is that you learn when you learn a language.

When you learn a language you learn to speak with people and carry on a conversation. If you are able to speak, that has something to do with the whole way in which you live, and it cannot be part of something that you are doing just on one particular occasion.

But why should this be? That is what is hard to show. Why *must* there be that connexion with the way one lives? as opposed to the particular techniques which one may or may not exercise? (They do not have the same sort of essential connexion with 'the rest of one's life'. You might say that the particular statements which you are making here and now have not either. You may never have occasion to use just these terms or make these remarks except when you are engaged in this rather special job or game. And yet the fact that you are saying something there, and that you are making remarks at all, does bring a connexion with what you say on other occasions.)

Learning to type and learning to play the piano have no internal connexion with one another. You may say that they are similar sorts of skills and even that you have to practise similar exercises in perfecting them. But it would have been possible to perfect either of these techniques without the other. And it would have been possible to develop either welding or lead burning without the other. Neither is what it is *through* its relation to the other.

But with the music you play, it is different. That *is* music through its relation to music and to singing. Otherwise it were comparable with the noises a child makes when it strums the piano. Or better: on the typewriter you make one kind of noise and on the piano you make another. And the case is clearer still in what you *say*.

But it is not only that. It is not only that there must be some internal connexion with other things you say. And perhaps the analogy with music is limited in this. For with language the matter of understanding comes in, and that brings with it understanding people – which is different from understanding a technique.

What is the difference there, though? What is there in this notion of understanding people? It is not simply a question of understanding 'how you do things', in the sense in which you may use that phrase in connexion with the performance of a particular job. It is not a matter of being able to do what they do, as I may when I learn to eat with a knife and fork. It is not even a matter of learning to kick the ball back when you are expected to.

In learning how to carry out a particular building job, for instance – or weaving – it does not matter much whether there is another man on the job with you or not. He may be replaced by a machine; and then I have to learn a few changes in the technique, but in the main I go on doing what I had learned to do before. Which shows something about the character of what I learned before. I understood what I had learned – and that was one reason why I could understand the new changes. This is because I was not learning to understand people.

You can understand people to a very large extent, and not understand music at all. (And there are people who do not understand much, and yet are 'captivated' by music. But I do not know that this shows much. Nietzsche at the end of his life; but he had learned music before his understanding suffered.) But you could not understand people unless you could understand language, at least such language as we have in gestures. And here I mean be able to speak that language yourself too.

It is because what you say now is connected with your understanding of people, that it is connected internally with other things you say. That is why it is different from the connexion between what you play or sing and other things that have been played or sung. For in the latter the connexion might seem to be more in the form – the 'shape' or the tempos of the melody – or in the composition: the way in which different works are related. I certainly do not mean that there is *only* a formal connexion even here. But in the case of what you say, that sort of form or shape of composition is really secondary. It is not because there is *that* connexion, that when the man makes the utterance here he is saying something.

One difficulty here: that as I am using the phrase, 'understanding people' is no *different* from understanding language – i.e. being able to speak with them. But one reason for emphasizing it is to bring out the reason why there must be the connexion with 'the rest of one's life'. People might be what they are, even if they never built houses. But they would not be what they are if they did not speak. But 'understanding people' can never be simply 'understanding the job that he is engaged on' or 'that they are engaged on'. And their communication with one another is not like the 'communication' that there might be between two or more controlling machines. Reacting to signals, even if they be very complicated signals – that is not what 'telling one another this or that' is. That is one of the difficulties with the suggestion that the relation between what is done here and what is done in other situations is one of family similarity; which it might be if we were considering the relation between various techniques. But so would it be if the communication 'belonged to what they were doing' in the way in which machine signals might belong to the work of machines. Language does not belong to the lives of people in that way.

CHAPTER 7

Language: a family of games?
(24.7.57–7.8.57)

I

There could not be a conversation which was the only conversation ever held. This is not because a conversation is a rule. So it is not quite like saying that there could not be a multiplication which was only performed once; or there could only be one calculation. And yet I do think there is some analogy. The point of the multiplication is that it is a rule. (Otherwise there is no sense in 'gives this result', and so on.) But the point of the conversation is that things are said in it, and they are said in language; and the understanding of the conversation depends on that. (Is there some analogy between this and 'the inference belongs to the language'? Although there it is really 'the inference belongs to the language *game*'. The language is not a language game. And I do not think it will give quite the point if one says that the conversation must belong to a language game. For some reason that is not it at all.) I do not want to say that the conversation is an *application* of language, though. What I mean is that the conversation is connected with others and with other sorts of speaking.

'Belongs to the language' does not mean 'is the case of a general rule' (cf. the question of what it has in common with other things in the language). It is not like 'belongs to a calculus'. It is not like 'belongs to a game' either. It is perhaps more nearly analogous to 'belongs to a conversation'. But that would be wrong here too, because the language is not a general conversation; and Plato may have made this mistake.

'Belongs to the language': there is something of being a case of a general rule in this, though. How are you able to understand the conversation? You are able to take part in the conversation. But this is not *simply* because you know the vocabulary and syntax; because you can do proses. This would be why Plato referred to the growth of understanding.

Someone may reply by emphasizing the varieties of language games. He may insist that speaking a language is not just one thing and that it is futile to look for what makes it language, or what makes it saying something.

I agree that saying something is not just one sort of act or process; and that it would show a misconception if one thought the relation of language to reality must be one sort of relation. But if in spite of their variety we call them all *language* games, that is already something. There are analogies between language games and chess, but no one thinks you are speaking when you make a move in chess.

Speaking is not just one thing. But when you speak, you say something, and someone who understands you will know what you have said.

The question of the way in which language hangs together, or the ways in which the different ways of speaking or different language games are connected with one another, is important if one is to see what speech and understanding are: at least as important as the diversity is.

I do not think that Wittgenstein's account of this in terms of family resemblances is really adequate. And I think it is connected with his view that the use of language is something like the exercise of a technique. (He may have been misled by thinking so often of a calculus as a language; and by the fact that at one time he seemed to think that an adequate language would be something like a calculus.) I think that Plato had come to see the mistake of that sort of view. And in some ways Plato's idea of the unity of language is more satisfactory. On the other hand, if he thinks the unity of language *is* the unity of a dialogue – as though all dialogues were parts of some all embracing discussion, and as though all speech tried to be dialogue – then that is a misconception too.

I do not think you can answer the question of what a use of language is unless you consider this question of the way in which the different exercises of language or speech hang together. The use of language is part of a way of living. But just for that reason, you cannot say that the use of language is part of a skill or technique. You are under a misconception if you try to think of an ideal language as a language for an airless space. You can see what speaking is, only if you see it in connexion with what people are doing. But that does not mean that speaking is a way of doing something, in the way that laying bricks is a way of doing something. Or that you do something with language. Life is not a business or an operation. And carrying on your life is not carrying on a business or an operation.

Perhaps there is some confusion between life and a *way* of living (or form of life). The unity of life is not the unity of a form. Any more than it is the unity of a skill or of an operation. It seems as though a way of life were something you could describe – 'this is what people do' – rather as you might describe a game or a complicated technique; a performance of some sort. 'All these things form part of a way of life.' 'They do that. That belongs to the way they live.'

And then there is the notion of understanding a way of life. And it seems as though understanding language, or understanding what people say, were something like that; or at least that it were closely connected with it. I think there is something inadequate about that. If we speak of understanding *life*, and contrast that with understanding the way people live – that may be confusing and confused in other ways. But it is emphasizing something that is important. Understanding the language *is* something like understanding the way people live. Or is part of it; perhaps the most important part. But understanding what has been said is not the same, I think. 'I know when one would say that. I know what it means if someone says that. I know what he would be getting at.' 'No, in French one would never say that, if one wanted to . . .' Cf. understanding manners; understanding style. Those are parts of understanding the way people live. And understanding is part of them – as they are of understanding language.

Only. . . we have the question of the reality of discussion. (Almost: something which cannot be represented, in the way the form of living can.)

And this is connected with the difference between living and the way of living. It is also connected with the difference between particular and general.

Family resemblances are resemblances among persons: in appearance, for instance. And the point is that there need not be anything like a generic photograph which would give what is common to all the people of whom you would say that they share a family resemblance. There need be no special feature of which you could say, 'This there must be whenever there is that family resemblance.'

Similarly, we call lots of things speaking, and we can find connexions between them. But we need not say 'This there must be, wherever there is speech or language; this there must be, if it is to belong to what we call language (cf. belong to the family).'

The way in which language hangs together: like the strands or fibres of a rope. This goes with the idea that if anyone were to ask what language is, you might give him examples, and then say '. . . and things of that sort'. That would be a legitimate answer. Whereas if you were to begin by trying to give something like the essential function of language: or if you were to try to give a general account of what 'saying something' is – then at best you could describe something to which certain of our uses of language might conform, but others would not. You cannot, so to speak, describe the kind of game that 'language' is. What you can do is to describe various language games, and then say 'and so on'.

I think this is important, but I think it leaves the connexions between the different 'games' too external. And partly for that reason, it does not help us to understand why they are *language* games at all. I think the idea of the *reality* of language is important here. And I think that can best be understood by reference to the reality of discussion. There is something which I should want to call a connexion of understanding. I do not know that this can be quite that idea of the growth of understanding which I have ascribed to Plato. For that comes too near to making all speech – or all understanding of what is said – something which belongs to the understanding of a general discussion or general dialogue. But I would not dismiss the idea of the growth of understanding altogether. It is important to lay emphasis on the growth of understanding *within* a discussion. For this is one of the marks that distinguish a discussion from a game.

'It is through their connexion with understanding, that they are language.' On the other hand, it will not do to *overlook* the analogies with a technique and with a game, either. A language is something which has to be learned. And if a conversation cannot be repeated (except in a record of it: the participation by different people who were involved cannot be repeated), still, a sentence can. That is why it is possible to tell you what was said. If a concentration on the notion of the *growth* of understanding led us to neglect that, we should never see what there is in understanding *what is said*.

'I understand what he said, but I could not see the point of saying *that.* Why didn't he tell us that Napoleon lost the battle of Waterloo, or something?' So in one sense of 'understanding what he said', you did not understand it; or as we say, you did not understand him. It just meant nothing to you.

Discussion and growth of ideas. The growth of culture. If we are going to talk about the connexion of language with a way of living, it must have to do with this. (That is one reason why it is not like the connexion of one part of a technique with more general modes of operation, or with a wider organization.) You cannot understand what is said unless you have some understanding of the ideas with which the discussion has to do, and which it may augment or alter. Perhaps we can talk about the growth of understanding in that sense.

Plato was inclined to say that belonging to the language means contributing to understanding; and that learning the language is the same as growth of understanding. There is something that is wrong with that, but there is something important too. In the first place, there is the question of whether the *conversation* belongs to the language. And that is rather different from the notion of a particular expression or phrase, or perhaps a particular grammatical construction, as belonging to the language. And in this latter, we have the notion, for instance, that such a construction would have no meaning or no sense in another language. It is intelligible in this language (but not, of course, intelligible by itself).

Even in the case of Wittgenstein's builders, speaking the language is something that they do with one another. It is not like putting the stones in place, and that sort of cooperation. That of course was the point of Wittgenstein's analogy with a game. For participating in a game is not like taking part in the work of an organization, in which there is anything like a discussion of labour in the carrying out of some common task. (Such a joint performance might conceivably be done by a single operator; by an operator with a machine, for instance, or by a single machine; in some cases even by a very skilful person. 'We can do it better together.' But that is not something that makes sense in connexion with speaking. What we are doing when we are speaking to one another – that is not something which might conceivably be done by a single speaker. As if the point of our doing it together was that we could accomplish it more quickly that way; or more efficiently.) (It may be that when I have been trying to think something out for myself, I would like a chance to discuss it with

someone else. But that is a different point. The actual carrying on
the discussion – talking together – is not a cooperation in carrying
through something.)

What the builders say is not a game – if only because it is
connected with other things they are doing. It has a point; there is
something that they are wishing to accomplish by speaking like that.
And if it were not for the connexion with the work they were doing,
there would not be any point in their speaking at all. That is what
may make it look as though it were like the pulling of a lever, or
something; though it is not like that, obviously. Anyway, it is not like
stopping and having a little game. It is connected with what one is
doing, as that could not be. But all the same, it is not like the way in
which the different moves of a team on a job, for instance, are
connected with one another. You might say that when that happens
there is not any need for the language. What they do has a point,
and you might say that the work of building could not go on without
it. They would be stumped there. This is connected also with the
other matter that when they speak they are talking about something;
whereas the game is not about anything. Or at least: the different
moves that the players in the game make, their participation is not
about anything. Even if you stop and have a conversation, that is not
like stopping and having a game. Because the conversation has to do
with other things in your life.

It may be that I have been confused in what I have said about the
impossibility of their speaking here if they spoke in no other
connexion; partly because I was thinking of a conversation as having
to do with other things in your life. But I do not think it is only that.
I think the point is that in both cases – both in the conversation and
in what the builders are doing – it is different from a game in that it
has to do with what you are doing. Even in the conversation: when
you stop and have a conversation, it has to do with what you are
interested in, and in a way you could say it has to do with what other
people are doing. It might seem to many people pretty trivial, but it
would be about something. That is a way in which you can make it
look as though it were something like an instrument. And yet, where
there is a conversation or a discussion, it is not that the discussion
does anything – except perhaps that it enables the people taking part
in it to understand. If you say that the conversation has a point, by
the way, it is important to insist that what that refers to is the fact
that the conversation is about something, not that the conversation is

in order to pass the time of day, or in order to amuse people, or anything of that kind.

But how does that bear on the question of whether that could be the only conversation? Note that the conversation is not anything that is repeated, whereas the orders the builders give may be. The fact that the conversation is not repeated has to do with the point that it could not have been the only one. And that consideration does not apply in the case of the builders. Saying something to one another is not like a division of labour. The sort of example that Wittgenstein gave, of one person supplying the information and the other drawing the conclusion or assigning it to a particular pile, or something of that kind – that does make it look like the carrying on the work of an organization. But that is not what the speaking to one another consists in. It may be done in connexion with a division of labour. But the communication, the participation – the both joining in – in the sense of understanding and speaking and so forth: the one perhaps asking the other to repeat what he had said – that itself is not like taking part in a common task.

Even in cases where I say I will tell you what I find, and you write it down; or I'll tell you what I find and you assign it its proper place, and Wittgenstein might want to say that your understanding *consists* in writing it down or assigning it its proper place – no, it is your doing it in this connexion, in connexion with the other things you are doing; and also, *nota bene*, in connexion with the other things you would do if you were asked. Otherwise we should have the mistake of behaviourism. But there is the difference in that an electronic machine could be *conceived* to do something of that sort; and it would not have been understood.

The point all along was that what they are doing has to do with building and with the work of the building. They need not be discussing anything. And it is not like playing a game, just because it has to do with the work of the building (as a game could not). But all the same, it is speaking to one another.

II

If you understand a language, part of this is simply a matter of knowing the vocabulary; and that already includes a good deal in the way of knowing the grammar, in the sense that you have to know the difference between colour words and numbers and names of physical objects and so on; also, the difference between a substantive and a verb (you may not be able to say what the difference is, but you have to be able to recognize it – to tell what makes sense in this way, and to see that the use of a substantive as a verb gives nonsense). And under this heading of knowing the grammar, it also includes knowing the difference between using an expression correctly and using it incorrectly. That is the kind of thing we refer to when we speak of knowing how the expression is used. The difference between the one use and the other: a good deal of knowing what the expression is, consists just of that.

My difficulty is that knowing the language in those ways seems to presuppose an understanding of what language is; or of what an expression or a word is; of what talking is, and speaking; and so forth. Well then, suppose you asked what being able to understand consists in. You would not know what talking and speaking is, unless you were able to speak and understand. That is something you must have learned before you learned any of the differences between different expressions and grammars.

My question is of what is meant by understanding. I do not know that I want to say so much what is meant by understanding the language. But rather the question of what is meant by understanding what is said. If you were to ask which is prior – the understanding of the language or the understanding of what is said – I suppose it would be rather a silly question; at any rate very difficult to answer. In one sense it seems that you could not talk about understanding the language unless you could understand what is said; so the latter seems prior. But someone might say: neither could you understand what is said, without understanding the language, so that is prior.

There may be a danger in trying to separate these too much. And it is interesting that both Wittgenstein and Plato, though in different ways, seemed to try to bring them together. Plato seemed to want to speak of understanding the language as a kind of expansion of understanding what is said; as something that you do not learn all at once. He would speak of it as understanding discourse. And perhaps he would say that there is no sense in talking about understanding the language apart from that. (I am not sure whether he would say that or not.) Wittgenstein seemed to want to put it the other way about, and to suggest that understanding what is said is a matter of understanding its role in the language game. But when he introduces that whole idea of language games, he is getting away from the notion of understanding its role *in the language* simply. And the question of the relation between the different language games becomes one that is interesting and rather difficult to answer. Also, there is the question of the difference between the role in the game – in the particular game that is being played – on the one hand, and the role in the language that is common to all the games. For in some sense there *is* a language which is common to all the games. And if one talks of the role of the expression in *that*, then one wonders what kind of business this is. Is that something like a role in a game, or is it something like a role in a calculus?

I think it cannot be the other, because that is not the way in which the different language games hang together. And in any case, if it were, then it would be very hard to find any connexion between the role in the language and the role in the particular language game. They must be connected in some kind of way. There cannot be that sort of division. (I have an idea that is the whole question of the relation between the particular and the general.) The connexion between the remark and other things that are said in the conversation is not of that sort: it is not the connexion of a rule. And the connexion of this particular game with the others is not either. (Cf. the criticism of the account of their relation in terms of family resemblance.)

For some reason, I do feel the inclination to treat understanding the language as a kind of extension of understanding what is said; and possibly as an extension of understanding what is said in a discussion or conversation. Otherwise there is the difficulty of distinguishing between understanding the language and understanding, say, a formal game. That would be a matter of knowing what to do with the various marks on paper, if you like. (And here the question of the *force* of the judgements, 'correct' or 'incorrect' would come in. 'That's the way to do it' or 'That's not the way to do it'. But it is not only that, when you just cannot find any sense in what the man has uttered; or even when you say it is plain gibberish. Or again: when you say yes, you can understand that. That's the sort of thing it makes sense for a human being to say.) Knowing what to do with the marks – or with the sounds – would not be language, any more than it would be mathematics for instance. The point is that the difference between correct and incorrect should be a difference between what makes sense and what does not. And if you are to understand what *that* means, you have to understand what conversation is or what speaking is.

On the other hand I suppose one of my chief questions was what the difference is between a conversation and a meaningless jumble of sentences. That was what seemed to lead on to the question of understanding altogether. The growth of understanding. And to the question of scepticism, the distrust of understanding and the question about the possibility of discourse and the reality of discourse. The objection against any formalist treatment of what language is, might be similar to the objection against the sophistical treatment of language as a technique.

The objection is not quite the same in connexion with mathematics as it is in connexion with language. (Which is perhaps something that goes with the idea that mathematics is a part of language.) When you are asking what it is that makes it mathematics, this has to be answered in connexion with the way it is used in the language. And one has to lay emphasis on the connexion between the mathematical propositions and their application. The connexion between the conceptions that are employed in mathematics and the use of those conceptions outside mathematics. Whereas if it is a question of what is meant by saying something or by language at all, it is not like that.

I have put the contrast between speaking the language and doing mathematics, in the idea of the contrast between doing mathematics together and speaking together. In mathematics you are following a rule, but that is not like saying something to somebody, or trying to understand what the other person has said. When you understand the calculation, and understand what follows from it, that is not like understanding what has been said. I suppose one might emphasize here that in mathematics you do not say anything.

Thinking about an organization seems to be connected with thinking about a calculus; or thinking of the analogies between grammar and a calculus. As though, almost, ideally the differences between what is said were grammatical differences. And then you speak of the different 'roles' of the statements.

Somehow, that seems to leave out the carrying on of the language with one another. It seems to leave out the way in which it is something that people do with one another. And in that sense it leaves out the character of the language altogether. To some extent you take account of that when you compare it with a game. But then you leave out the reality of the language, the reality of the discussion, the fact that you are talking about something.

Even if one talks about the different roles that sentences play, that enters in connexion with the idea of the different roles in the language; and the differences between what is said as being accounted for by the different roles in language – almost different grammars. Whereas what I am concerned with is, if anything, the different roles in the conversation. Of course the different roles in the language, or the different grammars, seems to have a parallel here in something like the different roles in the work of building. And that is on the analogy of the division of labour.

But even if that did anything to account for the different meanings of what is said – and in a way it may: I do not want to question that – all the same, the fact that it *is* something that is said at all is not accounted for in that kind of way; and the fact that they are speaking together is not accounted for in that kind of way.

You might say that the role in the language is something you recognize if you know the language, or if you know the language well enough. And if you are concerned with the role in the discussion, then you have to be able to follow the discussion, you have to be able to understand the discussion. And *prima facie* that seems different from being able to understand the language.

How does all this apply to the primitive language of the builders, though? Ought we to distinguish between the roles of the remarks they make – the remark 'Beam', etc. – the role of such a remark in the language, and the role in the work they are engaged on? I have an idea that one should. And this may be connected with the notion that the language is not confined to that particular piece of work.

Suppose one of them at one time gives an order, and at another time asks a question. Would one call that a difference in the role that it plays in the work of building? I do not think one would. One might talk of it as a different role in the language, even a different role in that primitive language. Only, this kind of primitive role is independent of the particular work on which they are engaged. If one talks of a different function, well it is not a function in connexion with that particular piece of work, necessarily. And if it can be understood there, I suppose it can be understood elsewhere.

I want to say almost that you bring something to the conversation. This has to do with the fact that there are people taking part in it.

That is one of the differences, I think, between saying things in the course of their building, and giving orders to a horse or a dog; because they do not bring anything to that. Well, do the builders 'bring anything' in what they say? If the sense of what they say is confined to their building operation, then you might ask, 'What is it that they are bringing to it?' And yet I think it cannot be put quite like that. Bringing something to the conversation – that is the sort of thing you do when you begin, 'In my opinion . . .'. In a conversation there are various points of view. You might also say that that is the point of having a conversation. Whereas in the case of the builders, the differences are almost like the different roles that they have in the organization. And yet it is not without some sort of analogy to the 'In my opinion . . .' case. For the one builder tells the other something. Otherwise there would be no need for him to say anything. There is almost something like judgement entering into it. Where it seems different from the conversation, is that what he says is what anybody would say in these circumstances or in that position. He does not bring his opinion or his judgement into it in that kind of sense (does not offer his opinion, or tell you what he thinks).

But he is not *just* someone in that position on that job. This is the point that they could not be leading the lives of human beings at all, if their life consisted simply and solely in performing the different functions in that job. Then they would be machines. And I think they would not be able to speak or tell one another anything, any more than machines could. It would be like having a bell ring automatically (as the bell on my typewriter 'tells me' when I am nearing the margin of the page). I dare say that in that particular building operation, what they say might have been taken over by some sort of automatic control, some sort of automatic signalling, if you like. But then that would have been different from having the man say something. There would not have been the possibility of making a mistake in the same kind of way. If you found that the machine was not registering properly, you would look to see what was the matter with it; but it is not like that with the human being. You may want to know 'What on earth are you trying to do? What do you make that kind of silly mistake for?', and so forth, but the machine does not make a silly mistake at all (even though it may be registering more 'wildly' than the man is). That difference is rather important.

That is what I am trying to bring out when I emphasize the

difference between their understanding one another and their simply reacting. It is not simply that the one is trained to react when the other one makes that particular signal. For if that were so, it would be on all fours with what the various machines might do. 'Machines controlling machines.' 'Instead of men minding machines we have machines minding machines.' (If the one builder says something to the other, he is not simply 'minding' him – as he might be minding a horse, in giving orders as they are needed.)

There is a considerable difference – between men minding them, and machines minding them – as far as this business of speaking and understanding is concerned. If they do say things to one another, if they have anything like a primitive language, well that is something they do with one another, which is unlike the coordination of different machines or different controls on the job. That machine does not tell anyone anything – does not say anything: that is the important point here. Whereas the other builder, no matter how primitive the language, does say something. And our question is regarding what that means, what that comes to.

If you want to bring out what the difference is between a man's saying something and a machine's making a noise or reacting, you have to do it in terms of what the man might do or could do or would do if you asked him other things. That is one of the principal reasons for saying that it would not be language, *it would not be saying anything, if this was the only thing he ever said* (or could say?). I think that is important; just as important as this would not be a multiplication if that were the only occasion on which it was ever performed.

The difference between a man's playing chess and a machine playing chess. The man is not set to play chess. He can leave the game and do something else, without having any particular adjustment made. And that goes with the fact that he brings something to the game. He is somebody with whom you can play. Which I think belongs with the conception of playing at all. And there is some parallel to what we were saying concerning the conception of speaking at all. If you play chess, I suppose it is not simply a matter of being able to guess and reckon possibilities and probabilities and so forth. It is also the fact that you are playing with a particular opponent. It would not be a game of chess otherwise.

Has this anything to do with the reality of discussion and the way in which different remarks are connected with one another? I think it has. These connexions depend upon the fact that people know the language, and the connexions also with other things that are said in the language. The remarks in the discussion are not connected with one another in the way in which the moves of the machine are. It is not a mechanical connexion, nor a logical connexion either.

Once more: if he says anything here at all, then that cannot be the only thing he says. There is nothing quite parallel to this in the machine, because this is connected with the fact that he is saying something here at all, that must be connected with other things that he might say, for instance, and also others that he has said. That is *not* quite the same point as that he is saying this rather than that: 'beam' as opposed to 'bracket' or 'brick' and so forth. And yet I think it is closely connected with that. And that latter has to do with the fact that language 'allows for' other possibilities. If you can say anything at all, then there are other things which you might say. Otherwise you are not telling anyone anything in what you say. And that is connected with the fact that he brings something to the conversation.

The reality of the discussion, and the reality of the discourse depends on the fact that people are speaking it. It depends on the connexion with life, and in that on the connexion with what they are doing. That I would certainly never question. On the contrary, the only question I have raised concerns the sort of connexion that it *has* with what they are doing.

It is because things are *said* in the discussion – because the people are talking about something – that it is possible to learn something from the discussion. Whereas it is not possible to learn that way from watching people observing rules – as one might watch the traffic, or a dance or even a game. There is no parallel to a discussion in any of that. This goes with the point that what you say is connected with what you are doing, or with other things in your life. It is not the motions of the discussion itself that are important.

CHAPTER 8

Understanding what is said
(7.8.57–29.9.57)

I

Discussion, language, is connected with people and with what they are doing, and with the lives they have led and are leading. (Both of those seem to be important.) It will not do simply to say that it is connected with a *way* of living – with how people live – or with a form of life. If they have a language, then they have a common life, in some sense; common ideas. But the point that they engage in conversation is more fundamental – is fundamental to that. You cannot say that it is because they have a common life that they are able to engage in conversation.

Unless you do see what the connexion is between language and life, you will never see what understanding language is. What Wittgenstein's builders say: understanding that. It is because of its connexion with the rest of the language that any of their utterances is connected with what they are doing.

Philosophy and language. Language as discourse, and understanding language as understanding discourse; understanding what is said.

I can imagine someone's saying that the phrase 'understanding what is said' is ambiguous, since in one sense you can understand what is said if you can translate it, even though you may get nothing out of the remark at all. The connexion of understanding with discussion (seeing the point of the remark). And the connexion between discussion – getting something out of the discussion – and the growth of understanding. It is that notion – 'the growth of understanding' – which bears difficulties that are the matter of philosophy. These enter with such questions as 'Understanding *what?*' The possibility of language – or the intelligibility or the sense of language – depends on the possibility of understanding. Or perhaps: on the reality of understanding. This is what is questioned in scepticism.

Suppose one asked what language is concerned with, or what discussion is concerned with. Perhaps that would have no sense. But if there were any, it would probably be that it is concerned with understanding. Almost as though one might say that the point of language is understanding. Even when one agrees that understanding is not just one thing – that there is a difference between understanding mathematics and understanding poetry, for instance – that answer might hold. Would there be a puzzle about the *connexion* between understanding mathematics and understanding poetry, though? This is the question about 'belonging to a language'.

The point that there are no principles of language or discussion, in the way in which the principles of logic underlie the possibility of investigation. There is no single principle on which discussion proceeds, and no fundamental form either. If we are interested in the possibility of language or the possibility of understanding, well that does not mean that there is something (some principle) which the possibility of language depends on. We cannot say that there is something which is fundamental to all discourse. If we said that the understanding was in some sense fundamental to discourse (and I would not recommend such a remark) that would mean something different.

The question of understanding the language can be a real enough question: you want to know whether the person understands the language or not. To do that, you may want to test him. And in that, you may try to find out whether he understands what is said in a particular connexion. But that is what is done more or less *in* a game; in a test, in something artificial like that. And you are getting away from the reality of language, the reality of discussion, and the reality of understanding.

If you understand the language, you can understand what people say. That is trivial, but it should be remembered when we are inclined to distinguish between understanding what is said and understanding the language.

If you are to understand what is said, you have to understand the language. That is certainly true. What is hard, is to see clearly just what the connexion is there. It becomes misleading if you say that if you want to understand what is said, you have to understand its role in the language, or something of that sort. Wittgenstein was moving away from that when he said that you have to understand its role in the language *game*. That introduced important changes.

Still, you could not understand the language game unless you understood the language, because understanding the language seems to *be* understanding what is said. And that makes it look as though the sentence were a tautology. Obviously it is not. Seeing the sense of a remark; knowing whether a remark makes sense. Seeing that a conversation or a discourse hangs together. The difference between that and a jumble of meaningless sentences. None of that is a matter of seeing that the remark is in accordance with the rule; or something like a move in accordance with the rules of a game, even. I think it is also somewhat misleading if you say that it is a matter of seeing what the man is trying to do with it; as you might see what the chess player is up to, when he moves the pawn there. It is not quite like that when you see the point or sense of the remark. Here the point that the remark is *about* something comes in again. (Cf. 'The point of the conversation is what the conversation is about.')

The difference between what makes sense and what does not: this is not just the difference between what is in accordance with the rules and what is not. The connexion between the remark and the rest – what makes it a coherent discourse and not a meaningless jumble – that the connexion is not a matter of accordance with a rule. Speaking the language is not operating with the language, as you might talk of operating with a calculus. Neither is understanding the language anything like understanding a calculus. That goes both for understanding the language and understanding what is said.

It looks as though this problem of what we mean by belonging to the language is more puzzling than it seemed at first.

If you are to understand what is said, you have to understand the difference between one word and another, and the difference between one grammatical construction and another, or one grammatical form and another. And this may naturally be described as a difference in the way in which the word or the construction or the expression is used. Therefore it might seem natural to speak of the difference between the two words or the difference between the two grammatical forms as a difference in role.

That might be important, in connexion with the point that what you say is always 'this as opposed to that'. You use one word or one form rather than another; and if you were not doing that, you would not be saying anything at all. Perhaps that would lead someone to say that if it has any meaning, it must have a role of some kind.

But that does not help you to understand what it is to be a remark. And in a way, it does not help you to understand what it is to be that particular remark either. It does not help you to understand what it is for people to talk to one another. I am not sure how far you can give anything like an account of that. But you certainly have to refer to it and emphasize it. And the point is that the reference to the different roles in the language – if that is what we are going to say, and I do not like that – if we talk simply *about* different words or different grammatical constructions, it is better, it does not add anything if you talk about different roles in the language – is certainly not like different roles in the language game. If one is talking about different roles, one may have in mind something like the work of an organization. For some reason, Wittgenstein thought that that was very important. I suppose his idea was that different grammars or different sorts of things that are said can be understood on those lines.

Compare Wittgenstein's earlier statement that to understand a proposition is to understand the language. This seemed to mean that you had to understand the use of that sentence. And that meant – it was rather like saying that if you are to understand a proposition in arithmetic, you have to know the arithmetic of that proposition. If you want to know what it means, you have to know how it enters into the other calculation. And in that sense, what to do with it when you come upon it in connexion with other calculations. It does not mean, of course, that you have to go through all that. But nevertheless, I suppose if you wanted to test someone's understanding of it, that would be the sort of thing that was relevant. That seems to have been the kind of thing that he had in mind in saying that to understand a proposition is to understand the language. And that seems to me confusing.

It seems to me that it is true that you cannot understand what is said unless you understand the language; and furthermore, that if you ask what is meant by understanding the language, well it is a question of being able to understand what is said. But you cannot understand what that is (being able to understand what is said) by reference to the analogy with arithmetic, or by reference to its role, or knowing what to do with it, or how it behaves in connexion with other propositions in the language and in the calculus and so forth.

The point is that if we think of different roles in the calculus, then that is misleading as far as understanding the connexion between the different things that are said in speaking the language. They are not connected like parts of a calculus. Obviously the difference between this word and another that I might have used, or this particular form of speech and another that I might have used – supposing even that one could say that the connexion between those two is like the connexion between the parts of a calculus – it would still not be true that the connexion between the things that I am saying, the things that are said by the people who are carrying on the language, or with the things that I have said earlier or may say later – that that is anything like the connexion between the parts of a calculus. And it is not like the kind of connexion between the expressions in virtue of their different roles either.

But I do not think we can describe even the connexion with the rest of the language in that way. There is the way in which my remark in the discussion about capital punishment is connected with the other things that the people who happen to be engaged with me in the discussion are saying in connexion with what I have said and will say, and so forth; its bearing on that particular discussion.

That cannot have been the only discussion that we have been engaged on. And what we say there has connexions with the rest of the language; the discussion has connexions with the rest of the language too. In some sense or other, the discussion belongs to the language, otherwise it would not have any point, and so on. That is important. And it is something which I was trying to illustrate in connexion with Wittgenstein's builders by saying, for instance, that if you wanted to know whether any of them understood what was said – whether he understood the order – if you wanted to know whether he understood what he was saying, and was not simply repeating it like a parrot (the distinction between a person and a parrot is important here) you would find that out by reference to other things that he has said, and so forth. If he says something it cannot be the only thing he ever says. That is important, and it is connected with the point that people say things and that machines do not. So what they say here is connected with other things that they say, and it is connected with other things that other people say (I think that is important anyway). And that this *discussion* is connected with other things that other people say, and in that kind of way belongs to a language.

This may be what brings in the notion of common ideas. The ideas we live among.

The connexion with other things that we the participants say, or might say, and the connexion with other things that are said. The idea of the application of the conceptions that enter into mathematics is analogous to this. The words that we say here and the words that we use here have connexions in other circumstances. That is why they have the significance that they do here. Otherwise we should not be discussing anything at all; we should not be talking about anything.

But the idea that you are 'saying this as opposed to that' is important too, although it is not quite the same. And if you could represent that matter of alternatives, and connexions of meanings, and knowing possibly even what follows logically, – that would all seem to belong together there. But what we mean by the connexion with the rest of the language, or belonging to the language, is not only that. There is this other kind of connexion, which is much more analogous, I am suggesting, to the connexion between the various remarks that are made in the particular discussion that we are carrying on. If I know what you mean when you tell me that the towel has a red border, then I know the difference between red and blue. And this is important in the consideration of what it is that you are telling me. But the question of what it is that I understand, or whether I understand your remark, is not to be identified with that.

The unity of the language is not the unity of a system. It is not the unity of a game either. It is the unity of a common intelligibility; that is all. We can understand one another; we can understand what is said. The language hangs together.

The unity of the language is what makes it possible for people to understand one another. Or should we put it the other way about? Perhaps that the fact that people can understand one another is what we mean by saying that they are (still) speaking the same language? The 'still' in parenthesis there – for the statement would have held either with it or without it – brings out the connexion or almost identity of sense in saying that people have a common language, and of saying that when they speak in this way or in that they are still speaking in the same language. If you understand the one 'game' you should be able to understand the other. 'I am not speaking a foreign language, after all.' The unity of the language is the presence of some sort of common intelligibility. The way you can pass from one part of it to another.

Would that not be the sort of test that one would apply? There would be a common vocabulary too, of course. I suppose one might employ the same words – if you asked for a fairly extensive list of the words belonging to the language, you might be given the same list – and yet they might have different meanings. In a limited way this happens in some codes.

So how do you know whether they *do* have the same vocabulary now? Once again: how do you know they are speaking the same language? Certainly the presence of the same sounds and printed words would be a presumption that they were. But put it the other way about, then: what would make you conclude that they are *not* speaking the same language? 'You couldn't make anything of it. Gibberish.'

We have not a common language – the people who speak that and the people who speak as we do, i.e., when they do that, they are no longer speaking the same language. And it does not really matter whether they are the same people or different people. I think this is important for the conception of 'belonging to the language'. 'If it belongs to the language, it makes sense.' Objection: nonsense also belongs to the language.

Language is something that people speak together. That must come in again. If the people speaking in that way, and the people speaking in this way, are speaking the same language, then they must be able to speak together. That is prior to any conception of 'having the same vocabulary'. I suppose that is why I do not want to say that belonging to a language is being part of a complex institution; any more than it means belonging to a system.

What about the point that if you say something it must belong to some language (you must say it in a language). It cannot simply belong to a technique, or to some particular sort of work like building. Could the language be something which those two builders had *only* with one another – in spite of the fact that they carried on their lives in connexion with other people as well? That is what makes me wonder whether you would say that they were speaking at all, if they did it only in this connexion. (Any more than you would say that they were living human beings if they never did anything except take part in this sort of building operation. The building operation belongs to their lives. But their lives are not comparable operations.)

People have spoken of language as an institution. That would make it comparable with marriage, with family life, with parliament and with money, I suppose. You can describe how an institution works. And so one might think one ought to describe how language works; though it seems rather queer to speak like that.

Suppose one were to compare language and money; compare speaking and making a payment, perhaps. If you say something now, it is connected with other things you might say, and with other things that other people say. Similarly, if you make a payment, that is connected with other transactions: otherwise it would not be a payment. And so you might say that it is a payment only in an institution – the institution of money. (Compare also the conception of weighing as an institution, for instance.)

And yet this treatment of language seems to make it too external. As though people might carry on this institution without understanding. Or at any rate, without the sort of understanding that we have when you understand what someone says. It would make it too much a matter of understanding how the business is carried on; or understanding a game or a dance (cf. even understanding a ritual – though perhaps one would not speak of understanding there). Almost like knowing how to find your way about in it. Compare having a knowledge of the moves of the society in which you are living (Sitten und Gebräuche (morals and customs)). Then you will know how to get on with people, and you will avoid doing the wrong thing. Knowledge of *how* people speak might be something like that. Knowledge of local idioms and mannerisms, for instance. But that is not what you understand when you understand what they say.

If people *are* speaking, then no doubt they develop their own moves. And languages change from one age to another; and so on. Languages can be translated, though. What is said in one language can be translated into an equivalent statement in another. This is made possible – so the suggestion would be, I suppose – by the way in which what people say is connected with the way they live, or with what they are doing. This is one of the considerations which may have led people to speak about the *role* of the statement: it might have the same or an equivalent role in the lives of people who spoke one language and in the lives of those who spoke another. So it is possible to 'say the same thing' in another language. That is obviously an extremely important notion, although it is very hard to give an account of it.

I do think the conception of *learning* is important in this connexion; much more important than that way of putting it allows. Important for the notion of saying something, as well as for the notion of understanding. And here I think it is the notion of learning that goes with that of learning from a discussion – getting something out of a statement. That is different from learning what people do with it or learning what is done with it. One trouble with the emphasis on institutions and moves is that it neglects discussion. And in that way I think it neglects what it is for people to talk together. A person does not learn anything when he makes a payment. Or does not learn anything when he receives a payment.

It is in that way that language is differently related to life. And that understanding what people are saying is not like simply noting what they are paying, or taking account of the payment made, or anything of that sort. Just because one does learn from it.

You can see the difference between speaking a language and exercising a skill, when you see that people speak with one another. There is something they are talking about. That is why it is not a game. You would not know what talking is, unless you were able to speak and understand. And you must have learned that before you learned any of the differences between various expressions and grammars.

Is there a difference between knowing the language and knowing how to speak? It would be confusing to say that knowing the language is prior – unless you are thinking of speaking a *foreign* language. I am inclined to treat understanding the language as a kind of extension of understanding what is said. For it is not like understanding a formal game. That is why it is not just knowing the rules for the use of signs. The difference between 'correct' and 'incorrect' in a game or a dance. But if you can speak, you know the difference between what makes sense and what does not. And how do they become familiar with *that* difference? (By learning to speak *with* people, I think. And once again: this is not learning to play a game with them.)

The reality of language. The reality of discussion. You say one thing rather than another (otherwise you are saying nothing at all). 'So what you say, has a definite role in the language. That is what distinguishes it from something else you might have said. And it is through knowing this role in the language that it is saying something; and that it can be understood.' Compare various propositions in a calculus. 'What makes it this proposition.' 'The meaning is in the technique.' But in a calculus you do not say anything.

Suppose you do account for 'saying one thing rather than another' in that way, you have not shown what it would mean to say that you were *saying* something in either case. (The difference between saying something and doing a calculus, for instance.) Nor would you have shown what it is for people to speak together. I think those are really the same point. (If you answer, 'It is saying something because it belongs to a *language*', we are back where we were.)

If you understand French, you can read French, and you can follow what the man is saying. That is not like following a discussion. Learning a foreign language may be something like learning a game. But in a conversation you say something, you tell the person something. And there is not anything parallel to that in connexion with a game. In a conversation there are various people, and various points of view. That does not mean: various roles in an organization. 'What the builder says, is what anyone would say in those circumstances and in that position.' But the builder is not *just* someone in that position on that job. They can take part in the work of building because they can do other things. Otherwise they are part of a mechanism. And they could not say anything or tell one another anything, any more than parts of my typewriter can. The builders talk *with one another*, even in that primitive language. And that is not like the coordination of controls in a mechanism.

III

Someone might ask, 'Well, if you are going to talk about the language to which they belong, well what *can* you mean except the set or system or collection of grammatical structures, or, as Wittgenstein would have put it, of various language games?' I do not know whether anyone would suggest that that is similar to the notion of belonging to a vocabulary, for instance. But in both cases, whether one is talking about grammatical structures or vocabulary, the more fundamental idea seems to be that of having a language and speaking together. (Cf. what I said elsewhere about 'having the same vocabulary'. I do not know whether that needs revision in view of what follows now.)

You might say that the thing to do in investigating this is to consider what is meant by 'learning to speak'. Because I have suggested that there is some fundamental sense of 'learning the language' which is pretty well identical with that. You can speak with people if you *have* a language. 'Learning to speak' and 'learning to understand people' – those seem to go together. And I have been suggesting that is something which is different from learning a game.

In support of Wittgenstein's view, consider the case of a child who learns two languages pretty much at the same time. A child that is brought up to speak Welsh with its parents when it is alone with them, will very soon pick up English if there are English people coming to the house. And what is interesting is that the child seems to know the difference between speaking English and speaking Welsh, and does not to any great extent mix up the two languages. And, further, it knows the difference between talking English with its parents and talking Welsh with its parents.

It looks as though there were a certain way of talking that hangs together if you are talking English and another way of talking that hangs together if you are talking Welsh, or something of that kind. And I suppose one might raise the question of what this hanging together is.

Well, is that something like the unity of a game? I suppose there are analogies there; though I have been wanting to say that there are differences that are in many ways more important. The example of a child learning to speak is in some ways clear. And anyway, I wanted to consider that because of the importance of the question of what it is that you *learn* when you learn to speak. What is it to have a language? But as for hanging together, and the difference between speaking English and speaking Welsh, I suppose that would be as plain in the case of adults that are bilingual. You often times find people who speak two languages equally easily, and who sometimes speak the one with each other and sometimes the other. And that would suggest that the test of whether you are still able to speak with one another, will not suffice for whether you are talking the same language.

It is possible for someone to say something in Welsh and for the other person to answer in English; they may not even realize that they are doing it. They might even change from the one language to the other in the course of the same conversation. That is not like changing from one grammar to another in the way in which one talks about different grammars where there are different language games. Different languages are not different language games, in the sense in which Wittgenstein was using that expression. And if one can shift from one language to the other in the course of the same conversation, can one do so in the course of the same game? If so, what is the relation of the different language games to one another? Is that their relation to the language? It is not their relation to English as opposed to their relation to Welsh, apparently.

As far as the connexion of the different language games with one another is concerned, it *does* seem to be a matter of whether people can speak with one another or not. If the game were quite unintelligible – let's put it that way – what would that mean? Then it would not belong to the same language, it would not – man kann gar nicht mit ihm reden, es ist nicht die gleiche Sprache (one cannot speak with him at all, it is not the same language) – and in a sense people are talking the same language even when they are talking alternatively Welsh and English. It *is* the same language if they can talk together, if they can make themselves intelligible to one another. This is the business of talking with *one another*, rather than talking Welsh or English specifically.

There is something important here in the way in which all this hangs together; and in the way in which one has got intelligibility and understanding and the growth of understanding here, and the difference between a language game and a game like chess, for instance. I want to consider what 'belonging to language' is, but I am doing that only in connexion with the question about intelligibility and about understanding. I am trying to consider what is meant by saying, for instance, that you can understand a remark only if you can understand the language. (I have said that there is some difference between the sense of that in mathematics and what there is in ordinary language.)

What I have been trying to emphasize is that belonging to a language is similar to belonging to a conversation; at least that that is the sort of example that you have to look to as a kind of type. The question came up in trying to see what it means to say that you can understand someone only if you speak a language. It is there that this question of belonging to a language as a condition of understanding or as a condition of intelligibility comes in. And I wanted to bring in this idea that speaking a language is a sort of extension of this business of speaking with one another.

It would be a mistake to say that the unity of language *is* the unity of a dialogue or of a discussion. In some sense the various discussions and conversations which the various speakers who speak with one another carry on, belong to the language. That is not quite such a distinct idea from the idea of their speaking with one another at all, as it might at first sight seem. Furthermore, this belonging to the language is something that has important analogies with belonging to a discussion. And if one is to talk about the unity of a language, well at any rate one can say both of that and of the discussion that they do not hang together in the way in which a logical system does. The connexion between parts of a discussion is not a logical connexion, or shall we say the connexion between the various remarks. And the connexion between the 'parts of a language' (that is a misleading expression here), or the various discussions that are held by the people who speak the language, – that is not a logical connexion either. (Cf. making up the rules as we go along.)

If one talks about parts of the language, or if one talks about belonging to the language, there are certain misunderstandings that are likely to come in. For one may start thinking of the grammar of the language as something that can be seen by analogy with some branch of mathematics. And as we know, some people have tried to give an account of the unity of mathematics by showing that the different branches of mathematics are themselves all parts of one general form of calculus (or that they form one complete calculus), or of calculation. And we have found the same kind of thing in the way in which certain people have spoken of language. Now my point is that if you speak about the different parts of language, then one may think first of all of different grammars; or what is more important here, Wittgenstein's conception of different language games.

It is important to notice that when Wittgenstein does speak of that, he is really talking about different games in the sense in which chess and draughts are different games, and not in the sense in which one game of chess is different from another game of chess. And then if one raises the question of their belonging to a language, or if you like, of what one is to understand by 'the language to which they belong', the question may seem similar to the question one would ask for instance about the different forms of calculus and their all forming what you may call 'mathematics' (cf. Wittgenstein's question, 'What is there *mathematical* about this proposition: . . . ?');

or about the different *parts* of a calculus, for instance. And that is
why Wittgenstein introduces this notion of their forming a family.

The question does seem to be one, as it is being asked now, about
classification or systematization of, shall we say, different formal
structures, of different grammars. Because even the idea of different
language games is introduced in order to clarify the notion of
different grammars.

And what I have been talking about are different conversations,
where the distinction between the one and the other is no more a
distinction between different *kinds* of conversation than is the
distinction between the various remarks that are made within a
conversation. The relations between conversations, the relations that
I am considering here, are first and foremost the sorts of relations
that there are between different remarks in a conversation. And it is
in that kind of way that I ask about their bearing one on another.
And it is in that kind of way also that I am thinking about their
belonging to a language; because what I am concerned with now is
the intelligibility of the conversation, the understanding of the
conversation; and also of course the intelligibility of the remarks that
are made and the understanding of the remarks that are made in the
conversation.

And what I want to emphasize here is the understanding of the
remark, for instance, in the sense of seeing the point of the remark.
As distinct from understanding the kind of circumstances under
which such a remark might have a point. And similarly with regard
to conversations: it is not a question of understanding the kind of
circumstances under which such a conversation might be carried on;
or the kind of circumstances under which such a game might be
played, or anything of that kind. (What it would be like to play such
a game. Whether you could imagine a game of this sort.)

I suppose this question about the relation of the conversations and
the remarks to the language, which certainly raises questions of what
we mean by 'the same language' or 'belonging to the same
langauge', and in that way raises questions of the kind of unity that
there is in language, and of the way in which (as we have been
putting it) the different parts of the language hang together – the
question has a special importance when one is considering the
connexion between language and the growth of understanding. Now
I say the connexion between *language* and the growth of understanding, and there the point is the connexion between *saying something* and

understanding what is said and the growth of understanding. That is what Plato was emphasizing, and I think that he was putting something that is immensely important.

The point is that you understand something when you can learn something from it. And that goes for conversations as well. And there does seem to be some connexion between belonging to a language and the growth of understanding.

Once again: the question is of how the different language games hang together. Somehow they seem to run into one another; and something of this is probably meant when it is said that they constitute a family. And it seems also to be meant that they constitute a language; and the belonging to the family would be belonging to a language.

For it seems that a language game must belong to a language. (I would say: that something must be said in it. That is why chess is not a language game.) And further, that the language itself is not a game: that it has not the kind of unity that a game has. (Nor the unity of a conversation either.)

Well, the trouble is in the question whether it is the same language game – and perhaps even the same family of language games – in two different languages. Or put it so: if a language game must belong to a language (or to a family), what is it that is meant by that? What would be meant by saying 'These two language games belong to the same language?' When have we the same language, in that sense, and when a different one?

They seem to belong to the same language when what is said in the one has some sort of bearing on what is said in the other; or might have. That may be difficult if one is thinking of the games as structures or as formal – if one is thinking of 'different games' in the sense in which chess or draughts are different games, or in the sense in which we may be playing the same game on different occasions. And if Wittgenstein's account is inadequate, it may be that this has something to do with it. For then their bearing on one another would seem to lie in some sort of similarity of form, rather than in what is said in them.

It would seem as though 'saying something' has a sort of ambiguity, according to the game in which the remark is made. It would mean something different when you are giving a report of a chemical experiment, and when you are trying to explain that there was something wrong in the way in which he played that musical phrase, or when you are telling a joke. And the relations between different language games might have something to do with the *kind* of bearing that a remark in one situation might have on remarks in others: how we could still be said to be speaking the language, even though we were doing these different things. That is the way Wittgenstein would have put it: *doing* these different things. And that way of speaking is connected with this way of viewing language games as *ways* of talking with people. It is not like considering the bearing of what is *said* here on what is said in other 'games'.

Perhaps we could say that the question is still 'Why do you still call it "language"?' when the games are so different; or when you seem to be *doing* something so different in the one case and in the other? Or must there be something in common in what you are doing in the one case and in the other?

But that leaves out the connexion of one remark with another, on which I have been putting emphasis for just that question, of 'what it means to say something'.

'If you say anything, you must say it in a language.' Now for this something like a convention may be important; an 'accepted vocabulary' – though that is not quite as simple, perhaps, as 'an accepted coinage'. But that still does not give you what 'saying it in a language' is, I think. (The difference between Welsh and English may be almost like the difference in the colour in which it is painted; and for certain purposes that is important.) 'If it were like the difference between playing rugby and playing soccer, for instance . . .'

'If you play a game, you must play it according to certain rules.' There must be something which you call the rules of the game. That seems to determine whether in what you are doing you are still playing rugby or still playing soccer. Perhaps that is like 'speaking according to a certain convention'.

But that cannot be what is important about the 'saying it in the language' which is indispensable if it is to be saying something at all. Here the point is rather that it cannot be the only thing you ever said; and that has to do with the responses you would make if someone asked you so and so about it. Because there are things that could be asked about it; comments that could be made on it, and so on. Otherwise it is pointless and not a remark at all.

Also it is connected with other things that other people say; that is just as important, and I had almost said it was more so. But here again I mean that it is connected with them in the sense of *bearing* on what other people say; that what they say may be said about it, and so on. The builders could not say anything in connexion with that particular work of building if they never said anything else, in any other connexion. And you cannot put that by saying that it is all part of an accepted way of doing things.

It is in all this that it is *unlike* carrying on an institution. And anyway, if you called speaking the language carrying on an institution, that would make the whole thing external: it would leave *out* the connexion of understanding.

That is why if you say that the Welsh language is an institution, you are mentioning only one thing about it; and you have not said much unless you explain the kind of institution it is. Then I think you would have to say that it is an institution of *language*. And just for that reason you could not say that language itself is an institution. And it is not the following of an institution that *makes* it language, or that makes it speaking together or that makes it understanding.

There are different kinds of coinage, and you might say that British coinage is one institution and French another. But you could also say that money is an institution anyway. And that is what I think you cannot say about language. I suppose you might have a theory of money. But you cannot have a theory of language in that way. Any more than there are principles of language although there may be principles of banking and perhaps (I do not know) even principles of money. And the reason is just in this matter of *why* you could not say anything if you never said anything else. Of the way language hangs together; that is not the connexion of a rule. That is why language is the concern of philosophy. And the reason *why* you cannot have a theory of language is connected with this business of the growth of understanding. *Of what it is to understand the language, for instance.* The difference between this and understanding money or understanding banking.

IV
(10.5.58–16.5.58)

Learning to speak is not like learning to follow a rule. Or at least it is misleading to put it that way. And in the same way, it is misleading to describe learning to speak as a matter of training. Which does not recognize the difference between learning to speak and learning to do a certain sort of exercise, as you may when learning a foreign language, for instance. Nor is learning to speak like learning to play a game; although the analogy there is closer in some ways. A game is not 'about something', for instance, as what you say is. Learning to speak is learning to speak about things. Perhaps the matter can be brought out better by saying that the game is something that is fairly self-contained. It has not any internal connexion with the rest of what one does, or with the rest of one's life. And speaking has. This difference between learning to speak and learning a game is similar to the difference between learning to speak and learning a technique. For some purposes you might compare it with that, but on the whole it is more misleading than helpful, I think.

One of the most obvious and most fundamental features of learning to speak is learning to speak with people, learning to carry on a conversation with them. Unless somebody has learned to do that, unless he is able to do that, you could not say that he could speak at all. Neither would you say that he could understand the language.

That has not always been emphasized. If you thought of learning to speak as learning to obey orders, chiefly, this would fit in with the idea of the learning as a kind of training or drill. And learning the meanings of words would look like learning to follow a rule.

If you can speak, you can speak with people; you can engage in conversation. Now there are games that are in many ways similar to that. (And I am not questioning that you may use games in helping children to speak.) But if you were to think of carrying on the conversation as the playing of a game, or the practice of a game, then it will be hard to distinguish between understanding an imaginary conversation and understanding a real one. This is connected also with the difference between learning to speak and learning to translate; or to understand and to translate.

If you are simply playing at it, then you are not really understanding the people. Or better: you are not understanding what is said – although you understand what the sentences mean, and even how they hang together here. You might say: he understands the *language* when he understands the imaginary conversation, just as much as he does when he understands a real one. You are understanding the sentences in the same way that you might if you were reading a story or doing an exercise. And Wittgenstein's treatment of the matter does not allow that distinction to be brought out clearly enough, I think. In the same way I think it obscures the way in which what is said now depends on what is said in other circumstances and by other people. The way in which the intelligibility of any remark depends upon its belonging to the language. But that is already suggesting a kind of formal relation that I think may be misleading.

You might say that the intelligibility of what is said in an imaginary conversation depends on its relation to the rest of the language, in the same way that the intelligibility of any real remark does. And in that it seems to have the same kind of difference from anything done in a game that I was referring to before.

One difference comes in when you think of *understanding* the imaginary conversation. Because in a way that is set, just as a game is. And you do not bring in criticism, as you may when you are trying to understand the point of an actual remark. That, by the way, is one of the important differences between learning a game and learning to speak. Because in learning to speak the meeting with criticism of that kind or similar is an important part; learning to make yourself understood. And that is not what people following an imaginary conversation (or a game) are trying to do. They are not trying to make themselves understood. Nor are they if they are playing a game.

Suppose they are reciting an imaginary conversation; or composing one. They may be trying to say something that is *like* what people would say if they were engaged in conversation. And in that way they are trying to speak the language correctly. That is probably important here.

Perhaps the important phrase is – 'what is said here' must have an internal connexion with what is said elsewhere. And somehow or other the possibility of criticism is important in connexion with that. I wanted to distinguish between saying something and doing something. And at the same time I wanted to say that a real remark belongs with what you are doing, in a way that an imaginary remark does not.

Saying something, and understanding people: those somehow go together. Of course, if you think of belonging to the language in the other way you might if, on coming to something written or printed you say 'Oh yes, that's something in French', then this idea of belonging to the language will not give you any connexion with the lives of people. It will not help you to understand what is meant by saying that the remark is about something.

(I do not know whether the question of the connexion with the *past* is related to this; and the way in which that helps us to understand the lives that we are leading.)

When animals live in societies, this is not a 'way of living together' in our sense. When we speak of human beings as living together, we think of them as understanding, or trying to understand, and misunderstanding one another. We think of the tasks and difficulties and satisfactions of living together. And whether they can make a go of it, depends on whether they can keep some sort of understanding. But for animals there is nothing to understand, in this way. Animals may have regular companionship, as they may also have mates, and they may keep together or they may fall out. But there is no question of understanding here, any more than there is any question of discussion.

The misunderstandings of human beings are not simply fights or antipathies, and falling out in that sense. If they were, there would be no problem. Criticisms and questions and objections. 'What is wrong with us? Can't we find a way out?' 'I wish I knew what I ought to do.' Trying to explain; trying to meet the objections of the other person. Trying to get one's own grievances across. By the way, this is not just failing to understand what the other player in the game is up to. Wondering what he has up his sleeve, or anything of that sort. 'He's got me bewildered now; I just don't follow it.' That is not the sort of bewilderment that comes into the misunderstandings between friends. As though there were something which somebody could tell you, although he has not. Or as though the want of understanding came from a want of intelligence. 'Marriage counsellors.' 'Why do you always say the wrong things?' 'She loves him, but she has a genius for saying things that he is sure to take in the wrong way.' 'He ought to understand that in her, though; he ought to make allowances, and know how to meet it.' Maybe; but it is often not as simple as that. There is something that concerns him much more deeply, and he could cut right across that with the sort of thing that you call making allowances. And this is something which concerns the way in which he cares for her; concerns his relation to her, and why he thinks his relation to her important.

My point is that that kind of difficulty arises only where there is discourse and reflection. It is even a question of 'understanding what she is saying'. It is only because he gets that wrong, as she gets his remarks wrong. Why can't she *see* that what is bothering him is not . . . ?

Well, I suppose the reason why is just that she cannot see what he thinks any understanding must depend on or start from. The parallel with understanding the point of a remark; or understanding what is being said. They cannot understand what is being said: they cannot understand one another. Those two are pretty well equivalent here.

Notice here the difference between understanding an imaginary conversation – and failing to, being unable to follow it – and their understanding or failing to understand one another. And yet the latter is a matter of understanding what is said. (And yet without the possibility of imaginary conversations and understanding them, there could not be that understanding and want of understanding between people.)

Human beings live together in discussion. Or at least, when discussion is introduced, this is not a new element, something else coming in, putting them in a different relationship. On the other hand, you cannot understand what discussion is unless you know how human beings live together.

If people understand one another, they understand the language they are speaking. But there must be more than that. For each of them might know the language, and they might not understand one another at all. We speak of 'the way they live', and we may speak of that finding expression in art; or as characterized by a morality that belongs to it. The conception of what is good and what is bad; or wisdom and folly; of what is law and what is admirable; of what is difficult and what is important; of success and failure. ('What Eliot's characters lack . . . is the feeling of being alive, the sense of good and evil.') Here it is the question of being alive at all. But also the possibility of communication at all; of relations between people – 'the heart is dead, love is an attitude or a game'; of understanding or of saying anything – the latter being just as important as the want of understanding. The condition of human beings without that is worse than that of animals. That sort of deadness is as foreign to animals as culture is.

Where there is no difference between success and failure, for instance, then there is nothing to say, and there is no understanding. 'There is no sense in this life. There is no sense in being alive.' The thought of death as an expression of that. Where there is sense in that, we can speak of understanding it. People understand the life they are leading; or try to. (In the other condition they do not even try to, they do not think there is anything to understand.)

Where there can be no art or morality (no sense of good and evil), there can be no understanding, nothing to understand. Not that this is *lacking* in animals, as it is in certain human societies. But what makes it senseless to talk about an art in animal societies, is just what would make it senseless to ask whether they understood the life they were leading. Language without morality would be a wallpaper pattern or a formal habit (not even a ceremony).

In what sense is language public? Is it just in the sense in which a conversation is public? The idea of saying something to yourself (instead of saying it out loud). Connecting this with the idea of private meanings. This is important because of the conception of meaning that is involved. Protagoras: each has the criterion of these things within himself. The idea that the language is the same for everyone; it is what we all have to understand. Perhaps the idea that it is something that we all have to understand if we understand one another.

But understanding a conversation is not like that. And if the public character of the language is public only in the sense in which a conversation is public, then it is not much like the institution which everyone has to understand who works in it, or anything of that sort. And yet there is something of this idea of 'that's how it's done', which does enter into understanding what is said, and which differentiates that from any sort of understanding that dogs have of one another. The child uses imitation in connexion with his understanding; and the dog does not. In fact the dog does not imitate at all – not in that kind of way. And that imitation does seem to have much of the idea of 'that's how you do it', or 'I've seen them do it that way, and so I'll do it that way here.' And this does make it look like learning a dance.

And yet understanding something is not learning something in that sense. You cannot describe 'saying something' in that way; or at any rate you are leaving out what is important if that is all that you take account of. Think of the way in which birds join in flight with one another. Think of the sympathetic participation that there is there; evident emotion. And it may be that younger birds have to learn to do that. Perhaps there would be something like that when children learn to sing in unison, or even when they learn to join in a dance. With practice you can follow the movements of the leader, and so forth, better than you could before. The child may learn to play 'Pat-a-cake, pat-a-cake, baker's man' with its hands, and so forth, joining in with the adults; but learning to speak with them is something different from that.

CHAPTER 9

Wittgenstein's builders – recapitulation
(A version of 'Wittgenstein's builders' and notes 19.9.57)

I

When Wittgenstein says that an account of what language means
would be like explaining what 'game' means, he is thinking of the
account of language that would be given in philosophy. It is not an
explanation you would give to anyone in an ordinary way. And it is
not quite clear what it is; what kind of explanation it is. The
explanation of 'game' is meant to give an analogy, but it is never
more than that. And with any analogy there is the danger of carrying
it further than was meant. (I am speaking here of the analogy in the
idea of 'explaining what it means'; not the analogy between
'speaking together' and 'playing a game together'.)

Wittgenstein did not always distinguish between 'language' and
'speaking', and this sometimes brings trouble: if you try to replace
'an example of speaking' by 'an example of language', for instance.
Or suppose you say that 'speaking' covers a family of related cases,
just as 'game' does. And suppose you say then that language – or the
language we speak – is a family of 'language-games'. Here you would
not be saying simply that the games are all various instances of what
we call 'language' but that a language is a family of games: that is the
kind of unity a language has. But the distinction is important
especially in connexion with the ideas of 'a common language' and
'something said in the same language'. I will return to this.

You might try to tell someone what 'game' means by describing
various games to him. I suppose you would have come to the
conclusion that he had never played one. This would be queer, but
we may imagine it. And we could say that in this way he learns what
'game' means; or that he understands what a game is. But if you
were trying to explain to someone what 'speaking' means – it could
not be that sort of thing at all. I said you must have imagined that

the boy had never played a game, and this is why you begin your explanation as you do. But if you thought he could not speak . . . you will not begin by describing how it goes.

You cannot understand what speaking is, unless you can understand what is said. And understanding speaking is not knowing what someone does when he speaks.

When would you say 'He doesn't know what it is'? And when would you try to explain to him? (A foreigner may not know the word, but that is different and it is not relevant here.) If we saw someone speaking, I could not say 'Do you know what it is that he is doing?' – meaning *speaking*. I could not assume that perhaps speaking was something strange to you and wonder whether you understood it.

Wittgenstein recognized this, and in one way or another he referred to it often enough. 'Do you understand what speaking is?' would be comparable to 'Do you understand what understanding is?' – where one might reply, 'How do you expect me to understand what you are asking?'

You might have played games often enough without ever having tried to say what playing a game is. But although of course you can speak without ever having tried to say or asked yourself what speaking is – this is not really parallel. If you try to say what playing a game is, you try to give a general account of what people are doing when they play games. But if you tried to say what speaking is, it would not be that. If you look for a general account, then it will not be a general account of what people are doing when they speak; not even with a list of examples and 'and so on'.

What would an illustration or example of speaking be? Suppose I describe what the two men do while they are building, as Wittgenstein does in the *Investigations*. If this does illustrate speaking for you, then you must not only understand what they are doing, but you must understand what they say. My description must show that they speak a language which each of them understands – and also which you understand, if the illustration is to help you. (Wittgenstein imagines them using German words. He would say this is of no consequence, but I wonder.)

Whoever says anything, says it in a language. I suppose that is a tautology, for it means that if he says anything he can speak with people, and if people speak together they have a common language. I can understand, or at least try to understand what is said, if it is said in the language I speak.

This bears on what 'a general account of language' would be. The difficulty is not simply that we may wonder whether when we say 'Those are all cases of language' they must have some general features in common, since we use the same word. That would be like what we might ask about 'They are all games.' But the trouble is rather in this idea of 'the same language' or 'a common language'. And we may even want to speak of something like a 'common intelligibility' which the various remarks must have if they are made in the same language.

When Wittgenstein was writing the *Tractatus* he might have said that 'being in the language' meant simply being language or being a proposition. 'Die Gesamtheit der Sätze ist die Sprache.' ('The totality of propositions is the language' (*Tractatus Logico-Philosophicus*, 4.001).) And anything to be meant by a *common* language was covered, if at all, by this notion of being language or being intelligible; for he argued that all propositions must have a kind of common intelligibility or commensurability simply through being propositions or having sense.

That idea of 'belonging to language', like the idea of 'human language' (cf. 'ein bestimmtes Bild der menschlichen Sprache') ('a certain picture of human language') is a peculiar one, for you might ask when anyone learns *die menschliche Sprache*, and what is written in it. But that is just the question of 'what speaking is' once more. The difficulty is that the troublesome notion of 'all propositions' has replaced that of different remarks in the same language.

He has dropped that notion of 'all propositions' in the *Investigations*. But he is still interested in 'human language' rather than in the language or languages which people speak. He suggests that any language is a family of language games, and that any of these might be a complete language in itself. And he does not say whether the people who might take part in several such games would be speaking the same language in each of them. In fact I find it hard to see how on this view they would *ever* be speaking a language. But these questions are complicated.

Learning to speak is not the same as learning a particular language like French or English. This is very important. It is important to distinguish between what a child learns when he learns to speak, and what you learn when you learn a foreign language. It would be wrong, for instance, to suggest that a child can speak when he can go on doing what he has been taught to do, as you might be called fluent in French when you can go on doing what you have been taught in grammar exercises and proses and 'unseen' translations. It could be queer and misleading to say that when an English child is learning to speak he is 'learning English'; misleading, because the first point is that he is learning to speak – to speak with people – and this is what the child in France is learning too.

When Wittgenstein says that the child learns various language games, he is thinking partly of what his parents do with him when they are teaching him various expressions in the language. But Wittgenstein is also explaining what 'teaching him expressions' *is*: what it is to be an expression or to mean something; and what it is to have a language or to speak. Anything is a significant expression if it has a role in some language game. Anyone can use the expression significantly, or say something, when he has learned the game. It is in the various language games we play that we may be said to be talking about things. And it is by looking at the different games and at the different things we are doing in them, at the importance which the different words have in them and in what we are doing, that we find the relation of words and things. For there is no *one* relation of words to things, any more than there is one way of 'talking about something'.

There is a difficulty in this as a way of explaining the relation of language to reality. If we say that anything is a significant expression if it has a role in a language game, well what about the various games which are deliberately imagined and expressly made unlike any which plays a part in our lives? What is the difference between saying that an expression has a meaning and saying that it *could* have a meaning? If we are asking about the relation of language to reality – or words to things – will an imagined game illustrate as well as an actual one?

These are difficulties which arise when we neglect the point that the significant expression or anything that is said must be said in the language, as well as having a role in a game. Having a role in the game only (if this were imaginable) would not make the expression intelligible.

I suppose this is part of the difficulty about giving an illustration of 'language' or an illustration of 'speaking', of which I have said that I am often not clear what the illustration is meant to do. Wittgenstein wanted to give only an 'external' account of language; to try to give any other sort of account of 'intelligibility', for instance, would be confused and futile. The kind of difficulties we meet in 'understanding what speaking is' had something to do with this, I think. But it led Wittgenstein sometimes to suggest that if you want to know what a word is, or what makes it a significant expression, you should look *only* at what we do with it in some situations in which it is used. To ask 'What is a word?' is like asking 'What is a chess piece?' But can we really answer what a word is in that way? Would that kind of explanation really tell us what a word is? If I describe the game of chess and what we do with various pieces in it, you know what a chess man is. But we do not *say* anything with the chess pieces. And that is why it is not a language game nor even much like one. If they were expressions in a language – as they might be – it would be different, but then I could not tell you what they are by describing simply how they are moved in this game.

'A game we play with chess pieces' – 'a game we play with words or with remarks': we might think of something like a student debate. But in the *Investigations*, in the example of the builders, for instance (§§ 2, 8 and ff.), he describes an activity in which two men are engaged, in connexion with which now and again one gives a shout, and the other reacts by fetching a stone or in some other way as he has been trained to do. Wittgenstein does this partly because he wants to portray a situation in which language would be something like the picture Augustine had given of it. He wants also to make the point that a primitive language need not be 'incomplete'. And he wants also to show something of the connexion between the use of language and what people are doing. This probably had some relation to the question he had asked at an earlier time regarding the point of the connexion of language and reality ('Wo knüpft sich die Sprache an die Wirklichkeit an?'). ('Where does language attach to reality?')

Wittgenstein then suggests that the few kinds of expressions he has described, which are all used in giving orders of one sort or another, might be the entire language of a tribe; and evidently they would be used only in the situation he has described: only in this kind of building work. But I feel there is something wrong here. It is not that I cannot imagine a people whose language had such a limited vocabulary. The trouble is to imagine a people who had a language at all and yet *never* spoke apart from the times when they happened to be on this kind of building job. I do not think it could be speaking a language.

Incidentally, if the children were *taught* these shouts and the reactions to them, in the way in which Wittgenstein suggests, then the adults would be using them in teaching, and this would be different from their use on the actual job. If they belong to a language, this is natural enough, just as it would be natural for the builders to use them in referring to the job after they have gone home. But then understanding is not just reacting correctly on the job.

If it is an actual building job, it will not always go according to plan; there will be snags. But I suppose that when these builders come on a snag and are held up, then although they have been speaking to one another in the course of the job, they do not speak while they are trying to find out what the trouble is. They will not try to ask one another anything about that. What they have learned are *signals* which cannot be used in any other way.

It seems as though Wittgenstein has described a *game* with building stones, and not what people would do if they were actually building a house. In a game there are no snags of the sort you meet on the job. And the signals are part of the game too. But this is not what he wanted. It does not show how speaking is related to the lives people lead.

In any case, if they had learned only those shouts and those reactions, they would not have learned any distinction between sense and nonsense. They might be nonplussed if there were a shout to which they had not been trained. But this would be no different from the bewilderment they might feel if someone moved a stone in a way that was not part of the routine in which they had been drilled.

Perhaps Wittgenstein would have said that for those people there is no such distinction between 'that is not what we generally do' and 'that makes no sense'. Perhaps this would have some analogy to the way in which the people would make no distinction between physical possibility and geometrical possibility (*Remarks on the Foundations of Mathematics*, p. 189). They notice that when you fold the paper in this way, you get this sort of construction; and they never ask whether this is a geometrical relation of the figures, or whether it is a result of the physical properties of the paper. Similarly, these people would simply disallow or take no account of certain expressions; and it is pointless for us to ask whether they are rejecting it as nonsense or rejecting it because it is not part of the routine. It might be for them what an utterance in some language we did not understand would be for us.

But I do not think this would be satisfactory. Unless there were a difference between learning to move the stones in the way people always do, and learning what makes sense, then I do not think we should say that they were learning to speak.

Wittgenstein used to wonder whether there might be a people who had only an applied mathematics, without pure mathematics. Whether we could still say that they were calculating, and that there were proofs, although their proofs were like that in which someone shows us how to fold the paper to get a hat: and they would have others of a similar kind in connexion with numbering and herding sheep and so on. These proofs would have nothing to do with what he would call 'concept formation', as the proofs of pure mathematics do. We might suppose they used the proofs only for prediction: 'You can get it in this way.' So the proofs would not be 'normative', in the way the proofs of mathematics are. But just for that reason, their whole position or role as proofs would become obscure. 'What puzzles me', Wittgenstein said, 'is how these proofs are *kept*'. They are a set of techniques which are used in forecasts, but they do not form any system in which there is any kind of dependence. And it is not clear how people could be persuaded to adopt them, or what force they would have.

'That is just the way they do things.' Can we say that the sense or otherwise of what is said *depends* on that? What is going on with the building game 'in the same way'? Is it just a matter of habit? There is a criterion or standard in the language we speak, which comes in when we say he is not using the word in the same way now, or he is using it wrongly now. But I do not see how there can be any such standard in the game Wittgenstein has described.

In the *Remarks on the Foundations of Mathematics* (p. 133), Wittgenstein says, 'I want to say: it is essential to mathematics that its signs should also be used in civil life. It is their use outside mathematics, in other words the *meaning* of the signs, that makes the sign-game mathematics. Just as it is not a logical conclusion if I change one configuration into another (any one arrangement of chairs into another) unless these configurations have some use in language *besides* the making of these transformations.'

You might ask why this should make such a difference – the fact that the same expressions are used elsewhere. And one reason is that then the expressions are not just part of one particular routine. Their uses elsewhere have to do with the point or bearing of them in what we are saying now. It is the way we use them in other connexions that decides whether they make sense together here, for instance: whether one can be substituted for another, whether they may be combined or are incompatible and so forth. What the expressions mean, even in this game, is not to be seen just in what we do with them or how we react to them in this game.

The builders are not supposed to be drawing conclusions or calculating. But if they speak to one another, the meaning of any expression they utter cannot lie wholly in the use or the reaction that it receives in this job. The point about the logical conclusion was that if the signs had no use or meaning outside this transformation, that the transformation itself would be without any significance and it would not show anything. If people are speaking together, then the significance of this or that remark is not like the significance of a logical conclusion. But the remarks they make have something to do with one another; otherwise they are not talking at all, even if they are uttering sentences. And their remarks could have no bearing on one another unless the expressions they used were used in other connexions as well.

If someone learns to speak, he does not just learn to make sentences and utter them; nor can he merely have learned to react to orders. If that were all he ever did, I should not imagine that he could speak, and I should never ask him anything. When he learns to speak, he learns to tell you something; and he tries to. In learning to speak he learns what can be said; he learns – however fumblingly – what it makes sense to say. He gets some sense of what different remarks have to do with one another. That is why he begins to follow a conversation, or to carry on a conversation himself. Or rather: it is misleading to say 'this is *why* he does that', as though we had to do with a condition and what results from it. For in beginning to carry on a conversation – in trying to tell you something and trying to understand your answer – he *is* getting a sense of how different remarks have a bearing on one another. This is different from learning general rules, even though it does not go without that.

And because he learns to speak, or learns what can be said, he can go on speaking or go on learning. If he can speak with me here, or ask me something, then he will be able to ask me about something else later.

When I say that he learns what it makes sense to say, I do not mean that he learns the correct way of using various expressions: as if he were learning various colour words, for instance, or learning what pieces to call slabs and which to call beams. He does learn how such expressions are understood (whether or not we call this learning how to react to them). But I want to emphasize, in the first place, that he learns to *tell* you something, and you try to understand what you are telling him; so that he may naturally ask you questions in connexion with it, for instance. And this is not something to which anyone can be trained, as an animal might be trained to react to an order. (The word '*Abrichtung*' is what one uses when one speaks of training animals, in German; and Wittgenstein chose it with this in mind.) In the second place, my point was that he can tell you something, he can tell you other things. It is sensible to ask him questions to try to get clearer what he wants. And if he is speaking to you this morning, he will be able to speak too this afternoon, and about something else. This is why I say that, if you did speak of 'what he has learned to do', you could not describe it by pointing to the expressions whose uses he has mastered.

'What it makes sense to say' is not 'the sense these expressions have'. It has much more to do with what it makes sense to answer, or what it makes sense to ask ('to ask for what kind of answer'); or: what sort of sense one remark may have in connexion with another.

If he tries to tell you something, he is speaking to you; and this is connected with the ideas of addressing you and of greeting you. He would never do this unless he thought you could understand. And although it is something he has learned, it would not be natural to say that he has learned how to do it. Nor is it like learning a game. We may *use* something like a game in teaching him. We say his sounds back to him, and in this way bring him to imitate other sounds we make. And this is a game. But it is not what we are trying to teach him. And if all he learns is how to play like this, he will not have learned to speak. He will never be telling you anything, nor asking you anything either.

When he can speak, we may be delighted because 'He can say things himself now – not just repeat.' But what is important is that he can *say* things: not that he can construct new sentences – as it were in an exercise. You may set him exercises if you want to test his vocabulary. But this is not how you find out whether he can speak.

You might test his knowledge of a foreign language by setting him exercises. And it would be something the same if you wanted to see whether he had mastered a particular notation; or again, if you wondered whether he could do arithmetic. Wittgenstein used to speak of teaching a child to multiply by going through examples of multiplications for him, then getting him to go through these and through other exercises while you corrected his mistakes, and then saying 'Go on by yourself now.' But if you said anything like this about teaching a child to speak, you would have left out the most important thing. (It would be like training a very intelligent parrot.) The point, roughly, is that if he can speak he has got something to tell you or to ask you. In arithmetic it is different. 'Telling you things' is not part of his achievement when he learns to multiply, whereas it is his principal achievement in learning to speak. It is not just an extension of what he was doing as he repeated sentences after you. It is not 'going on' with *that* – although if he can speak he must be able to go on: i.e., to say that he never spoke more than one sentence in his life, would be as foolish as to say that he never understood more than one sentence in his life. We should not call it speaking.

If you ask, 'What *does* he go on with then?' ('Vous êtes le nègre. Eh bien, continuez.') ('You have the chores. So get on with it.'[1]) This is somewhat like asking 'How do you know he is speaking?', and one answer might be 'By trying to talk with him: perhaps asking him questions so that I can make out what he is trying to say.' It is largely the question of 'knowing what speaking is' which I mentioned earlier. My point has been that the question itself is puzzling and I would be foolish to offer a short answer.

There is a difference between learning to do exercises you may be set, and learning to play a game. And when Wittgenstein compared

---

[1] Faire le nègre: to be landed with all the chores. Faire comme le nègre, continuer: to carry on with what one is doing.

(The origin of what could loosely be called an ironical catch phrase is to be found in the seemingly pointless comment uttered by Marshal Macmahon, President of the French Republic in the 1870s. When visiting a military academy he asked a junior recruit what his functions were and when told 'Je suis le nègre', i.e., one acting as a temporary batman, Mac-Mahon, always lost for a word, simply said: 'Eh bien, continuez!', the French equivalent to the military: 'Carry on as you were!' (*Dictionary of Modern Colloquial French*, René James Hérail and Edwin A. Lovatt, London and New York: Routledge, reprinted 1987 (paperback), p. 206).) (Ed.).

learning to speak with learning a game, one reason was that you generally play a game with other people. This was important in various ways, but I think it still leaves out the idea of telling one another things. It was important to emphasize that 'what we learn is a game we play with other people', because Wittgenstein thought that the difference between using a word rightly and using it wrongly, the whole idea of the correct use of it, depended on this. And if there is any criterion which can decide whether you are using the word 'in the same way' as you have been taught, this is because in fact nearly everyone playing the game would agree in calling *this*, rather than that, 'going on in the same way'. The idea that in speaking we are playing a game with other people was important also as a way of emphasizing that when we do understand people we have to understand the game that is being played, and not just the meanings of the words and the formal syntax: think of ethical statements and statements in physics, for instance. In these ways the analogy does help us to see. But I keep thinking of Wittgenstein's own remark about the idea that mathematics is a game: 'Wenn die Mathematik ein Spiel ist, dann ist ein Spiel spielen Mathematik treiben, und warum dann nicht auch: Tanzen?' ('If mathematics is a game then playing some game is doing mathematics, and in that case why isn't dancing mathematics too?') (*Remarks on the Foundations of Mathematics*, p. 133). This is not really fair, because Wittgenstein would never have said that speaking *is* playing a game. But it is near to a difficulty which he did recognize, of why you should not call *any* systematic activity between a number of people a 'language game'. If I suggest that he has not shown what makes them all *language* games, I could have put the same point by saying that he has not shown how the various language games hang together. They have likenesses – and why not family likenesses? – with other things as well. They speak the same language in the one language game and in the other.

III

Not all discourse is conversation, but I do not think there would be speech or language without it. And if there were someone who could not carry on any conversation – who had no idea of answering questions or of making any comment – I do not think we should say he could speak. But one reason why a conversation is not like playing a game together is that the point of the various moves and counter moves in the game is within the game; whereas we may learn from the conversation and from what is said in it. Generally each of us 'brings something to' the conversation, too: not as he might bring a skill in making moves, but just in having something to say.

I want to contrast (a) the external relations of moves in a game, and (b) the internal relations of the remarks people make to one another in a conversation. 'Internal relations' has a technical sense in the theory of knowledge, and I am not thinking of that. But it does suggest 'connexions of meaning', and this is the point here; and it cannot be reduced to connexions in a game.

I have spoken of having something to say. The point about chess, for instance, is that the pieces are furnished for you – you do not have to find them, nor decide what they shall be. They belong only to the game and are, so to speak, determined by the game. Someone might then put the analogy by saying, 'This means that the sphere of *possible* reactions is limited in this game.'

If you are giving me a lesson in a foreign language, we may carry on a sham conversation to give me the opportunity of constructing appropriate sentences and giving appropriate replies. Neither of us learns anything from what is said in a sham conversation of this kind, because neither of us really tells the other anything. And unless there were the distinction between genuine speaking and sham or pretence, then speaking *would* be nearly like playing the game correctly. You could say what you have been trained to say without telling anyone anything.

Once more: if I know you can speak, then it makes sense for me to ask you what you mean, to try to get you to say more clearly what you want, and to ask you questions about it: just as truly as it makes sense for me to answer you. The example of the builders does not seem to allow for any of these. Neither could reply to the other – there is no such thing and it would have no sense. And there can be nothing like that so long as the meaning of the utterance is confined to 'what you do with it' in this particular connexion.

'Why should they not have a language which they use only in this connexion?' What would it mean 'to use language for something'? Granting that the child learns to use a certain expression when he wants to call someone, we cannot say that he learns to use *language*. It is only when someone has begun to speak, and so is speaking a language, that you can try to get him to use this or that expression.

And if we said that the builders learned to use those expressions in connexion with the different things they did, it would be meaningless, I think, to say that they learned to use language in connexion with their building; or that they learned to use language for any particular purpose at all.

Of course there might be people who used Welsh only for religious services, or French only for diplomacy, or Latin only for scholarship. But the question is that of learning to speak and learning a foreign (or special) language again. If the people who used Welsh in their religious services spoke no other language and never spoke Welsh in any other connexion – then I do not think they would be speaking in their religious services either, for all that they used Welsh words and sentences. It would just be mumbo jumbo. On the other hand, if they spoke English in all other connexions, and only Welsh in religious services, there would be nothing specially puzzling about this; no more than it would when English people living in France speak English together when they are at home and French when they go out. In the second place, when we say that they hold their religious services 'in Welsh' (which is what it means when we say that they use Welsh for religious services), we assume that Welsh is a language which has developed and is spoken *not* only in this connexion (and similarly, *mutatis mutandis*, for French and Latin). What makes no sense is the suggestion that they used a language only in this connexion, where this means that they never spoke ('used a language') otherwise. If Welsh is a language, then those whose language it is do not *use* it; in particular, they do not use it *for* anything.

We are back at the question of what it is to *have* a language, or what it is to speak. And this is what Wittgenstein is trying to answer in his analogy with games. He speaks of the games we play with this or that expression – with colour words, for instance, or with 'metre' and 'centimetre'. And one might ask, 'What is the objection to saying that the learning of these various expressions *is* learning to speak? There is not any *single* thing which is learning to speak – as though that were an operation too, perhaps something over and above what we do with these various expressions. But knowing the use of such expressions – being able to use them on the occasions in which they arise, together with other people – that is speaking.' (Cf. *Investigations*, § 23, for instance.)

I could only answer what I have tried to say already. I do not want to suggest that there is some one thing which he learns when he learns to speak – especially if this means anything comparable to 'some one operation'. This is why I have said that learning to speak is not learning how to speak or how to do anything; and it is not learning the mastery of a technique – although learning a foreign language might perhaps be called that, and obviously mastering a notation may. On the other hand, if it were really anything like my paraphrases have made it out – if that were all there were to it – then the child will not see the difference between a jumble of meaningful sentences and a sensible discourse. I have said that this is something that he learns, although it is not something you can teach him by any sort of drill, as you might teach him the names of objects. I think he gets it chiefly from the way in which the members of his family speak to him and answer him. In this way he gets an idea of how remarks may be connected, and of how what people say to one another makes sense. (But, I repeat: speaking to him; not playing games with words.) In any case this is not like learning the meaning of this or that expression. It is important that if he can speak, he can go on to say and ask other things. And this is not like going on with the use of any particular expression, or any set of expressions: although of course it includes that.

The different remarks do not bear on one another simply because of their functions in this situation – as moves in a game might. Rather it is *because* of what they say and what they are, that they bear on one another here. This is why they have to be *understood*, in a way that moves in a game do not. They hang together because they are understood, not just by one person (as one person may understand the different statements in an argument he is following), but because the people who make the remarks understand each other.

This latter point leads to matters which I cannot discuss here. In one of his most interesting remarks (*Investigations*, § 23) Wittgenstein says 'The word "language-*game*" is meant to emphasize here that the *speaking* of language is part of an activity or a form of life (einer Lebensform).' He said in another place that to imagine a language is to imagine a form of life. The idea was important in his later writings. But he did not make very explicit what might be included in it. Sometimes, as in the case of the builders, he is speaking of a way of *working*; as he also is when he speaks of an institution like money, or an institution like buying and selling wood. But I think this is confusing. There is clearly some important connexion between the language a people speak and the life or culture they develop. And it is important to emphasize, as Wittgenstein was doing, that to understand what is said in the language you must understand more than the vocabulary and rules of grammar. But the differences between one form of life and another are not like the differences between one form of some institution (say marriage customs or financial institutions) and another. And the activity of the builders does not give you an idea of a people with a definite sort of life. Do they have songs and dances and festivals, and do they have legends and stories? And are they horrified by certain sorts of crimes, and do they expose people to public ridicule? The description of them on the building site, if you add 'and this may be all', makes them look so much like marionettes. And if they do have a life, then to say that their speaking is part of that life would be different from saying that their speaking is part of this activity of building.

Language is something that can have a literature. This is where it is so different from chess. And if we include folk songs and stories, then literature is immensely important in almost any language: important for the way in which things said in the language are understood. It has to do with the 'force' which one remark or another may have in that language for instance. And in this way it has to do also with what is seen to make sense and what is not.

(It is not true that any two mates on a building job can understand each other equally well, just because all are equally conversant with the phrases that are used on the job.)

Of course there is much else that is necessary as well. If you want to understand them, you have to know what they are talking about. And for this you need to know how they farm and build, and their marriage customs and the rest. I do not say this is less important in any degree than, say, literature. I am saying simply that it is misleading if you describe language as a part of that – as a part of the way, or ways, of doing things; especially if it leaves the suggestion that the language that belongs to building is no more closely connected with the language which belongs to marriage customs than are the movements they make in the building and the movements that are made in the office. And that the language they use at home would have no other sort of connexion with the language they use at work than the way the home is run may have with the way the job is organized or the way the office is run.

The boy learns to go on speaking in a way that makes sense; just as he tries to get the sense of what he learns. This is true in whatever job he happens to be, or whatever he happens to be doing. In other words, there is a distinction between what we say and what we are talking about, which goes with the idea of a reason for saying what we do. Our sentences do not get their 'meaningfulness' merely from what we are talking about. And this goes with the fact that the same expressions are used elsewhere.

This does not mean that remarks made in the language form a system, and that they get their sense from that. But it does suggest something like a common understanding. The thought of language as a system, like the idea of language as a kind of method (cf. 'a method of representation', 'a method of projection' and so on), almost as a kind of theory – those ideas are wrong if only because language is something people speak with one another. In this way it is not at all like mathematics. And it would be confusing, for instance, to think that 'the language' is related to what is said in the language, as pure mathematics is related to applied mathematics; almost as though the language were something that might be written down and studied by itself. (At the same time, the way in which being able to calculate in what you do – the difference between that and a purely empirical technique (a way of bending sheet iron to make sure that you get an even bend) – a way in which this depends on the existence of a pure mathematics, can throw some light on language and what is said.) At the same time, the comparison does suggest something. And when I speak of a common understanding, I do not mean simply what Wittgenstein used to call an 'agreement in reactions' which makes it possible to talk about using the word in the same way or using it correctly. It has rather to do with what is taken to make sense, or with what can be understood: with what it is possible to say to people: which what anyone who speaks the language might try to say.

'If you want to understand the proposition, look at what we do with it' – look at how it is applied. But can we say this of *language*? Can we speak of the application of language? Is 'Look at the various language games' meant in this sense? So that, to the general question of what language is, we answer: 'Well it is this sort of thing, and that, and whatever is like these.' Then we might say, 'Understanding the various games is understanding the language.' Or: 'If you have a general idea of the *application* of language from these and these examples, then you will be able to go on, *i.e.* you will understand it.'

When Wittgenstein speaks of 'our language' he means *human* language. Which nobody ever speaks; and in the ordinary sense nobody understands it either. Wittgenstein thinks of understanding it as understanding what language is. This is one reason why, instead of speaking about understanding the remark that women are fickle, he speaks of understanding what happens when someone says that women are fickle. And this leaves out the language in which it is said. When Wittgenstein spoke of the application of language, as he sometimes did, it was associated with the idea of a general rule, and, in this measure, with a general account of language. But the ideas both of 'rule' and of 'application' may become ambiguous in this kind of discussion. Clearly we cannot speak of an application of language as we should speak of applying a rule or principle in mathematics or in physics. He used to speak of language as something analogous to a system of measurement, almost as though one were applying a measuring instrument, and spoke of applying it to reality. It was a way of speaking of how language or propositions have meaning: or of what you are saying when you say they do have meaning. This relation to reality is what makes it possible to distinguish between sense and nonsense. The suggestion that the meaning of a proposition was in its method of verification was in the same line, in many ways. And it was still sprung from the idea of an *Abbildung der Wirklichkeit* in the *Tractatus*.

When people were saying that the meaning of a sentence is the method of its verification, they were bothered by the question of what you verify, since the sentence apart from its meaning is just a set of marks or noises – which is nothing anyone could even *understand*, let alone verify. I imagine that this was connected with the same trouble that is bothering me here, and that it comes from unclarity about the kind of 'understanding' Wittgenstein had in mind, and about the idea of 'having meaning'. I suppose the point was that *if* the sentence has meaning it *can* be compared to reality. And this does not say: you cannot know what it means until you know how it could be compared. It is an account of what it is to say *that* it has meaning, or that you understand it (not of what you are saying when you assert the proposition itself).

In an ordinary way, to understand a proposition or to understand what is being said, does not mean 'to recognize that it has meaning'. Wittgenstein knew this well enough, of course, and he said much the same thing himself. But in some connexions I wonder if he has not confused the idea of an application of something that is said, like a proposition in engineering, with application in this other sense: the application of language – of which we might want to say that it is not an application at all.

Again, if we think of a rule which I may follow in building a house, or a rule which I keep when I am playing a game, then the idea of a 'rule' on which any correspondence with reality depends, is nothing of either sort. If Wittgenstein sees no difficulty in suggesting that learning to speak is learning the meanings of various particular expressions, is this because he is thinking somehow that learning to speak is learning how language means: which is learning how words apply to things, of what we do with them?

IV

We have to put this idea of understanding in contrast with the mastery of a technique. We can do this only by showing how understanding one another in speech is fundamental. Such understanding is not only not a case of understanding how to go on, but it is something which no understanding of how to go on could possibly lead you to. (Which is not to deny that it may depend on understanding how to go on in some way.) Understanding one another is very similar to understanding a dialogue.

If you were to say that understanding is a matter of knowing how to play a game, then you could leave out the whole question of the growth of understanding. You would leave out what is central in the whole idea of understanding; and therefore also the idea of intelligibility. I do not believe you would ever see the connexion between understanding and the problem of life in that way.

Understanding a game – that is generally something you can carry on without speaking at all. That is rather important. As we have seen, this emphasis on games leaves out the distinction between an imaginary and a real one. (Which belongs together in the way in which Wittgenstein treats the subject.) You do not have this distinction here. Probably that is the same point that we have made in saying that a game has not any particular connexion with life. It is not about anything, and it is not of concern to your life. One of the differences, one of the reasons why we say that real speaking and discussing is not a game, is just that it is not a matter of doing it according to the rules in the way in which one does it in a game.

There are rules in the game, and that is what makes it a game, that is what takes it apart from the ordinary business of living.

Contrast a game and an investigation for instance. If you keep to the game you keep to the rules. If you keep to the investigation – well no doubt there are rules in connexion with it, but the main point is that you keep to the subject, you keep to what it is concerned with. And there is not anything like that in connexion with a game. No doubt you do understand one another in the sense that you can 'play ball together'. But that is much more like being able to work together on a project; being able to get along together. Whereas in speaking it is this understanding what is said and understanding the dialogue that is fundamental. And one might almost say that the understanding of the rules was incidental to that. In other words, what is important is seeing the point of the remarks. If you just learned the rules and learned how to construe odd remarks, or if it were really something like learning a game, and your teacher said 'Now let's play. I'll move here . . .' etc. or: 'Now let's play. I'll say this. Now what are you going to say?' this would be a game, all right, and what you say would be determined by what is possible according to the rules, and by what you could think of. But there would be no reality in it, and neither of us would be telling one another anything.

And the point I want to emphasize is that the rules have quite a different importance there. They are what make the game what it is – and they are what in a way keep it external to the players. They determine the kind of course the game may take. Whereas in the conversation it is not like that. No doubt there may be surprises in a game, and there may be a development which was unlike any you had ever seen before. But note that you would never speak in this way of surprises in the course of a conversation. I think this goes with the fact that you are not considering possibilities in the same kind of way.

'For the professional player the game is not a diversion.' All right. But all the same, what happens in the game is not *about* – it does not have to do with, *it does not get its sense from* – what happens in the rest of his life. And in that sense it is something 'apart', in a way in which a conversation is not.

If you want to see the kind of role that rules do play in speaking with people, you have to consider the way in which the various remarks in the conversation are about something; the way in which people are talking about something when they talk together. That is what makes the big difference. It is why their connexion with one another is rather 'internal', in a way in which the connexion of moves in a game is not.

PART FOUR

Belonging to language

CHAPTER 10

Conversation and institutions
(7.2.59)

I

The principle question has been regarding my reasons for saying that you could not have one conversation unless you had others. I have been wanting to suggest that this was a logical matter; a logical impossibility. But I am asked for a clearer exposition of what sort of things they would have to be. If I give the example of the two women having a conversation over the fence about the illnesses of their relatives, I have been wanting to suggest not only that there must have been other conversations but that there must have been conversations of other sorts. One of the questions that was put to me was, 'Would it not be possible for them to have had several other conversations, but all of them about the illnesses of people?' And I questioned this, because I thought that it was necessary if they are to speak and understand the sort of things that are said in that conversation, it would be true that they would speak in other connexions in the lives that they were leading as well; and this has something to do with the fact – or rather had some sort of parallel in the fact – that the concepts which are employed in mathematics must have been employed outside mathematics if mathematics is to have any force at all and not be just a wallpaper pattern.

In this case: there must be something of that kind if their conversation is to be a conversation at all and not something like a dance, for instance. Cf. the question of whether the rules of a dance could be called laws of thought. All of this had to do with the question of their understanding one another in that conversation; with the fact that the remarks that are made in the conversation are seen to have such and such a bearing on one another and such and such a bearing on the topic of the conversation. I might even question whether you could talk about the topic of the conversation at all, if this were the only topic. One of the points I made was that conversation – being able to speak to and understand one another – is much more of a personal matter than that. By which I meant, for example, that if they could speak about anything, then they, for instance, quarrel with one another. And this has something to do with the sense of the things that they are saying. That the sense of the things that they are saying does not lie simply, for instance, in their function or role in that particular conversation. But this is a difficult matter to get clear, because in one way I want to say that it is only when they are taken in their bearing on that conversation that they do have sense. But my point is that that is a different kind of thing from having a role in that conversation in the way in which a move in a game might. Part of what I had in mind was that you have to be familiar with the sorts of things that people say, if you are to understand how the statement is to be taken. Questions about irony and sincerity come in here.

With regard to the 'personal character' of what is said, the point is that the two women would be trying to understand one another. (*Per contra*, what either of them says would have sense if it were said by someone else.) This would be something different from trying to counter a particular move, for instance. Agreeing that what we call debating is one form of conversation – although it is a matter of trying to make an impression on somebody else than the person with whom, or against whom, you are talking – it is not even clear to what person you are talking, so that a debate in this way is not a conversation in one sense at all – but even here the different debaters have to understand one another in the sense of understanding the things that are being said; and this has connexions with other things that are said in a way in which the moves in a game of football, for instance, do not have connexions with moves in other games. And I want to say with regard to speech that it *essentially* has connexions of that sort. But this is the matter which I was asked, and rightly, to develop and bring out.

(In football the player may try to remember how one game was played, the moves that were made at particular junctures, and to be guided by it in the present game. It may even help him to guess what his opponent is up to. But he *could* judge the importance of the other move by considering it in the present game, simply. No doubt he must know something about the game, and probably he has played before. But in language it is different, since I would say that he cannot even 'see what move it is' – see what is being said – unless he is familiar with the sorts of things which people say.)

I am trying to show that it is not a matter of a lot of different games which just happen to be similar to one another in some ways. This is why I said that it is almost a matter of playing a game with the language.

I have an idea that all this is connected with the question of 'What is the child doing when he tries to understand you?' or 'when he tries to make himself understood'. If I could make that clear, then I should have made clear, I think, why it is that if he can ask questions here, in this connexion, he will go on to ask questions in other connexions as well.

'Asking questions and answering them – can you describe this in terms of a particular game?' Certainly you can say it is not the same as following instructions and issuing instructions (which Wittgenstein would have called one sort of language game); and in a way it is more fundamental. I should want to say that the two women could not carry on that conversation unless they did other things. There could not be a life which consisted simply in that. If you ask, 'Why not? Surely it is logically possible?' then my point is that if that were so, we should not regard what they are doing and saying as intelligible at all. It is only because they are human beings who are speaking and such that it would be sensible for us to ask them other questions about other things, that we can notice and record and set down what they are saying. And it is for this reason that we speak of them as having a *conversation* there. I imagine this is the point which I ought to underline.

A general account of language is largely an account of how the things that are said hang together: how they bear on one another, or how they belong to the language. And here we found a certain ambiguity in the point that a sentence would be said to belong to language even when it is not being uttered. This has analogies with the idea of the meanings of particular expressions. And the notion of the ways in which different language games belong to language, and so in knowing the games, and possibly in knowing how they hang together, you know the language. This is all connected with the difference between speaking and doing exercises. Cf. responsibility and taking part in a play.

In any case, you do not give an account of belonging to language, and in this way you do not give a general account of language either, by showing what the different propositions or the different things that are said have in common. As though a general account of what speaking is would be a general formula under which every statement would fall, or of which every statement would be a particular case.

II
(24.9.57 – 25.9.57)

For all the revolution in Wittgenstein's later thinking, he does seem to have kept, in much of what he said anyway, to the idea of a close parallel between mathematics and language. He certainly does not want to say that language is a calculus. But he does not seem to want to make any difference of principle between mathematics and language. Perhaps he would want to say that mathematics is a particular department of language – a particular kind of game, if one likes, a kind of language game. That is already getting to be misleading, because in mathematics it is not a game they play with one another in the way they do in connexion with conversations. But what this brings out is that for him, then, on that kind of view, language just is a 'family' of such games. This kind of family relationship seems to be for him simply a kind of resemblance among a set of different techniques; at least that is the way in which he sometimes speaks; all these techniques then being apparently regarded as *ways* of doing things. That is the importance of speaking of it as a game in this way, I suppose. A game and an institution – there are important parallels here.

If one is speaking of games and institutions the importance of rules seems fairly prominent. In legal institutions the importance of legal rules is obvious. If one speaks of language as an institution, as something that governs our lives in the way legal institutions do, it is misleading. Language does not play this part, or even a parallel part, in our lives; even if the peculiar rules, grammatical rules or what it may be, of a *particular* language, Latin or English or French, could be said to do that.

When Wittgenstein said that there is not a necessary form of language, that bore on what he had to say about the unity of language too, and that was why he wanted to speak of it as a family or almost a collection. And I suppose this went with his idea of making up the rules as you go along. (There may always be new developments – as we may add new quarters to a town.) It also went with what he had to say about logic and about things like the law of contradiction: whether a contradiction *could* not work, and in general the whole question of the relation between logic and intelligibility.

But what I wanted to emphasize now was the connexion with the idea of the *unity* of language. In what I am trying to say about the growth of understanding, I want to emphasize the unity of language in a way which possibly Wittgenstein did not. In doing so I am not reverting to anything like a common form of language. What I am doing is raising the question of what is meant by speaking the same language. And that is something that would have to come up when one was considering the different language games too – because they are in the same language. That is where the business of intelligibility and understanding comes in. And I think that Wittgenstein does neglect it in the way in which he tries to give an account of language in terms of games and techniques, and so on.

Being the same language does not mean having a common form. It means pretty much what is meant by speaking together. Speaking together – intelligibility – is not a matter of form. It is not a matter of the relation between the sign and the reality in the way in which Wittgenstein once talked about that. But understanding the language is not understanding an institution either.

Cf. knowledge of the ways of banking. Becoming an experienced man in the field. It is not really like that when one speaks of the child as being better, or as understanding more than he did. There are analogies, but this idea of 'becoming an experienced man in the field' is important, and I want to bring out the idea that it is far more external in that case, than the kind of understanding that goes with language is.

Understanding and the growth of understanding – that is what I am coming back to again and again. The growth of understanding is not like the growth of proficiency. Neither is it a matter of becoming more experienced. It certainly is not a matter of becoming more familiar with institutions.

I do not like talking about 'the institution of language' anyway. Even if one were to call a particular language like French or English an institution. And if you like, a particular vocabulary. Still I would not call *language* an institution. Parliamentary institutions, economic institutions; the institutions of property. It is in connexion with legal institutions that the expression is particularly at home. For the same sort of reason I should not want to call language a custom or habit. Because that leaves out understanding. It leaves out that it is something we do together.

But to talk about language altogether as an institution would be misleading; just as much as it would be if you talked about thinking as an institution. *Speaking* as an institution.

Perhaps you might call mathematics an institution. That is the kind of thing Plato would have questioned (because of his views about mathematics and understanding). And the reasons for which Plato would have questioned it are probably the reasons why Wittgenstein wanted to insist upon it. And one can see the importance of that insistence in connexion with mathematics. And in a measure also the importance of it in connexion with language. If one wants to emphasize that the way in which we speak is not responsible to anything like the nature of reality as a sort of ideal standard, or the form of the proposition. This goes with the point that there are no principles of language; which goes with the discussion of the foundations of mathematics. Well, I see the importance of all that.

Even if you did say that speaking was an institution, still understanding what people say is not a matter of understanding an institution. And I suppose partly for that reason I balk at suggesting that 'saying something' means 'carrying on the work of an institution'. Understanding what people say – that is understanding what they are talking about, rather than understanding how the institution works.

I was almost going to say there that it is understanding what they are talking about, rather than understanding that they are talking about so and so. If somebody tells you that the train has been delayed, you understand what he is saying. We say that you understand the point he is making, and so forth. (You do not ask 'Well, what do you want to say that for? Why do you tell us that?' which might come roughly to 'Are you crazy?' or 'Don't talk nonsense; if you have something to say, say it.') That is something rather different from understanding what the sentence means. That is why one is inclined to put it as 'understanding *him*'.

Understanding what is being said; not just understanding what the words mean. Objection: 'Those are synonymous.' I do not think so. You can understand what the words mean even when nothing is being said. (Cf. 'how you would say so and so.') This is almost like being able to translate them; being able to tell someone what they mean. As opposed to: explaining the point of the remark.

Understanding the remark he is making is not simply a question of knowing English. It is a question of finding that he is saying something intelligible, that he is saying something sensible. And what do you have to know, in order to see that? What do you have to learn in order to understand him in that way? It will not do, just to say that you have to learn the language (know the language), if that means that you have to acquire a kind of equipment. Just as you might have to know addition and subtraction and multiplication, if you are going to be able to give the correct change; or something of that kind. Because learning the language itself presupposes being able to understand what people are saying.

I say that understanding what they are saying is not simply a question of understanding what the words mean – in the sense in which someone who knows English but who did not know when or where it was said, might understand what the words mean. Perhaps one would call that a general understanding. Something which Wittgenstein might have called knowing the sort of circumstances under which they might be used.

I have agreed that being able to talk about something at all depends on the fact that the people with whom you are talking share what you might call a common way of living. The idea of saying something, and also of what you say, is bound up with that. But here we might note first of all that that seems to be constant, whether you say one thing or another. And also, the whole business of saying something and making a remark requires that you are talking with people and that there is something like a conversation. That you are making yourself understood and understanding the other person. And this is something over and above this business of having a common way of living.

Certainly he has to be the sort of person you can talk to. This may not be much different from what you presuppose in a great deal of your behaviour towards him, as distinct from talking with him. And the whole business of saying something is something over and above that.

I do not want at all to deny the importance of the other. I do not want to deny that this whole business of a way of living – and you

may call that an institution if you like – or a custom – that that is
indispensable. And it may be an idea that is more important and
sheds more light than anything like the nature of reality. But it does
not quite fulfil the same role as that other did either. The reality of
the remark and the reality of the discussion seem to be left out.

Perhaps I should make a distinction between behaving intelligibly
and speaking intelligibly. Behaving intelligibly covers whether he is
the sort of man you can talk to. But he is not saying anything in that.
That is the kind of distinction that we are concerned with here.
Behaving intelligibly does seem to be more or less like living under
an institution; following certain rules, and so on. Almost like using
intelligible expressions. But it is not like speaking intelligibly, just
because it is not saying anything. You have to be familiar with the
way of living (with the institution) if you are trying to understand
what he is saying, or if you are to see that he is saying anything at all.
But that does not mean that understanding what he is saying is
something like being familiar with the way of living. This bears on
the distinction between learning to speak and learning to read, I
think. It also bears on the question of *how* you learn to speak; and of
whether learning to speak is a matter of learning how it is done. I
want to argue that it is not.

Certainly there is a lot of learning how it is done in connexion
with it. And also, there is a lot of learning how people live; the
growth of understanding seems to depend on that to a considerable
extent.

And yet the growth of understanding is not a growth of understanding how people behave; like the growth of understanding of
banking, for instance. It is being able to understand what is being
talked about or what is being said. And I agree that that *depends* to a
considerable extent on being familiar with the way in which people
live and the sorts of things they do and care about and so on. (The
importance of literature.) This is already taking us away from the
learning of rules, and much nearer to the understanding of people. It
is probably important to notice how these run into one another.

Being able to understand what is being said in the sense of being
able to talk to people. This is what is important. I do not think you
could understand what is being said, in the sense of following a
conversation in which you were not taking part, unless you were able
to talk to people. Neither would you learn to read unless you can talk
to people. Understanding what he is saying, is not simply knowing

the *sort* of thing he is talking about; and I almost want to say it is prior to that. This is where being able to see the point of the remark comes in again. And it is in that that we have the growth of understanding. That is why understanding what he is saying, is not simply knowing the sort of thing he is talking about.

CHAPTER 11

Language and generality
(17.5.58–27.6.58)

I

When you understand what is said – what is that? Is it like understanding a technique? Is it like understanding what people are doing? Is it like understanding a rule? Is it like understanding a game? I suppose one would have to answer 'yes' to all these. And yet one would have to insist that there are differences, which are often so important that one may want to say that it is not like any of these.

Why is it that understanding what is said, or why is it that understanding people, seems to be connected with understanding the language? The trouble is partly that we are not even clear what understanding the language is; and the relation between that and learning to speak. I think that is one of the main points.

What is the difference between learning to speak and learning a language? You do not learn to speak by being trained to do exercises. On the other hand, there can be no speech without language; that is in a way trivial, but it is important. And the possibility of saying anything on any occasion and under any circumstances depends on the fact that what you are saying then has some sort of connexion with other things that are said on other occasions and by other people.

There cannot be a private language. I should not think there could be a language of only two people either. And it is somewhat similar to that if we say that there could not be a language which was confined to the practice of a particular technique in which perhaps only two people were engaged.

This all has a bearing on the sense of the statement that when you say something you say it in a language. That is simply an attempt to analyse or clarify what 'saying something' amounts to. And I think it leads to a consideration of the connection between saying something and intercourse between people or what is meant by living among people and understanding one another.

The difficulty in all this comes from the fact that you can learn a language, and you can understand what is written or told you or repeated in a language, when it is not anything that anyone is saying to you or that you are saying to anyone else; when you are not speaking with people or trying to understand anyone. This may be akin to understanding people when you listen to them speaking to one another. And of course unless that were possible, then this connexion between your saying something and other things that are said would not be there at all.

You can understand what is said even though it is not said to you; you can understand what is written here although it was not written for you (and has nothing to do with the situation in which you are); you can understand what is told in a story or what is recited in a play, even though it is not written or uttered for anyone in that sense at all.

And I say this creates a difficulty, because it makes it seem as though learning to understand – or learning to understand what is said – is *not* like, or need not be like, learning to understand people.

You may want to follow the instructions that are written and it does not matter to you who has written them. And yet: if you leave out the connexion with understanding people, then I do not think you have grasped what understanding language is. You have not seen the difference between that and understanding a scheme or mechanism. Or we might say: you have not seen the difference between a language and a set of rules (cf. a calculus). Perhaps that is why it seems as though a language were like the learning of a game. And if you do not see that difference, then you will not be able to see why people should not speak – have something which we should call a language – in connexion with a particular building technique, even though they had nothing of the sort in any other connexions in their lives.

This is connected with questions about the unity of language or how language hangs together or about the relations of inter-dependence of various parts of it. This was the kind of question that Plato was raising; for instance the question about whether the unity of language was the unity of a system, for instance. (Cf. also Parmenides on the unity of discourse.) Or whether it is of another kind, as Plato thought it was; and I think he is right.

Some writers have connected this question with questions regarding the conditions of the intelligibility of the statement. And it has been one of the reasons many have thought of language as analogous to a calculus, I suppose, and of belonging to a language as something analogous to belonging to a calculus; and of understanding a language as understanding a calculus. There is much that is sound in this analogy. And probably there is something that writers, including Wittgenstein, were trying to get at there, which was lost in his later conception of language as a family of various language games. In this later view he was emphasizing what you might call the essential incompleteness of language. And these various language games seem to be in a measure independent of one another. The idea of family likeness seems to give you an external relation between them; and you would not need to know or understand the one in order to understand the other. And yet the question of belonging to the language cannot be answered on quite those lines. There is some sort of internal connexion there, which differentiates the way in which what he is saying on one occasion is connected with what he or others say on other occasions, on the one hand, from the way in which a game or technique which you can learn or apply on one occasion is connected with a game or technique which you learn or apply on others. There are analogies and perhaps essential similarities too. But it is not essential that it should be connected with other games or other techniques in that sense, in the way that there is in language. That is why Wittgenstein in his early days did think there was an internal connexion there, something like there is in a calculus.

Part of the difficulty about the particular and the general, or the particular and generality in language has to do with grammar and vocabulary of course. When people are speaking, they are always saying something which, so far, seems to be as particular as the particular steps they take or strokes they strike. And on the other hand, they say it in this vocabulary and grammar.

If you say anything now, it is connected with things that have been said. With things you have said yourself, or that people have said to you; and with things that people have said to one another. This is because speaking is connected with understanding people and living among them. When you understand this person, that is connected with understanding other people as well. At least, you could not understand this person unless you *could* understand other people as well.

It is this which gives the appearance of generality. Almost as though you could learn to speak and understand people (or learn to *say* anything) by learning vocabulary and grammar. Almost: 'It is because this man is saying what other people might say – and only for that reason – that you can understand him.' But that is the wrong way to put it. (a) Because it is not in that way, chiefly, that the connexion between understanding and understanding others is important. (b) Because it neglects the distinction between seeing the point he is making, and knowing what the sentence means. (a) and (b) are not really separate.

Understanding people, and living among people. How would you describe people living together? Not by referring to a *way* of living. (You do not describe what language is when you refer to various ways of speaking. 'Ways of *what*? Why do you call them all *language games*?' Wittgenstein's question, at one stage, of whether forms of regular activities, not using words, could be called languages as well. The importance of what he said about laws of thought: that you would not call the rule a law of thought unless it went through the whole of your life.) This sort of thing – the sense of speaking of people living together – is allied with what is meant by 'being a language'.

The *difference* between this and understanding a routine. And 'organization' – or role in an organization – does not give the conception of *the point* of a remark either. It is *because* people go about among one another, that understanding them is not understanding a routine. ('My station and its duties' *per contra*.) Because a man may have various jobs, for instance. Because he is not *essentially* connected with any one job or any one post. It is not the various roles in an organization that you have to understand if you are to understand what is said.

Other people may repeat what Leonidas or Caesar or Napoleon or Bismark said on a particular occasion. But they are not making the remark themselves. Even where similar situations recur and people say the same thing ('Will you marry me?'), then in one sense it is not the same remark.

What is there in common in the different things people say when they speak the same language? 'It must be something they both understand; at least if someone explains it.' Here the contrast is with *privacy* or with 'private meanings'. (Is that whole question connected with the idea of the *unity* of language, then?)

What is the relation between the language you use – or the *meanings* of the words you use – and what you say? Suppose I repeat Caesar's remark. 'It is because the words have those meanings, that you have only to repeat it in order to tell me what he said.' The words which Jesus used on the cross were the words of Isaiah. The words which the judge uses in pronouncing sentence. An exclamation like 'Fire!' The repetition of a proverb (A rolling stone gathers no moss). 'I know the meaning of the sentence, so I know what you are saying.'

If I say something and you answer me, we are speaking the same language. 'You could not have used words, nor grammatical forms, that were entirely new. You could not do that (use new words and new grammar) every time you spoke. It would be no language at all then. And there would be nothing to understand.' I must have been familiar with the words and the grammar you used. One almost wants to say that there must have been some relation between your words and mine. But can this be anything more than the fact that I am familiar with both?

It is not enough that *I* should be familiar with both. The language is something that is spoken – that various people speak with one another. There would be no sense in saying that I was familiar with the words unless this were so. Otherwise it would be just a familiarity with certain sounds. What is it that you are familiar with when you are familiar with the words? You know what they mean. And you have met them often and used them yourself. You have met them often. They are common in the language that people speak. (And that is something they do together. It is not like saying it is a habit everyone seems to have.) That is what you are familiar with – people using the words in intercourse with one another. That is why you can understand what I say; why we can understand one another. That is how 'belonging to a common vocabulary' comes in. And it is nothing different from belonging to a common language. That is why it is not helpful to refer to a common vocabulary in order to explain what a common language is. We are speaking the same language. Our words belong to the same language. (The connexion here is the connexion in the lives of those that speak it.) We are speaking a language that other people speak. ('Yes of course; what did you *think* I was saying?') A language that other people understand.

But that is not to say that what you understand is a rule; or that what you are familiar with is a rule. That would make it too much like being familiar with mathematics. I must be familiar with mathematics if I am to understand when you talk mathematics – introduce mathematical expressions or give a mathematical explanation of something. But the familiarity with words is not like being familiar with the way something is done – with the difference between correct and incorrect in that sense. May we say that the distinction between understanding the words and understanding what is said has no clear parallel in mathematics? The nearest would be the distinction between knowing the rules – which amounts to knowing the *subject* – and following a particular calculation or proof. Seeing how the rules are exemplified here. (Cf. the sense in which a proof in pure mathematics does not *tell* you anything. 'That is really just what you had before' etc. It may be held that when you are puzzled by a man's mathematics, you are puzzled to make out what he is up to. But then it is not *merely* a question of whether what he has done is mathematically correct. And what you need to decide it, is something more than a knowledge of the methods of mathematics. It is familiarity with discussion, I suppose.)

II

He is speaking in the recognized language. He is paying in the recognized currency. Certainly it would make no sense to say 'I use a currency which no one else uses.' The idea of making use of a convention or an institution. As though one might say that he makes use of language.

People could get along without money. They could barter. It is not like that in language. Language is not like a common currency. Making payments, or making any sort of exchange, is not trying to understand one another. Nothing is being *said* in the money you give or receive. And although I may question whether you have given me the right amount (for the articles bought) or the correct change – this is not like criticizing or questioning what you have said when I am trying to understand you.

Coins are not words, nor anything like them. The currency is common in the sense that I accept the coins from you because I take it for granted that others will accept them from me. The idea of 'validity'. But it is misleading to think of language in this way. As though words were something that were given or taken in exchange (Cf. again the idea of discourse as the common measure). Words do not have 'value' in that sense, and they are not taken in exchange. (If something is given in conversation, it is not like that. There is nothing bought or sold. Unless you come near to the sophistic idea of language as something through which you gain points or lose them. There is no question of giving up anything and receiving anything. Cf. 'I do not take money for my teaching.')

The point is that there is in conversation something which one might call an 'exchange' of some sort. But in this the words and sentences do not play at all the role of a currency. They are not even what is exchanged. Perhaps it is for this sort of reason that you could not have a conversation purely in the form of a calculation. You can have a discussion concerning a calculation, of course, and calculation may form part of a discussion. But this is something connected with the idea of *measure* which seems to be out of place here.

Neither are words something that I give you in *place* of something, although you might say that about money. It is because I can give money in place of anything that can be bought and sold – because it enables us to dispense with barter – that is one of the points in speaking of it as a common or universal medium of exchange. And money *does* fulfil something like the role of a common denominator, in that way.

It may be that some people have thought that words were a substitution for pointing to things. And if it were like that, then the analogy with currency would be closer. It may come in also when we say that 'all I can give you is the words; of course I cannot give you what is really before my mind.' The idea that each of us *translates* his private experience into words, which are the common currency. It is in that sense of the publicity of language that the analogy with a currency comes closest. And I expect both of them are equally far from what it is that we mean when we say that the people who speak together must have a common language. Or when we say that speaking is 'something public'.

'Wie bezeichen sich die Wörter auf Empfindungen?' ('How do words designate sensations?') The idea of 'standing for' them; or for things. And so you need conventional signs. Learning a language and learning a notation. And of course you can speak of *using* a notation. 'Saying it in a language' and expressing it in a particular notation. Turing's machines. A notation that will 'do everything you want'. The notion of an ideal notation or an ideal language. The universality or generality of mathematics, and the generality of language.

If we talk of the universality of mathematics, does that mean the universality of the propositions in a system of measurement? The idea of grammatical statements. But somehow this is getting away from the generality of language – or not directly. It does come in when we consider the nature of the distinction between correct and incorrect, no doubt, or why it is that we call this the correct way to go on. In other words, it would be absurd to talk of a private mathematics.

The confusion seems to come in when you consider whether a notation will allow you to do everything you want to do. 'If you adopt that notation, you have to keep to it.' 'Anyone will understand you who understands – i.e., can follow – that notation.' It is here that we have the connexion between understanding and being able to follow a rule. And the point then seems to be that you have to try to understand the notation *before* you can understand what somebody is trying to state in it. Compare the idea of private languages: you must have adopted the conventional signs before you can talk with people. 'The meaning of language lies in what the words stand for.' Reaction against this, with the view that 'language must take care of itself'. It is not responsible to anything to which it must be 'adequate'; and so on. But then the conception of language as a game lies only too near. 'The relation of words to meanings is not like the relation of money to the things we buy with it, but like the relation of money to the *use* of money.' It is hard to work that out, though. Language as a medium of exchange. (Because we cannot barter our ideas directly.) So we depend on its being universally recognized. I suppose the conception of language as a game was intended partly to avoid that. But I do not think it is quite satisfactory to make this a matter of whether one can give oneself a private rule.

What is important is rather the conceptions of 'saying something' and 'understanding'. This has to do with understanding people and understanding the lives they are leading; perhaps with their understanding one another. Anyway, the point is that the 'type' of publicity here is that which we have in a conversation. It is because it is there that we have speaking and understanding, and that there could not be anything intelligible about something which 'only I can understand'.

I know that if I put it in this way, and place less emphasis on the notion of a rule, then I may be neglecting the 'abiding' element in language – in the sense in which an institution might also be said to be abiding. And that is why I should want to emphasize also the fact that the language is something that is spoken by several people, and not just by these two (the builders); that there could not be just this conversation either. That is a matter which I want to bring out, if I can; the point about the language of the builders is connected with it. And I have an idea that Wittgenstein's treatment of the question about private languages in terms of a private *rule* may be one reason why he did not see (as I take it) the impossibility of that. And also why he did not think the unity of language need be anything more than the unity of a family resemblance.

In other words, I think he did not bring out the connexion between the intelligibility of what is said and its belonging to a language; although he was certainly correct in insisting that it must belong to something that people speak together – as he would have put it, it must have a role in a game that we play with other people – if it is to be a word or to be intelligible at all. Well, what *is* the point, then? What is the belonging to a language? What is the 'being part of the discourse which people carry on with one another'? And what is the difference between this and being used in accordance with a recognized rule?

Certainly it is important to bear in mind the difference between public and private here, because anything we mean by the generality of language or by a common language is connected with that. On the other hand it is misleading if you think that its being a common language is something like its being a public institution; and that its universality or generality was something like the universality of an institution like money – or a particular currency. We might say that that was universal, in the way in which certain more specific institutions or special offices are not. If we do speak of a common language, the point is that we can understand one another. That is the point I must keep repeating.

If it is a common currency, the point is *not* that we can understand one another; not in that sense. The point would be, perhaps, that we both accept it; and the 'acceptance' includes the recognition that it is the currency which others will accept. But if I understand you, or if I tell you something, there is not here the question of 'accepting' the words or the sentence in that sense. Yet I could not understand you, in this sense, if you were the only person I understood. Here the publicity is important. And that is why one might want to say, 'But it is not just that I understand *you*; I understand what you are saying.' Other people could understand you if you spoke to them. Otherwise you would not be *speaking* to me.

A child might be brought up by its father, in isolation from everyone else, and learn to speak from its father. Here again we should have to say that he comes to understand what his father is saying; and this is different from understanding simply what his father is up to, for instance. On the other hand, I do want to say that it is not like learning rules from its father; nor like learning mathematics from his father, for instance. What the example shows is simply that it is very difficult to see how the generality does enter in. Or what it is that the child is 'familiar with' for instance. A child might be brought up in isolation by his father to play the violin. But that would not present the same problems.

What his father tells him is not: how the other people say so and so; or how to speak the language. (Linguaphone records. At a later stage he might learn *that* from the machine, but the machine would not be saying anything.) The boy does not simply understand *him*; he understands what he is saying. If the boy learns to speak from his father, he will be able to speak with other people. (That follows from the proposition that he is able to speak with his father – to say things to him.) This (the connexion between speaking with his father and being able to speak with other people) is not merely an empirical connexion, in the sense that we know as it happens that the language he learned from his father is a language which other people speak too.

III

Compare the knowledge of mathematics that enables you to understand what he is doing; the knowledge of chemistry that enables you to understand what is going on here. Those are different, but they are more alike than they are like the knowledge of the sorts of things people say, which enables you to understand that cryptic remark. 'Trying to understand what he is saying.' 'Trying to understand what he is doing (in the calculation).' In the latter, the point is that the mathematics may be too complicated and difficult, and at times you may feel out of your depth. Or perhaps he is going too fast for you, or perhaps you could have followed him if he had introduced certain intermediate steps that are not really necessary for the cogency of the proof. There is something like this in arguments given outside mathematics too; in legal arguments, for example, or arguments in economics.

But in all these cases, you recognize that the trouble comes from want of knowledge or skill on your part. You do not think there is any question – any real obscurity – about what he is saying. Whereas in the sort of case I am considering you do not think that someone with a better mastery of some subject or other would be better placed than you are. It is not a question of your being out of your depth, or of your having missed something that you could have got if you had been quicker. (Cf. the understanding of Blake's poetry, perhaps.) I am thinking of trying to understand what a child is trying to say, for instance. But there are plenty of examples when I find it awfully hard to see what an adult is trying to say, perhaps because he is hesitant and cloudy in his words himself. And my point is that the difficulty here is not like a difficulty in understanding what someone is *doing*: any more than it is a difficulty in understanding what is going on.

Understanding what he is doing is much more a matter of seeing the formula or the law which applies here. (So it would seem that Wittgenstein did keep to this idea.) Cf. trying to find the right word for the colour of the sky now. 'What is the word I want? What is the word which applies here?' That is also much more akin to trying to remember the word in a foreign language. But I do not think it is widely characteristic of trying to say something; and certainly it is hard to see how it fits in with 'trying to understand what it is that he is saying'. (When I try to understand the words of Jesus or of Saint Paul perhaps.)

Being familiar with the sorts of things people do in mathematics. In so far as this is relevant to your facility in seeing what he is doing now, they may be doing these things with the same face. Whereas that is not irrelevant when it is a question of how 'familiarity with the sorts of things people say' helps you to see what he is saying now, the things that are said have various sorts of importance for the people concerned. They say them in various characters and colourings. This is how it is unlike mathematics, and how it is unlike a game, too.

'What he said was clear.' 'What he said was obscure.' Cf. the contrast between 'beautifully clear' and 'needlessly complicated' in mathematics. I do not think there is a very close analogy here. (Why does it seem to be significant that he is not *saying* anything in mathematics?) It is not connected with other things that you say, in that way. That is part of it. ('A game does not go outside itself.') For some reason, that is why what is done (in chess or mathematics) is not 'alive', as something that is said is. The way in which what he says may be enlightening. 'When he gives a proof in mathematics – showing you something you had not realized before – is he saying something then?' That is where mathematics comes closest to it or has seemed to. (Plato and others seem to have suggested that a mathematical proof was the only really intelligible form of statement. And I suppose you would only really understand what someone has said, when you had a proof of it.) The proof may be illuminating, and this seems like a statement sometimes. Also, the illumination lies in seeing the connexion between the proposition proved and other parts of mathematics. A new insight into the subject. Cf. a new insight into the possibilities in chess.

And yet in one sense the man who gives a proof is not saying anything. In the same sense as you might say that you do not learn anything – it only shows you what you knew already. (Anamnesis. The circle of the same.) (The way in which sameness and difference must be combined when you learn anything. Analogy.) I have the feeling almost of: 'The man who is working out the proof is not saying anything; he is doing something for himself.' More like a sculptor working on a statue. 'Suppose someone shows you the solution of a mathematical problem. Then he tells you something that you want to know.' And yet that is an unnatural way of putting it, because it suggests that he is in a position to tell you something which you could not find out for yourself.

We see connexions between different parts of mathematics. But the different parts of mathematics do not have different faces. When it is a question of being familiar with the sorts of things people say, you do take account of the different faces. (Talent and peculiarities.) How things are said, the way people bring them, how they take to them. But the main point is that you have known and spoken to various people. (And that is *essential* for the type of understanding we are considering. The difference if you had never known or read but what one person says – no matter how gifted he may be. We must exclude even what he might tell you of other people's ways. The difference this would make to your understanding of new people when you did meet them.)

It is not anything one could learn from a machine (even if one could learn to sing a tune correctly from a machine). A machine might conform to the requirements of a notation. But the machine would itself make no attempt to understand or tell anyone anything.

'How do you know the machine does not understand? How do you know it is not trying to tell you something?' This is like 'How do you know he is not an automaton? How do you know the stone does not feel anything?' Would that mean 'Is there any way of telling the difference between a man and an automaton?' or 'Is there any way of knowing whether someone is hurt?'

'Perhaps a machine is really trying to say something and *never* shows it' or '. . .really trying to understand, and never shows it.' (What would it mean to say that the machine was wearing a dead-pan expression, though. We use the expression 'He doesn't show it' or 'You can't tell anything from his face' in a way that makes no sense of a machine; and makes no sense except of the sort of beings that sometimes do show it. What would it be like if the machine *did* show it? Unless you can answer that, it means nothing to say that it doesn't show it. Doesn't show *what?*)

'Maybe the man gets his ideas of understanding etc., from conversation with others. But the *child* cannot know this. The child only has the sounds and the motions. Well, it might hear sounds and watch motions in a machine. Is there anything *more* that he gets from the human being?'

The child tries to understand. And above all, he tries to say something. The way this is received by his father is different from the way it *could* be received by any machine. For one thing, how could the machine know, or show, that it had understood the child correctly, or that the child has understood the machine correctly? That is important. For it is not a question whether the child has given one of certain *expected* responses – so that something clicks in the machine.

Notice that this is not a question that arises in the playing of chess. That is important too – important incidentally for the whole question of the analogy between language and chess. Cf. here the question of 'being familiar with the sorts of things people say'. But this is more a question of being familiar with *people* than it is of being familiar with the sorts of moves or the sorts of play that may be made. Because when you are 'familiar with the sorts of things people say', this is a matter of coming to *understand* the sorts of things people say. And you can tell this – you can tell whether you have got it right or not – from the people and what they do and say and look. And there is no general criterion that will serve in the same way for everyone with whom you may be talking. You have to depend on your nose, very often.

Is there anything here comparable to the feeling for the way a piece of music ought to go? Probably. Cf. generally the conception of 'that is exactly right' in aesthetics. The objection is that this applies only to special sorts of statement and special sorts of understanding; that it does not apply to someone's question whether it is raining, or to the statement that the grocer could not supply the goods you wanted. Well certainly I do not want to say that the understanding here is a matter of aesthetic judgement, or that you have to have a sense of style before you can tell what someone is saying. The analogy that interests me is in the way in which one *acquires* such judgement. For I think that the standards which guide you in 'being able to tell whether you have understood him rightly' are more like the aesthetic standards (by which I do not mean that they *are* aesthetic standards) than they are like the rules which enable the beginner to judge what is correct and what is incorrect arithmetic.

The case of the feeling which an accomplished mathematician develops – when he is doing research in pure mathematics, for instance – the feeling for 'the way in which certain expressions behave' is different, and this may come closer to the aesthetic judgements. But if it does, then I think it is 'from the other side' and that it is not so much like the sense that enables you to tell whether you have understood someone correctly.

It is not like the question whether he has presented the correct solution to a problem (which the machine might show). How would you set a machine to change its behaviour when it has understood, or when it has understood correctly? (Repeat: this is not like changing its behaviour when it has reached the solution of a given problem.) You may set a machine to work towards and reach a given objective (under the guidance of negative feed-back). But suppose the objective is to understand what the man is saying. How would you set a machine to reach that? (Like a game of Twenty Questions? I suppose a machine could play that. But that *is* a game, and it is not like a conversation. In a conversation you might ask him what he meant and he might tell you, and then there would be the question of whether you had understood *that*. The possibility of pretence and deceit.)

The Socratic questioning is something different still – though there is something artificial about the conception of one of the speakers who *only* questions; and there is a good deal of suggestion in the questions that are asked. That is one of the considerations which makes it plain that this would be even further from anything that a machine could do. Anyway, Socrates' questions have almost nothing in common with the questions in a guessing game; it is not a matter of coming nearer and nearer to it in that way. (Though it is doubtful whether there could be many cases in which a machine could achieve even that nearer and nearer. For how do you measure whether one guess is further from the mark or nearer to it than another – except when it happens to be 'partly right' perhaps?) I have an idea that this is important for the question of what kind of objective it is; and for the distinction between this and finding the correct solution of a problem.

IV

Referring to reality. Does this happen by rules and conventions? Relation of atomic propositions to general propositions. That seems connected with fundamental questions regarding the relation of what is said here and now, to the generality it must have if it belongs to the language. 'Saying the same thing.' 'Speaking the same language.' 'All expressions are general. (Otherwise words would not mean the same for both of us; or the same on two occasions.)' 'How can we talk about what is continually changing?' 'We cannot express what is individual or particular.' Cf. Plato's forms and the theory of participation. 'How can the general meanings refer to what is particular? Or have any bearing on what is particular?' ('What was *purely* particular would not be intelligible.')

The suggestion of general and particular *objects* seems a bad confusion. The idea of logically proper names. This seems to go with the theory of descriptions. ('How can general meanings refer to what is particular?') So presumably it goes with the idea of the proposition as a 'representation' (showing what things would be like if it were true). As though what 'this' *means* were what you were pointing to. A different meaning each time. But that is nonsense. The idea of a name that *shows* what it means. (And so presumably could not be misunderstood.) Cf. 'I know what this means to *me*. It means *this*.' 'If you understand it, you know what it means – to yourself, at any rate.'

The theory of private language is connected with this false theory of meaning and understanding. (And the ideas of interpretation, a common medium etc., that go with that.) But then some misunderstandings about the generality of language must spring from that as well. We think of general laws and particular cases. I suppose the emphasis upon rules helps to foster this. Particular cases to which the general rules apply. As though, perhaps, the 'application' of language to things were something of that sort. 'Application of language' is queer. Difficulties and confusions of 'class membership' and 'class inclusions'. As if the particular thing of which you are talking (or 'to which your words refer') were a particular case of what your words mean.

But getting away from the 'genus–species', 'abstract–concrete' business, consider the application of a formula; or membership of a series. 'The conception of "function".' 'Does not the formula say something about the particular case that falls under it?' If it does, then 'saying something about it' is not the same as 'applying to it'.

'Oh yes, I see what that is.' How it goes on. You are saying something about the series when you say how it continues. This is rather like explaining the *meaning* of some expression. It is not like saying something about a concrete thing (that the jug is broken or the milk is sour). The theory of descriptions and logical constructions seems to have been an attempt to amalgamate the two (to amalgamate saying something about a particular jug, and saying something about the meaning of 'a particular jug' or 'this jug'). Analysis of judgements of perception: analysis of what it is to talk about a physical object; in terms of what the expressions refer to.

The contrast between language and what it refers to (what we are talking about, what we are saying) *is not a contrast between general and particular.* The contrast between a general formula and a particular case is a contrast *within* language. And it does not lend any sense to speaking about the generality of *language*. Which would at once raise the question 'generality as opposed to what?' Cf. the distinction between 'formal propositions' and 'mathematical propositions'. The idea that very general propositions cannot be material so they must be formal or grammatical? That seems to lead towards saying that the peculiarity of logical propositions is that they are very general. ('Nothing could falsify them.' Or verify either.) There is something misconceived in all this. It goes with the idea of propositions as truth functions of atomic propositions. 'Propositions as possibilities.'

Well, what of the distinction between grammatical and empirical propositions, then? Does this question arise when we are considering 'all'? And when we are considering the notion of a 'general concept'? Whether it is a 'mögliches Prädikat'? ('possible predicate'). When Wittgenstein was questioning whether the distinction between grammatical and material propositions was as sharp as he had earlier suggested, he was also questioning the idea of generality that comes into a logic like Russell's; and he was questioning the account of a general concept as a possible predicate.

Pure mathematics and applied mathematics. And, I suppose, the idea of the application of mathematics. Certainly the application of a formula *within* pure mathematics is very different from the application of mathematics to physical things.

Frege and Russell giving the analysis of number in order to show how it is that mathematics is applicable. Wittgenstein was questioning whether that analysis of number did show that. And his emphasis on the relation of the concepts of mathematics to what is outside mathematics seems to have been part of this same discussion.

The idea of *use*. And this idea of *grammar* that goes with that. A rule of grammar as a rule of use. Well, if the use is the kind of application that you have of a rule or formula *within* mathematics, then this does not tell you much about the use or application or sense of mathematics itself. This is one of the points Wittgenstein was emphasizing towards the end. 'Was ist mathematisches daran?' ('What is mathematical about it?') Trying to describe both the use and the dignity of the office, and so forth.

Mathematics itself does not apply to things in that way. Or: the relation of pure mathematics to what is outside mathematics is not of that sort. (It may be that Russell had imagined that it was. That his analysis of the concept of number and the rest would show both what the procedures within mathematics were, and also the relation of mathematics to the world. 'Mathematics refers to some reality. It is responsible to some reality.' I think Wittgenstein wanted to show that there was something wrong-headed about that.) This might be one reason for rejecting the idea of grammar then. And the revision of the view regarding the distinction between grammatical propositions and others would go together with that.

The question of the relation of language to things is part of the same story. And remember that the earlier view of that rested on the idea of the analysis of the meanings of statements in terms of sense data.

The idea of talking about something. Well, the difference between that and talking about words will still be important certainly. That is the point we are making when we emphasize the difference between the application of a formula within mathematics and the application of mathematics to things.

One other point would be that the application of mathematics to things is not just the same as talking about something. And it would be unnatural to speak of the latter as the application of language to things. If I am talking about Snowdon, or if I am talking about juvenile delinquency, it would be unnatural to speak of this as the application of language to Snowdon or the application of language to juvenile delinquency. On the other hand, I may say that a particular statement – perhaps that it is dangerous to climb – is one that applies to Snowdon and would not apply to certain other mountains.

What is said applies to Snowdon. When I said that, I was talking about Snowdon. This is not much like the application of a proposition in mathematics. (Perhaps because the notion of 'interpretation' does not come in in the same way.) And if we say that *what is said* applies, is this the same as saying that *the language which I used* applies? Could one speak of 'what is said' in mathematics? Is not the point that the rule of calculation applies? Whereas if I say of Snowdon that it is a dangerous climb (or that it is not) well there is no question of applying a rule or applying a calculation here. And I want to say: I am saying something, not doing something. And I think that is important. And the idea of *understanding* what is said, would be different too.

This question about application is much the same as the question I have been considering when I ask what is the difference between an actual conversation and an imaginary one. To distinguish between talking about things, and talking about what words mean – this seems always to have been very difficult.

My chief problem is still regarding what knowing the language is, and the sense in which that is essential for understanding what someone has been saying. I want to make clear if I can the difference between what you know when you know the language and what you know when you know mathematics or when you know, in the sense of being familiar with, a notation; or when you know – are used to using – a system of measurement.

Is all this connected with the matter of the way in which people live, and the need to be familiar with that if you are to understand people? This seems to involve the question of the unity of language; the way in which the language hangs together. It is that vague phrase 'hangs together' that is the source of much of the difficulty; or rather, contains much of the difficulty. I suppose this matter of the bearing of it is important here.

Only, I wanted to get away from an over-emphasis on the idea of rules of language, and perhaps that understanding language or understanding what is said (that is the main point) is something like understanding the rules – understanding the rule that applies here. It is an understanding that you have to get much more by going among people (although reading would be one form of that). That is what makes language alive, in the way in which mathematics is not alive. That is what makes it a language; and that is why mathematics cannot be a language. That is why it says something, and why mathematics cannot say anything. (That is why what you say has a face.) That is why language is so constantly surprising, I suppose. The person who had not gone about among people would be awkward; would not understand what is being said. That is why it is so different from the matter of knowing mathematics and knowing the rules. He *could* do that. My point is that he would be constantly misunderstanding things. And that is not like mathematics. The misunderstanding is of quite a different sort. He would be constantly misunderstanding things, not because he did not know the rules; not because he was not sufficiently familiar with exercises and examples, for instance.

What you have to know, in order to be able to get on with people. This is different from the sort of experience that you have to have if you are going to be a successful engineer. In engineering you cannot get along just with the theory either; you have to have had experience. Or for any sort of construction in a work shop. But that is not like what you have to know if you are going to get on with people. And there may be some point in emphasizing the analogy with aesthetic judgements here. And this may be at variance with the sort of thing that Plato seemed to be trying to say. The question of learning to be able to understand people is very different from a question of learning to be able to solve problems.

There are other questions or problems that are connected with this, such as the matter of interpreting a notation, for instance. My point is that where it is a question of whether you have interpreted the expression correctly – which is much more like the question whether you have the correct answer to the question of what series he is writing down – this is something that is generally pretty different from the question whether you have understood correctly what he is saying. I mean that the idea of correct and incorrect, in the way in which you determine whether it is done correctly or not, is a different sort of thing in the one case and in the other. The idea of language as a notation, or as a medium for the exchange of ideas – it is probably that that is at the root of a good deal of this way of looking at understanding: as though it were like understanding a foreign language or translating.

v

On this whole question of generality there may be some confusion between a general proposition and the generality of language. The idea seems to be that a general proposition in some way holds of, that in some way the possibility of general propositions rests on, what other more particular propositions have in common. Think of the way in which Wittgenstein speaks of elementary propositions as though their being elementary propositions at all is itself a guarantee of there being a perfectly general proposition.

The notion of a general proposition, as he develops it there, seems to be connected with the idea of an operation; with the conception of 'and so on'; with the way in which it is possible to pass from one proposition to another; and the way in which various elementary propositions, for example, may lead to a result.

It may be that the general proposition is then thought of as a function of those elementary propositions. The idea of a function seems to have gone together with the idea of an operation, in Wittgenstein's view at the time. That would have something to do with the way in which you can pass from one of those elementary propositions to another, I suppose. And there would enter here also the notion of a possible argument of a function, or possible value of a variable. The idea seems to be that if these different elementary propositions can have a bearing on one another, then they must all be possible arguments of a common function. (Did Plato hold that the soul, or discourse, is a process according to a measure or number? 'If it can be understood it has to be covered by this operation.') (This idea of a function is not very clear yet. The example that comes to mind is being members of a series; or illustrating a common or general formula.)

The point is that if they are all propositions, and if they are all in that way intelligible – I almost want to say 'intelligible *to* one another' – then they must be manageable under a common operation. Almost as though this were the operation of understanding. Almost as though this were the operation of using language: I dare say that is what comes in here.

What is obscure in this whole position is the notion of *using* language. And there the idea of an operation – particularly the operation of a calculus – seems to have been introduced just in order to afford an illustration, an example of what using language – using perhaps an elementary proposition – would be.

Possible values of the variable and possible subjects of an operation. The fact that they belong in that way to a common system of discourse – that is where the idea of a common system of discourse seems to come in; that is the way it is supposed to illustrate what a common intelligibility would be. And it is this idea of a common intelligibility that leads on to the idea of something like a common medium, I suppose. I suppose that seemed to be covered by the idea of a common formula, and in that way belonging to a common system. The idea is that if they are all propositions, if they are all in the same sense intelligible, if they are so to speak intelligible to each other – and therefore if they all belong to the same language – well for that reason they must have something in common. That therefore they must in that sense be values of or be instances of a very general proposition.

All this suggests that it is this notion of common intelligibility, of being able to speak with one another, that is important here. When people do say things to one another, they say quite different things, and at first sight to suggest that they have something in common or that there is something in common seems rather startling, and it does not seem to have much foundation. But the idea that we have here is just that of belonging to a common language; but that seems to *mean* just that they are intelligible to one another when they say these things.

One of the difficulties with trying to take this in terms of being values or arguments of a general operation, is that this seems to suggest that the bearing of these propositions on one another, or their relevance to one another, is always a matter of *logical* relevance. And that is obviously not so.

The question of whether there can be any very general proposition seems to be much the same as the question of whether it is possible to say anything about all propositions; or whether it is possible to say anything in a general way about all propositions. (The question whether you can do anything except give an example and add 'and things of that sort'.)

But is there not something queer about that idea of generality? The idea that there should be some highest degree of generality which is about all propositions. Or even the question whether generality in a given field – a very general proposition about moving bodies or about plants or numbers even – the idea that this must be a proposition about other propositions, or perhaps that it is a function of other propositions, seems to have something queer in it. Perhaps Wittgenstein was recognizing this in his questioning of the idea of a general concept as a possible predicate.

Does the possibility of a general proposition depend on the structural similarity between more particular propositions? That kind of general proposition would certainly be a grammatical one, would it not? For it seems then to be a proposition regarding the structure, and I suppose that means the grammatical structure, of the other propositions. Perhaps the idea would be that if they are not of a similar grammatical structure, then you cannot in any way come to a general proposition; perhaps because you cannot make a general type of assertion. And that is important. There must be some kind of similarity between the general proposition and the special cases that fall under it. They must be the same or similar type of assertion, in some way.

On the other hand I suppose it is clear that that kind of thing is not necessary if, as we have been putting it, the different propositions are to be intelligible to one another. Which means, I suppose, that we do not have to look for that kind of generality if we are to agree that they are all propositions; or perhaps, that they all belong to the language.

The reason for supposing that there was something of that sort seems to have been connected with the idea of an operation, and with the idea of 'and so on'. And perhaps one of the reasons why I should *not* want to think of intelligibility in that way, one of the reasons why I should *not* want to say that the question of whether something can be understood is a question of whether it is a possible subject of an operation – a common operation in that sort of way – the reason lies in the difference between *learning a mathematical calculation* and *learning to understand what somebody says*.

What makes it a proposition? What makes it intelligible? Certainly part of the question here is: what kind of bearing can it have on other things that are asserted? If it did not have *any* such bearing, then it would not be a proposition and would not be intelligible. But can you put this in terms of a general operation, in that way?

If there is something wrong in the idea of generality, and in particular if there is something wrong in the idea that had been put forward about what having a common language is, what there is in common to the various things that people say to one another, so that they can understand one another, for instance – what this whole business about belonging to a language – call it a 'system of intelligibility' even, if you like – if there is a misunderstanding about that, then I suppose there would be something correspondingly wrong with the notion of 'understanding', and I suppose therefore of what a proposition is, for instance.

That is why it has seemed to me that we have to tackle this idea of understanding one another, of trying to understand what is said, of trying to get someone else to understand. And the kind of mistake that there seems to have been in the *mistaken idea of the generality of language*. This seems more and more to be the central issue here. The kind of mistake that there seems to have been has to do with and makes itself apparent in this question of *whether it is like learning a rule*, or even of whether it is like learning to do mathematics.

This may affect the conception of the use of 'all', and the whole conception therefore of logic. But in this way it also affects the conception of *the relation of words to things*. The difficulties that have come up about the generality of language, and of how general meanings and general concepts can yield you knowledge about particular things, for example – perhaps the *trustworthiness of abstrac-*

tion and the rest – all that seems to be in a way wrong headed. And the idea of speaking a common language seems to be what we have to put central.

Why did Plato insist that discourse must be about what is? I imagine it was because he wanted to insist that the distinction between *sense and nonsense* was not arbitrary. He wanted to counter Protagoras' ideas there. And especially that the distinction between *valid and invalid* argument was not arbitrary.

This got him into queer difficulties, partly because of difficulties regarding generality. This suggests that this question about generality is fundamental for the question of what talking about something is. Or we might say: When Plato says that discourse must be 'about what is', that is raising more questions than it answers, and the question is what that 'about what is' comes to.

Plato was thinking of discourse as a measure. And that affected his idea of the relation of discourse to reality. It affected his idea of how it is possible to talk about something, and what talking about something is. Which would run into the question of what 'saying something' is; or understanding what somebody else says. And I dare say that some of the difficulties about being and becoming, which certainly Plato had inherited from Parmenides, are rooted in that same trouble.

If you think of the relation of language to things, if you think of talking about something, as an *application* of language; and especially if you have as an analogy there the application of mathematics, I expect there is a whole nest of troubles you have brought with you.

Cf. the idea of the comparability and the intelligibility of things, as though there was something similar to the comparability and the intelligibility of propositions. In fact the way in which Wittgenstein speaks of the various elementary propositions as having something in common in as much as they are capable of being subjects of an operation and producing a result, and so forth – their bearing on one another in that sort of way – that is reminiscent of the way in which some philosophers seem to have spoken about what things must be like if we are to be able to study them and discover the bearing of one thing on another. Even things like causal relations, for example, might fall under this.

Plato and Aristotle had questions about participation and about general concepts, realism and nominalism. But the way of the expositors of logical analysis, phenomenalism – that seems to be the same sort of thing. There again it is the suggestion that there must be in things the kind of comparability and intelligibility that there is between statements.

Compare also Plato's conception of coming to be and passing away as a kind of discourse. Discourse is the only thing that you can understand. Therefore if we understand the things that come to be, that must be a kind of discourse.

VI

Trying to understand him. Is this like trying to find the answer in a guessing game? Or even like trying to find the answer to a riddle?

The importance of questions and criticism. This is not like the criticism of what someone is doing, or of the way in which he is going about trying to reach a recognized objective. Where a more skilled and experienced worker can give him tips, for instance. There is no clear analogy to that in connexion with trying to understand what he is saying.

In Twenty Questions it is the person who is *asking* the questions who might be criticized. And he is not trying to *understand* anything the other person has said at all. Where one is trying to understand, then in *that* connexion one may ask questions; and the questions may go together with a criticism of what the other person has said. 'I don't understand. Surely that can't be right – surely you can't mean that – because (that would land you in these and these consequences).' Or: 'But surely that is not true . . .' This is not like criticizing his attempts to reach an objective: 'Look, you're trying to get there, aren't you? But you see you've gone off here. What you want to do is . . .' Or: 'That would have been much better if you had done it like this . . .'; perhaps adding 'you get a much better finish then' or 'the thing sits much more tightly then'. In such cases there is no disagreement about where we are trying to get; though the instructor may have a better view of it than you do. In any case, he is not trying to understand *you*.

Trying to understand him. This is not even like trying to find whether what he said is true or not. 'That is an interesting idea; it hadn't occurred to me. But I wonder whether it is really so.' Here I am not trying to understand him, for I assume that I do. If I do criticize him, it may be to get him to give up the idea. But it is not because I am trying to get at what it is that he is trying to say.

Criticism of someone's play in a game. 'It just doesn't make sense. I don't see what he's trying to do.' Is this analogous to 'I don't see what he's trying to say'? I do not think the analogy goes very far. In the game the point is – so it seems to the critic – that he can't possibly reach what he's after that way. It does not fit in with any strategy at all. Anyway, the point is that here we have a standard of what is good play and what is not; or above all, of what is skilful play and what is not.

Now in connexion with language, there is certainly the judgement of whether that is an intelligent thing to say (not the same as whether it was well expressed, but connected with the question of whether it really tells you something) or whether it is a stupid thing to say. And it may be that these standards do enter into a good deal of the question of whether you can make sense of what he is saying or not. 'He can't have meant that; that would have been just silly.'

All the same, that is not the main consideration when I am puzzled to understand what is said in the scriptures, for instance. And if I raise objections and criticisms, it is not because I think that what I read there is stupid; although it may be because I cannot see clearly what the difference is between what is said there and something that *would* be stupid, or at least open to obvious objections. 'What a queer thing to say.' ('Whether he can speak – that is not so much a question of whether he has mastered a certain sort of skill, as of whether he shows a certain sort of intelligence.') Why do I say 'He certainly can't mean that'? And if he replied, yes that was just what he did mean, I should say 'No, that just makes no sense; he just has not understood the conversation.' (Would that mean that he was not really saying anything at all?) And in certain circumstances – as with a person completely deranged, where nothing he said had connexion with other things he might be saying or doing – I might say 'Well, it is pointless to try to understand that: there is nothing to understand; he is not capable of understanding anything or of saying anything at all.'

This is the kind of thing Plato might have had in mind if he thought of the growth of understanding. It is also what gives sense to the phrase 'Trying to understand *him*' in these connexions. And it indicates how the criterion is not of how what is said can have a role in a system of calculation. It is much more connected with other things *he* says and does. Trying to see what he means. Trying to see the wisdom of what he says. Or if he said 'Well, that is just what I do mean', I might answer, 'Well then I just do not understand what you are talking about at all.' I would not try to understand him if I thought what he was saying was just stupid and pointless.

'Belonging to the same language': does this mean subject to the same operation, or subject to the same rules? Notice that these two ideas seem to go together. That is what Wittgenstein was getting away from in his conception of language games, and his insistence that each of the 'systems of human communication' is complete and independent. This was also connected with a tendency to question whether any language need be translatable into another.

In the earlier view he raised the question of what makes it a proposition, and suggested that this rests on some sort of structural similarity. There we should have to say that where there are propositions, they all belong – not, in one sense, to the same language – but that they all belong to 'language'. And that seemed to suggest that there was communication between the one and the other. And when he came to question whether languages need to be translatable into one another, this was what he was challenging.

I suppose this raises the question of what understanding one another is, and of what understanding the language is. (Cf. the notion of the necessary and the arbitrary parts of language.) (Which is reminiscent of the idea of 'the structure of thought'.)

There are reasons for that idea; just as there are reasons for the idea of structural similarity, which seems to be the same as intelligibility. Just as there are reasons for asking what it is that leads you to call them all *language games*. Or if you say that there are other languages which cannot be translated into ours or into one another: what is it that leads you to call them all 'languages'? And it seems to me that the analogy with 'what it is that leads you to call them all games' is not quite satisfactory.

You might say that if you call them all languages, part of what you mean is that they could be understood or could be learned if you did try to learn them. And Wittgenstein seems to have been saying at one stage that this was like saying that it is a game that could be learned, or an institution that could be learned, or perhaps a way of life which you could have followed if you had grown up in it, or something of that kind. And that all seems in some way or other to make the matter external.

Are we justified in extending this idea – of the way of life which you could have followed if you had grown up in it, and the rest – to the various language games which are supposed to make up one language? Wittgenstein may have been misled here by the persistence of the idea of 'language' as opposed to a particular language; and of 'belonging to language' in that kind of way. Because the different language games that he thinks of, although he speaks of them as complete systems of human communication (note the 'human': almost as though there were no essential difference from the 'systems of communication' which animals may follow) – he thinks of them as forming one language. Well, you do not have to translate from one to the other; in fact he could say that there could not be any question of that. And where you *are* translating from one language to another, for that reason is not quite similar. And the different language games do not belong to different *ways* of living.

This has a bearing on the question of the relation of logic and language, and on the idea of laws of thought. Rules which belonged only to one game, or to one dance, for instance, would probably not be called laws of thought. They are that when they go all through our life. And here the notion of 'our life' seems to be the central one; the unifying one, if you like. If we say that for the unity that there is in *that*, there are various games, activities, institutions – I do not think you could say that their cohesion, their being of the same life, was a matter of family resemblance or similarity.

In this matter of 'resemblance' we seem to have a descendant of the earlier idea of structural similarity: that there must be . . . Wittgenstein was substituting the idea of a family similarity or a family resemblance for the idea of a structural resemblance, which he had thought earlier was a requirement for belonging to the same language. (The idea of 'structure' persisted too, only here it is the structure of the game rather than the structure of the proposition.)

Being subject to the same operation; being a continuation of the same operation; this is still the operation which we were performing earlier; we are still speaking the same language. It is here that Wittgenstein brings in the notion of family resemblance partly because he wants to speak of freedom – I suppose he wants to emphasize the unpredictability. One of the big revolutions he was making was in the rejection of the idea that you cannot have any new form of proposition, that one ought to be able, from what we know now about propositions, to deduce any possible form of proposition. This is what he was questioning later. (I suppose the notions of the necessity of logic and the necessity of mathematics – what it is that makes this proposition mathematics – both went with this.)

If you and your friend are engaged in one language game, and I and my friend are engaged on another, still we *could* understand one another – all of us could understand one another. And when we say this, it is not like saying that as a matter of fact we just happen to be all of us able to speak these several languages (so that if we switched from one to another it will not matter). The point is that your being engaged in that language game, and our being engaged in this one – those hang together. There is some sort of essential connexion between the language they and the language we are speaking – and the fact that we are all able to speak the same language. In other words, I should question the conception of 'complete systems of human communication' here. This is the point about the builders and the possibility that they should speak only in that performance and not elsewhere.

But I would raise further objections. If Wittgenstein is going to call using a different grammar – using language in a different way – playing a different game, then I do not think that it is plain that the person with whom I am speaking need be playing the same game – that what he offers in his reply, for instance, or what he may offer by way of comment, need be the same sort of grammar or the same sort of game. This is connected with the point about the ways in which the different language games do hang together. It is not as if we have different groups of people playing their different games, and passing from one game to another. It is almost as though each of us were playing a game with the language. (Cf. 'going about among one another'.)

That is why it would not be possible – and I would emphasize this – for anyone to play or to understand the game I was playing, unless he understood the language. Somehow the sense of that game, or the intelligibility of that game, depends upon its belonging to the language. (In this way, of course, it is not like a game, in a literal sense.)

There is some connexion between our understanding each other in this game, and your understanding each other there – there is some connexion between that and the fact that we are all able to understand one another. There is some essential connexion between the language we arc speaking, and the fact that we are all able to speak the same language; that we are all able to understand one another. And I want to suggest that the 'understand one another' here is in some way fundamental. ('Common language' – the generality of language – the same language.)

I think it is misleading to put the emphasis upon the common vocabulary and the common syntax. The point is partly that the various people do not just *happen* to have a common vocabulary and a common syntax.

Is it not possible that a foreign language should have part of the vocabulary and syntax that is involved in these two language games? And if we were able to understand that part of the foreign language – there is something queer about that – this does not mean that we should be able to understand anybody who was saying other things that might be said in that language. And this is in some way important here. It is connected with the point that the builders could not have used language just in the circumstances in which they did.

It is not even clear what is meant by saying that they 'have a common vocabulary' or a common syntax. Because, how far does this go? In one sense we were saying that they had a different syntax: 'complete systems of human communication'. On the other hand, you might say that the people who are speaking have a common vocabulary and a common syntax, and that would mean simply that they happened to know those words and those structures. But that is not the point, for this would make it exactly similar to saying that they happen to know so and so many different languages. That they could understand one another if they spoke those languages, and so forth.

The point is that what they say *belongs* to a language, in some way or other. And that leads one to say that they belong to a common vocabulary and common syntax. But that is why I want to say that the vocabulary and syntax that they are using belong to the lives of the people.

What is important here is that those two are speaking the same language. And this may lead one to say that it belongs to the same *way* of life; which may even lead one to want to speak about institutions, though I think that is misleading.

And I suppose that question of what one learns when one learns to speak or learns the language comes in here.

Remember that that notion of 'the same language' raises the

difficulties about the generality of language; and so, I suppose, about intelligibility altogether. There may be similar difficulties about 'the same way of life'.

The question of the standards of what makes sense; the standards of what is an intelligent thing to say, and the relation of this to the question of whether one has understood correctly or not. Statements that belong to the same language: statements that are intelligible to one another. Intelligibility in the sense of what seems intelligent, as contrasted with intelligibility in the sense of what is formally correct.

CHAPTER 12

Language, speaking and common intelligibility
(18.5.58–5.8.58)

I

If you ask what we learn when we learn the language, the easiest answer seems to be, 'the rules'; just as that seems to be the easiest answer when you ask what we learn when we learn the meaning of a word. In this latter case, we seem to want to answer the question 'what is it that we teach a person when we teach him the word?' Wittgenstein saw that there was something misleading in that, when he came to write the *Brown Book*; and this is why he introduced the idea of learning a game and an *Abrichtung* (training). Probably he wanted to distinguish between knowing how to go on, and knowing how to use a word, on the one hand, and being able oneself to supply the explanation or tell someone what the rule *is*. It is not as though you should be able to supply someone with the formula, or anything like that. This was one of the important points he was getting at here. But all the same, I think he was closer to that question – the question of what it is that we teach a person when we teach him to speak (or what it is that you understand when you understand what is said) – than really is healthy.

This idea that you learn a rule is connected with the point that you learn 'how to go on'. This was important because in distinguishing between the picture and knowing how to use it, he was laying emphasis on the importance of '. . . and so on'; you could not teach him what it meant, because that is something he would have to understand if he were to understand any teaching. (I think that this gets its force partly from *starting* with the assumption that learning what the word means, or learning how to speak, is above all or essentially a matter of learning how to go on – of being able to learn from examples, and so forth.) If you have been thinking about this – which means: if you have been thinking about language in fairly close analogy with mathematics – then this point about the fundamental character of '. . . and so on' seems very forceful. But, for instance, I doubt if learning to speak does consist in learning from examples in that way. And I expect that the fundamental character of '. . . and so on' belongs especially to learning at a later stage – such as the learning of a notation, for instance.

I am not sure how far this idea of the fundamental character of '. . . and so on' fits in with the notion of *Abrichtung*. Does the dog understand '. . . and so on'?

If you suggest that this '. . . and so on' is what is involved in learning to speak – in a way comparable to that in which it is involved in learning arithmetic – then this suggests too much the idea of learning an operation; or learning by having someone show you, and then be told to do what he does.

It is not even like *Abrichtung*, in the sense that when it is learning to ask questions and answer them, you cannot be brought to this by being trained to it, as a dog might be trained to obey orders or to do complicated tricks. Or as you might be trained to do multiplications.

The general point seems to be that there is something that is important and something that is plausible in this idea of learning how to go on. Or: putting the answer to the question of 'what you have learned' in terms of knowing how to go on. And what I want to emphasize is that there is something wrong with that question regarding what you learn when you learn to speak. (Objection: well, you do learn to speak. And if you are asking what speaking is, then you are asking what it is that you have learned.) And yet I still think there is something wrong with this. This is partly the general difficulty of 'explaining what speaking is', or 'giving an account of what speaking is'. And it may be connected with older difficulties about the growth of understanding – 'Understanding what? And is this like the growth in proficiency of some sort?' Or we might say: if you do ask what speaking is, it is so very hard to see what you are asking. Here you *may* want to give examples of it, and follow with 'and things of that sort'. (Suppose you want to explain why you would not say that a parrot is speaking, for instance.) I can understand why Wittgenstein thought that this is the only sort of reply that makes sense.

The ways in which we speak about 'understanding' also seem to suggest this business of understanding how to go on with the word; understanding how to use the word. Think of the expression 'knowing how it is to be taken', for instance (and of 'he has mistaken it', or 'he has not taken it in the right way – that is not what it means'). If it is a word that means something, then it is a word that is to be taken in one way or another. This means that there is a right way and a wrong way of doing it (there is use and misuse). If there is to be any sense in talking about understanding 'it' – what does that mean? I suppose the only answer which seemed plausible was that it is understanding how it is to be taken, how it goes, how it works. That is what we seem to come back to again. It is so much understanding the mechanism. And if we have the analogy with 'how the calculus works', this analogy with the mechanism would hold.

We seem to have the same sort of idea in the suggestion either that it is understanding the game, or that it is understanding 'the role of this expression' in the game. Cf. understanding the move that he had made in chess.

But is there something misleading about this idea of 'how it is to be taken'? And is there something misleading in the suggestion that learning to ask questions and to answer them is something like learning how the game is played? For if it were like this then you ought to be able to show a person how to ask questions and to answer them. Can I show you what you have to learn? I do not deny that imitation does play a role; that if the child did not watch and listen to other people speaking and asking questions, he would never have learned to do that himself. All the same, there is a difference between his imitating the questions which they are asking, and his asking a question himself when he really wants to know something.

This idea of really wanting to know something – it is the development of this which is involved in learning to speak. And I do not think it can be accounted for in terms of learning how it is done. (Neither has it much analogy with anything that is done in a game, I think.) (The distinction between real and imaginary conversations.)

Now if you cannot show him how to ask questions and to answer them, I think this is connected with the point that learning the language is not a matter of learning to go on in the same way. Or rather, I think it is connected with the point that belonging to the language is not a matter of going on, of being a continuation of some sort of rule.

It is part of what the earlier view was getting at when it suggested that the various propositions . . . that if they belonged to a language,

then there must be some operation by which they can be transformed into, or that one proposition can be translated into another,
through some operation. Where this idea is at home is in the
propositions which all belong to the same calculus; the same system
of calculation; in which case, I suppose, they would all be said to
have a meaning or significance in the same sense. There is some
common intelligibility that goes through them there. And when one
is talking about a calculus, it seems natural to express this in terms of
the possibility of transforming one into another, or the possibility of
translating one in terms of the other. (Cf. the idea: 'some method of
passing from one proposition to another'. And the question: 'But can
I not pass as I like?') Or at least: it can be transformed into other
expressions or propositions, into more than one set of them – which
do belong to the same calculus; and this must be some sort of bond
that holds throughout. It would not mean, of course, that any two
propositions of the calculus must be equivalent; that would be
nonsense.

There is something in the idea of their all belonging to the same
system of calculation which does seem a tempting kind of model,
when one is trying to think of the way in which the different
propositions of the language belong to a kind of common intelligibility. But I think that it is a misleading model.

Or we may speak of the different propositions as being intelligible
in terms of one another. And then we are bringing in the analogy
between language and a system of measurement. To assert propositions in a language would be to treat them in accordance with or in
terms of a system of measurement; treat them in terms of a common
sort of commensurability. Otherwise you might say that the various
remarks that are made cannot have anything to do with one another.
And the conversation then would not be a conversation. It would not
be an exchange of remarks. (I was going to say it would not be an
exchange of ideas – which is all right, except that it may mislead by
suggesting the idea of a medium or currency in which ideas of the
mind are made public.) It would not be an inquiry. It would not lead
to anything.

II

If you are speaking now, you will speak in other connexions; and you
might even say that if you are speaking with this man now, you will

speak with other people in other connexions. That is not just an internal connexion there. It is not just that we infer, but that it would not make any sense. You could not be said to be speaking now unless that were so. You would not be saying anything. The expressions you are using now would not be saying anything, or would not be intelligible apart from that.

This is something connected with the idea of the unity of language, simply because it suggests that there is some internal or essential connexion between what you are saying now and other things said. And it has to do with the equivalence of the expressions saying different things in a language. Nothing could have been the only thing that were ever said. Neither could there have been just two remarks. This is why it is not a necessary relation to this or that particular remark that is required for intelligibility. There is a puzzle about that, because it does not make a great deal of sense to talk about the completeness of the language, or the incompleteness either. You cannot say that if there were not certain things said – if Mr Green had not made those remarks to Mr Lewis on that occasion – then what you say here could not have sense. And that would hold of anything Wittgenstein calls a language game; because he is thinking of a game that *might* be played and might be repeated. Here is the general difficulty that what is said on one occasion might be said on another occasion. 'He said the same thing time and time again.'

If you are considering the way in which actual statements – the statements which people have actually made and are making – are connected with one another (and in some way or other they are: that is one of the points I am trying to emphasize), then the insistence that there is an internal connexion there lands you in queer results. It seems to suggest that you would destroy the sense of any one of them, if none of the others had ever been made – or were to be. Or it might suggest that you could deduce the other statements from these two or three. If you really know the language, and if you really understand what is being said here and now, then you should be able to deduce everything that is ever going to be said.

That leaves out the time and the temporal order of the statements; and also their relations to one another. For their relations to one another in a discussion or a conversation, for instance, are not their logical relations – whatever those may be. That is of capital importance. In the way I am trying to speak of it, there cannot be any sense in any statement except in its temporal connexion with other things that are being said and with things that are being done. (Though somehow it would not have any connexion with the things that are being done if it did not have any with what has been said or with what people might be expected to say.) We might even want to say that temporal connexions cannot be internal.

Is there any sort of parallel here with historical studies and the understanding of events in history? It is through their connexions with other events in time that we find them in some way intelligible, or that we are able to learn from them. And this is not a matter of being able to predict or infer; any more than it is a matter of being able to give a causal explanation.

That may be why the kind of insight that you get has sometimes been thought of as religious. In any case, the temporal connexion is not seen here as an external one, but somehow as prior to that. And yet if we say that this event is internally connected with others, that leads too easily to absurdities. I suppose this is one of the big questions in the philosophy of history, and it accounts for some of the queer lines that have been taken by philosophers. It is connected with difficulties about 'historical significance'.

I have even been suggesting that the understanding of the past – through historical study or through myth – has something to do with the understanding of what is said, too. And I must return to that. The question is whether there is something like the internal connexion in language. This is getting hopelessly vague, but I am not sure that there is no analogy at all.

Consider the sort of internal connexion that there is in mathematics. There again it is misleading if we try to think of the whole of mathematics as a complete system – again with the suggestion that every new branch of mathematics is something that could have been derived from certain fundamental principles.

Even if we consider different structures – that notion, as Wittgenstein uses it, seems to be connected with the notion of different language games – here again we have the point that although it will not do to speak of the interconnexions of these, what it is that makes you call them all *language* games, as though that were in terms of likenesses comparable with the likenesses between different techniques, still we do have to take account of the development of different ways of speaking, new ways of speaking, new grammatical structures and so forth, the development of what Wittgenstein would call new language games; and on the other hand we cannot say that what we mean in the way we are talking now, the grammar and the sense of what is said in this game, would be entirely lost or entirely altered if that other game had never been there. So again, if we say that there is an internal connexion, or if one says that there is an essential connexion – the fact is that . . .

With regard to language games, there, probably what we mean by the unity and the connexion with other things that are said is precisely the point that we are making when we say that language is not a game, and that you could not speak only on one occasion or only in connexion with one particular technique. That, I think, is obviously so. But it does not mean that there is any particular sort of game or technique besides this one, that is essential. That is why I am inclined to speak of connexion with life, I suppose. Speaking generally must belong to your life. And speaking generally is not a technique which has a particular application or a particular use. Plato may have been trying to make this point, against the rhetoricians, for instance. (Why the development of language comes through the writing of stories and poems and plays. The differences between Greek and Hebrew.) (The use of language for particular techniques seems to be derivative – shall we say parasitic – on that.)

If we talk about the unity of the life that people are leading, and that seems to have something to do with the possibility of discourse, or with the possibility of their understanding one another at all, that is not the same thing as talking about the unity of a *way* of life. It is not a sort of conceptual unity. (I wonder whether Aristotle's criticisms about real and conceptual unity had anything to do with this. I expect it did not.) If we think of this possibility of understanding, then the point is that people do carry on this discourse and have this understanding or misunderstanding (and where there were no understanding – where they were absolutely foreign – there were not any misunderstanding either). We think of it then as occurring in time.

The difficulties about being able to say the same things on various occasions. If we are talking about the way in which the intelligibility of what is said depends on its relations to what is said on other occasions – that does not mean the intelligibility of this sentence depends on the intelligibility of other sentences; at least I do not think it does, but the trouble is that that comes into it partly – if one talks about the unity of language, or the internal connexions, is one thinking of the intelligibility of various sentences, or has it to do with the routine of speaking, what goes on in time when people are speaking the language? Plato: it is only in time that discourse can be intelligible to us.

'Being spoken by the same people' – belongs to the life they lead together, with which they go about among one another. Belonging to their understanding of one another. (But what is it that is the same? What is the connexion?) This is not like sharing a common property – as there might be a common property in what people are doing if they are making the same noises (or tunes written in the same key).

Not the connexion of remarks in a conversation, although I think it has something to do with that. It is not even like saying that someone else could have said the same thing. No, the point is that people are speaking the same language there, and so you could understand them. It is that latter point – the possibility of understanding – that is important more than the fact that they may have been using the same vocabulary and the same grammatical constructions. I say that the connexion with what has been said there and by those people is essential for its being a remark or saying something here at all. But if you ask '*what* connexion', the temptation is to fall back on using the same vocabulary. (Music written in the same key and for the same key-board.)

Living among people is something different from being one of a herd, partly because of the important role that history plays there, I suppose; because of the conception of developments – that is why it is prior in a way to any possibility of institutions. Cf. why it does not make sense to speak of institutions in an animal society. But in a way that is pushing the question further back, or else it is circular. This appears when we ask why it has sense to think of history in connexion with human societies and not in connexion with those of animals.

It is important to make clear and admit that we are not talking about something that all language has in common. And Wittgenstein's pointing this out was extremely important. Cf. the idea of a fundamental contract in society, or perhaps some sort of fundamental institution. Almost as though society itself were an institution – though if language is an institution, then why not? Wittgenstein wanted to say that there are not any all-pervasive axioms or all-pervasive rules, as regards language and understanding. And that that is not what makes it saying something. I do not question any of that. At the same time I do want to emphasize that belonging to a language is something that is more important than his notion of a family of language games seems to make out.

I should certainly agree that you cannot talk about one language game. That would get you into the same sort of difficulty about completeness. And although you can talk about belonging to a game, I think that living among people and understanding people is prior to that. A conversation is not a game, and there could not be one limited conversation which was the only conversation you ever had in your life. But for all that, the connexion that a conversation must have with other conversations that you may hold and that other people are holding is not that of belonging to or being parts of a conversation. Certainly, if you want to try to give an account of what living among people is, or of people living together, then you have to bring in the carrying on of conversations with them; because if that were totally absent, it would not be what we call living among people. But all the same, that does not mean that if you want to give an account of such association, you can speak of it as taking part in a conversation. (It has to do rather with the way in which conversations may circulate past and around one another.)

Neither can you say, I suppose, that it would not be a remark at all, or that it would not say anything, unless it were connected with other remarks in a conversation. If Plato fell into misunderstandings here, it was probably because of the way in which he narrowed the idea of 'understanding' which there may be between people – though their only relations were relations of their several professions or trades. This led him to unify the sort of understandings and misunderstandings, the sort of communication, which people may have with one another, in an illegitimate way. Perhaps there is an analogy if you think of all use of language as operations with a calculus. (Overlooking the difference of persons; emphasis simply upon the difference of roles.) Although I think that carrying on a conversation is more important for what we mean by speaking and understanding than this account so far has brought out.

III
(7.8.58–20.8.58)

I find the difficulty in saying what language is or what speaking is or what propositions are, very queer; I find it hard to grasp just what the difficulty is. And I do not know why.

'How can there be an investigation of language?' 'How can there be an investigation of logic?' This parallel may help show what some of the features of the question about language are. For one might wonder why there should be any difficulty about an 'investigation' of language. After all there is the whole study of philosophy for instance.

There might be an investigation of logic, in the sense of an exposition of the principles of logic – the construction of a logical calculus. More important: the discussion of what you regard as the criteria by which to judge or criticize any such calculus that may be put forward.

There are certain difficulties which go together with the fact that logic is called a normative science. Any investigation here would be an investigation of standards, in some way. (The same would be true of certain sorts of investigation of mathematics – as opposed to doing mathematics.) Is there something of this sort in connexion with language as well? If you ask what language is, then what is puzzling is the notion of intelligibility; which connects with ideas of understanding correctly.

One might try to understand the position of logic in connexion with different forms of discourse. The sense in which all investigations and proofs depend upon logic, for instance. We might put this by asking what sort of principles logical principles are. We have here the parallel to which Wittgenstein referred between grammar and geometry. You can criticize and study or examine a calculus or any formal system, for its consistency or freedom from contradiction. And anything like a judgement – anything like the bringing of criticism, the raising of difficulties or the meeting of them – seems to employ the logical principles. And it is hard to see what it would mean to criticize – test, study or examine – these principles themselves. You cannot carry out an investigation to discover whether any principles of investigation are trustworthy.

One might speak of an examination of the reality of them. But this does not tell us much about it. (Certainly it is nothing like an examination of a theory. There can be no question of a correspondence with reality in that sense. And there cannot be anything like a logical hypothesis.) In connexion with language: Plato and others have discussed 'the conditions of the possibility of discourse'. Here the difficulty is not quite like having to apply principles of logic in order to be able to carry out any criticism at all (so that you cannot ask whether the principles which you are using are valid or not). But there is some important parallel which it is hard to express. 'You cannot discuss the question of whether any discussion can be understood.' 'You cannot seriously raise the question of whether there is any sense in asking anything.' 'You cannot try to understand the intelligibility of what one is saying.' Unless someone knows what language is – unless he can see that something is being said, and understand it – you cannot discuss anything with him, nor explain anything to him. 'So that question: what language is, is not a question which can be discussed.' You cannot ask whether it is possible to say anything.

Plato may have seen the connexion much closer, since he may have made the connexion between following what is said and following an argument much more internal. Understanding was connected with criticism and testing. This may be the reason why people have talked about 'the calculus of language'.

Suppose one were asking what logic is: or what the force of logic is. The ideas of adhering to logic, or going contrary to logic, would be connected with this. If you went contrary to logic, what difference would it make? Would you have made a mistake of some kind? The temptation to think of a parallel with grammar: if you went contrary to grammar what difference would it make? And so the idea of 'speaking correctly' – which is connected with the distinction of sense and nonsense. If you speak correctly, it is intelligible; if you do not, it is not.

If you want to find out what a particular remark means, then you ask for an explanation; or you may carry out your own investigation to try to make out what he means, as you do when you are studying an author, for instance. But this is something different from investigating the conditions of sense and nonsense. It is also something different from asking whether the remark means anything at all. Anyway, it is not clear that if you want to find out what it means, the proper method would be something that you could call investigation into grammar. This goes together with the question of whether understanding what it means is understanding the rules.

'The way in which logic hangs together.' The difficulty of showing the difference between logical principles and contingent principles – how far is this like the question of how logical principles form a system? Cf. 'How can there be *many* logical principles? Why do they not all reduce to one?' (Parmenides. Leibniz.) ('If you can say anything, you can say many things.' But in logic you do not say anything anyway.)

'What about the logic of the system itself? That is not something which is established *by* the system.' – Could one say that this *is* the question of how the system hangs together, or how logic hangs together? And yet, whatever the answer, it cannot be like the attempt to say how *language* hangs together. There is no question of under-standing comparable to understanding what is said.

Nobody can teach you the logicality of logic. ('It is something that you learn when you learn the language.') Nobody can demonstrate to you the logical force of logic.

The difficulty of saying how language hangs together is closely bound up with the relation between logic and language. It is so much a part of this trouble of seeing the way in which logical principles are and the way in which they are not principles of understanding. Is the difficulty partly that you cannot put in general terms what the understanding of what is said depends on? And you cannot put in general terms the way in which what is said here hangs together with other things that are said. One of the difficulties which might be raised is that this would make the whole thing seem arbitrary – whether you understand or not; or a matter of personal caprice. And I suppose this is the kind of idea that does help to make men think that the intelligibility of what is said is a matter of the effect which it actually has; and that you cannot give any general account of this except in terms of an empirical generalization. This is clearly wrong headed in some way, although it may be rooted in a real matter.

'A logical symbolism will make clear which *forms* of propositions are permitted and which are not.' The idea of the general form of the proposition. Correct this by remembering that 'generality is not the mark of a logical proposition'. Tautology is. And yet the general form of the proposition is the only genuine primitive sign, from which the possibility (or impossibility) of all combinations of symbols can be deduced. What has this to do with truth and falsity by the way?

The distinction between what can be said and what cannot be said. The importance of this for understanding what logic is. The propositions of logic do not say anything. The truth of logical propositions can be seen from their expression in their symbol. This brings again the point that certain combinations of symbols are possible and others are not. Generality through combination (disjunction, conjunction) of elementary propositions.

The difference between talking of 'all propositions of astronomy' (and I suppose you might give someone characteristics of them) and talking about 'all propositions'. The idea of tautology as 'that which is common to all propositions which have nothing in common with one another'. What is the sense of this? Partly that you add nothing to a proposition if you assert a tautology in conjunction with it. But probably something more definite than that.

Obviously, the account of tautology isn't the same as the account of the general form of the proposition. I do not know that there is any 'formula for tautology'; anyway, Wittgenstein would not have said that this was one with the general form of operation or with the logical constant from which all forms of proposition (i.e. non-logical propositions as well, apparently) can be derived. I suppose there are different forms of tautology. And the point would be that the general form of the proposition must cover all of them.

The conception of all propositions as truth functions must depend on the general form, somehow. And in this way the conception of logical propositions as 'true in virtue of their form alone' would also.

One thing that 'cannot be said' is the relation of logic to reality. Not even in the sense in which you can speak about the relation of empirical propositions to reality (a connexion with verification, for instance). 'The proposition shows what it would be like if it were true.' But a logical proposition does not show that (and 'if it were true' – a 'logical hypothesis' – would mean nothing here). The only postulate is the postulate that it is possible to say something. And for Wittgenstein this means: that there *is* something, or that there is a world. This is necessary, because if the proposition has sense it must refer to reality. It must make sense to think of comparison with reality. And *this* means that there must be elementary propositions, demands of the possibility of sense. 'But could we not get along without logical principles even so?' You could not calculate. Is there anything more to it than that? Is there any way of *proving* which forms of proposition are possible (in what ways is it impossible to say anything)? Is there any *theory* to which you could have recourse or make an appeal in this kind of question?

'All right, but why is this question of the possible forms of propositions important?' Knowing what you can conclude, and how to verify this. Has it something to do with the *applicability* of logic and mathematics? The possible forms of proposition and the possibility of any criterion for distinguishing between sense and nonsense. (It is not nonsense just because you cannot understand it.) The possibility that what you say is *intelligible* – i.e. that it really tells you something about the world. The idea of 'the limits of language'. (Limits of understanding.) There can be no language if *anything* goes.

IV
(1.7.58–31.7.58)

Language games, and the unity of language. Wittgenstein might have agreed that a proposition in a language must be intelligible to one another. It is because you are familiar or versed in one game, that the other games are language to you, and you can see that they have sense.

What is the point he is making in talking about the various language games as each of them a 'complete system of communication', though? What is the sense of 'completeness' there? His main point is that they are not to be called *in*complete, since he does not want to suggest that they form parts of a system; nor, perhaps, that there is any one way of speaking which is fundamental, and that the others are derivative. Cf. what he says about 'elliptical' expressions, for instance. This all bears on the idea of a necessary structure of language. Relations which propositions must bear to one another if they are to be intelligible, and so forth. And this is connected with the point that the relation of the remark to the language cannot be put in general terms, for the most part.

I think he might have held to that, and still avoided the suggestion that any one of these which he is calling 'games' might be speaking and understanding one another in that particular task (which, for all he says, might be performed rather seldom) although they never spoke with one another or with other people at any other times. I do not think that that is merely unlikely; I think it is impossible.

If we speak of the language as a family of language games, and if we think of the language as spoken by people engaged in their various pursuits, then we might, I suppose, say that at any time there are various language games being played or spoken among those people. But it were a misleading picture if we should imagine something like a lot of different games which were being played simultaneously by different teams or sides: soccer here, rugby over there, hockey further on, and so on. As though you could speak about the set of people who are playing this game, and the others who are engaged in another. Now certainly there are some who are engaged in business, some who are engaged in a surgical operation, some debating in parliament or in a law court, perhaps some in a religious service, and so on. And in many ways the use of language will be different. The point of making remarks at all will be different. But in the first place, these people would not be doing that – they would not be using language at all – if they never used it on other occasions; it would not be language; and we should certainly have no occasion to speak of using it *differently* in the one case and in the other. All of these hang together with the lives people are leading in other connexions. And in this way they are unlike so many different games.

Suppose we speak of the people as being engaged in different occupations. Even here, these hang together; that is why we speak of them as different occupations. And it is not the same as it is when we speak of different games. For the occupations are connected with the lives the people are leading, and with the other things they do; and their games are not. The occupations are connected with the other things that *other* people do, as well. And the point they have depends on that. The meaning of what he says – what I understand – is not its place in the system or its 'role' in the language. And the sense of the life I lead – what you may understand – is not its role in society. ('Doing my bit.')

Certainly I would not say that they all form a system; and still less that they are parts of some all embracing enterprise. Perhaps Wittgenstein was emphasizing that, and I very much agree.

Neither can we say that there is anything which is the point of living with people (no more than we speak of the purpose of language). Not a task which he has to fulfil. But there is not that in language either: calculus, perfect intelligibility. At the same time, we can say that there is a point in the lives which the people are leading together (even though there is nothing which is *the* point for everyone 'otherwise he would not be there'. There is nothing like my station and its duties). But it is not just that people happen to be interested in this game now, tomorrow it may be another, and so on. More important, perhaps: living together is not playing a game together. Nor is it doing a particular job together either. That is why there is some sense in the idea of understanding one another. Or rather: there is some sense in what they are doing vis-à-vis one another, in the lives they are leading vis-à-vis one another; just as there is some sense in what they are saying. The idea that there is some meaning, and so some connexion in the things people do. Not only a connexion of the various things in my life, but a connexion in the lives of people. This is possible in spite of the fact that they are not all joined in an enterprise. Or rather: the 'in spite of' is out of place there, since association in an enterprise would be something entirely different, and would not give you what we mean by living together.

There is something similar which holds for speaking. The different games have in some way a meaning in relation to one another; and the main point is that they have a meaning in the language that people carry on. If we play a different game in the things that are said in a surgical operation and in a debate in a law court, this is because they *are* connected with one another or might be. (It is that kind of game vis-à-vis the rest of language.) It is in this sense that they have a meaning in the lives that people are leading. And this is not a meaning in the sense of being a serviceable technique. This is the point I want to emphasize. If it were like that, then it would be the sort of connexion that there is in the parts of a system or parts of a technique.

I think also that the way in which the intelligibility of one depends on what goes on outside, in the rest of the language, is different from what we find in Wittgenstein's account. The analogy is not to be found in 'going on in the same way' in the following of a rule; or in 'oh yes, I see what that is'. The difference between seeing what the sentence means and understanding what he is saying, comes in here. But that would come in when we distinguish between one language game and another anyway; since I suppose the same sentence might come into different language games and in different senses.

If you are talking about the various games that go to make up the language (however misleading that expression may be), you still have not made very clear what understanding the language is; or what it is that you learn when you learn to speak. Because you do not just learn one of those games. (And if you *use* games in teaching a child to speak, still that is not what you are teaching him; nor a series of them either. That is not what you are trying to make him able to do.)

The unity of language and language games. The question of what way it is that knowing the language is important for the intelligibility of what is said under any circumstances. Being familiar with the sorts of things people say. This cannot be reduced to a matter of being familiar with the way in which this particular game may be played. This may be rather important. It is not a skill in this particular game; nor experience in this particular game. (And there is nothing parallel to this in connexion with experience in football or in chess.) This is once more the difference between knowing a language and knowing a technique. It is not comparable to the kind of thing you expect in an experienced footballer or an experienced chess player, or anything like familiarity with the sort of strategies that may be expected or may prove useful. It is much nearer to aesthetic judgements than that.

This is important for the general question of the 'completeness' of the language games; and to what extent you can put the understanding of what is being said in terms of the understanding of a game like that.

When Plato emphasized dialogue, he was emphasizing what he called the reality of discourse; the reality of the distinction between sham discourse and real discourse; and also the universality of discourse – the generality of discourse. And those two were closely connected, because he thought that the reality of any discussion depended on – or lay in – its relation to discourse. Its relation to discourse particularly in the sense of growth of understanding. He seemed to think that dialogue or discussion had something important to do with the unity of discourse. And you could understand what was meant by the unity of discourse – having a common language, and so understanding one another (the conditions of the possibility of discourse) – if you understood the nature of dialogue.

I think the character of discussion is important in this connexion. And also the kind of relations that various discussions have to one another; and more particularly the kind of relation that discussions have to the rest of language. But I am not sure that Plato has brought that out very well.

What it is to recognize something as language, what it is to recognize something as discourse. The difference between this and recognizing how it goes, or knowing how to go on. The question about the possibility of understanding and the question about the reality of understanding. Scepticism. If it were simply a matter of techniques, how should that kind of question have arisen? or what sense would it have? In part it is just the question between genuine discourse and sham discourse, I suppose. ('Well, if *anything* goes . . .') And Plato thought it particularly important to be able to recognize discourse: to be able to recognize when something is being said, and to tell the difference between this and the imitations that were offered by the rhetoricians and the sophists. If you teach someone to speak and understand, what is the difference between teaching him that and teaching him a skill or a craft? (Conferre: teaching him to play music with understanding. Teaching him to paint with understanding. The difference between that and teaching him to go on as he has been taught. The awakening of understanding in him.) The child has not begun to speak until he has something of this. By 'speak' I mean 'speak with people', of course.

The distinction between genuine discourse and sham discourse, for Plato, is very much the same as the question whether there is a distinction between discourse and convention. And here the point is that there must be a distinction between what is real understanding and what passes for understanding. In this, I suppose Plato is distinguishing between understanding what is said, and understanding the language in the sense in which the rhetoricians had spoken about it. And yet Plato would want to deny that there can be no distinction between understanding what is said and a *real* understanding of the language or of discourse. In all his emphasis upon dialogue, and in his insistence that what is said is intelligible through its *temporal* relations to other things that are said, and not on its formal or logical relations simply; in all his distinction between what is intelligible to us and what is intelligible 'in itself'; and in his reference to the best account that we can understand as something *like* a truly intelligible account – Plato never does do away with the distinction between what is intelligible – even 'to us' – and what 'goes down'.

Certainly there are difficulties in the suggestion that everyone might think a given system of communication was intelligible and all of them be wrong; or that people might go on over years thinking that they were speaking a language when they were not. And the idea of some criterion for intelligibility, or some definition of a language, which is behind or beyond what people actually practice, seems pretty confused. Protagoras would have been right in rejecting that.

But what about some particular thing said in the language – the question whether that is intelligible or not; whether it belongs to language or not; whether it is a proposition. Plato would be reluctant to say 'If it passes for a proposition, it is one'; or (what is perhaps not just the same) 'If people think they understand it, they do.' (Just as he might have been unwilling to say 'It means whatever the generality of people think it means', and *therefore* 'It means whatever it is taken to mean.') And Plato's objections here would have come from reflections on mathematics, largely. And here there does seem to be a method for determining what it really means; or for determining whether it is really intelligible. And the man who knew mathematics could decide this, and the important generality of men could not. So the generality of men might be wrong.

This is connected with the idea that you really understand it when you know the proof of it, and can give an account of it in that sense. And this is like trying to see what it means in itself. 'Learning is recollection', and does not depend upon experience. 'Unless you recognize some general or universal criterion, *anything* goes.'

It is misleading if we take mathematics as a model or even as an example here. Whether it is sensible to look there for some guarantee of consistency within a system – or even for some more precise and general account of what consistency is, so that we may be able to determine by a clear method whether something can belong to the system or not – that is a question on its own account. But there is certainly no criterion in *this* sense by which you can decide quite generally whether someone has understood correctly what another man has said. I do not mean, of course, that there is nothing you can do to find out; for in most cases there is. Plato's point that it is a temporal relation is important, especially if one has begun to think in terms of structural similarity or of family likeness.

Wittgenstein sees that when we ask whether there is something common to all conversations, then at least we cannot think of anything that they *have* in common, any common structure, for instance. We do not even have to say that they belong to a common grammar. We are not concerned with anything like a fundamental grammar running all through them.

On the other hand, we do speak of them as being conversations in the same language. This is not quite the matter that Wittgenstein was considering, because he spoke rather of language games, and it is not always perfectly clear what he did mean by that. But Wittgenstein might say that the fact that the conversations belong to the same language is certainly important for the intelligibility of each of them, but this is all one could say. What they have in common is that they do belong to the same language. (Perhaps: they do not belong to the same language *because* they have something in common. For that would be like saying that it is something they have in common which makes them all intelligible. And this is the point that there is no criterion of their belonging to the same language. Here I suppose the analogy with the notion of 'going on in the same way' – and that is connected with the older question about 'and so on'. And here the point is that there is no *criterion* which tells you that you are following the rule correctly. 'How do you know that this is red?' 'How do you know that you are still using 'red' in the same way?' The idea of a structural similarity does not help. 'How do you know that it is a proposition?' – although this is not really parallel: 'all propositions' is not a specific class. Wittgenstein was leaving the view that various propositions are like so many geometrical figures that might be brought under a common formula. At the same time, there is the fact that they are all intelligible in some way. I am not sure that Wittgenstein in his later work comes to terms with this question, quite as directly as he might.)

I do not think it will do to say that they are said in a language game. They are said in various language games, and in all those cases you are speaking of them as things that are *said*. And Wittgenstein seems to think that you can give an account of this by reference to the sort of similarity. If you can understand what a language game is – and he seems to think you can convey this sort of understanding by reference to the sorts of examples of primitive language games that he offers – if you can understand that, then if somebody says 'and so on' or 'and other things of that sort', you should be able to pass from this primitive case to others that are more complicated; perhaps rather in the way in which Wittgenstein does in the early parts of the *Brown Book*. But this is just what I think is misleading. (Is Wittgenstein still with the idea of an analysis of language? Cf. the idea of what a language game *could* be: 'We could even imagine such a case . . .'. Thinking of alternative possibilities, so that we may look on the existing practice differently: so that we may see that there is no necessity or inevitability about the way we do it, for instance. Or again: constructing language games for the light they may throw on certain features of our language.)

These primitive games do not give you what is meant by speaking, because they do not give you what is meant by belonging to a language. And this suggests that there is something inadequate in his whole account of belonging to a language – that you cannot do it simply in terms of family likenesses. As though you could simply point to that kind of language game, and say 'That, and other things of this sort.' (The reference to those games is all right in reminding someone who is already familiar with what a language is. But if you want to know what is the difference between speaking and the use of other techniques – and that is the kind of question that does come up in Plato's dispute with the rhetoricians, I suppose – then this way of doing it will not serve.) You can quite reasonably take that course of offering examples and saying 'and other things of that sort', if you are trying to answer the question of what a game is. But it will not quite do in connexion with 'saying something'.

This goes with the fact that people have faces. And what is said is very commonly debatable. Cf. the sense in which one may be said to understand a conversation; know what it is about, and follow it; the sense in which one may, or may not, find any sense in the conversation. But you cannot say '*This* is what anyone must understand if he understands the conversation correctly.' This holds especially when the conversation is a discussion. We should say often that you cannot understand a remark unless you can see its bearing in a conversation or discussion in which it is made.

It is doubtful if we can give an account of understanding in terms of the analogy with understanding a game or understanding a technique in the way in which Wittgenstein tried to do it. And if we do say that 'understanding is not always the same thing', it may not be enough to remind us that the mastery of one game is not the mastery of another. The ways of speaking and understanding seem differently related than this analogy suggests.

My point just now is that if we say that different remarks belong to the same language, this means – or part of what it means – is that they have a kind of common intelligibility: one remark might have a significance for the other. On the other hand I suppose we ought to take account of the fact that there are many remarks belonging to the same language that seem to have no bearing on one another at

all; and this may be commoner than the other. I shall have to return
to this. This is the kind of thing that suggests something like
interlocking language games of which Wittgenstein may have been
speaking. If we are considering 'speaking the same language', then
the point seems to be that the remarks or the statements that are
asserted by me can be understood by you, and vice versa. That is the
sign that we are speaking the same language.

The idea of what I have been calling 'an interlocking intelligibility'
may be important here. It would seem that the idea of people
speaking the same language is the more fundamental here –
fundamental to that of different remarks as remarks in the same
language. When you learn to speak, you learn to understand people.
And if we ask then what it is that you have learned, you have learned
to speak with other people who speak the same language. And the
dependence or interdependence – or shall we say 'inter-intellig-
ibility', common intelligibility – that there is among things said
which has to be put in quite a vague way: this is one of the essential
points here, and it is one of the reasons why the language is thought
of as general: you have to put it in the vague way of saying that you
will be able to understand other things, without specifying what
those other things are. Some people have said that you can specify,
and must be able to specify, the form or the possible forms in which
the things could be said; they must have that sort of intelligibility.
But you do not specify what the remarks are. And this is part and
parcel of the point that you will be able to understand the remarks
that other people may make. This has something to do with the
relation of particular to general: the *particular* remarks that people
may make. One wants almost to say that in the nature of the case
these could not be deduced from remarks that have been made up
before. And yet you will be able to understand them. This does not
commit you to saying that you will be able to understand *all* the
remarks that anybody may make. But at any rate you will be able to
understand other remarks than these, and other remarks than any
you happen to have heard. You would not have understood anything, if this were the only remark that you could understand.

Here we have the idea of the connexion between what is said here
and what is said on other occasions. But the fundamental idea seems
to be that of understanding other *people* speaking the same language
on other occasions. It centres on the notion of a common intelligibility in the intelligibility of people to one another in their conversa-

tions. And the common understanding would belong to the fact that people do speak the same language, and can understand one another, rather than to any method of interpretation of propositions, or anything like a general method of the solution of problems, or anything like a general method of analysis of propositions for example.

On the other hand, if you do put it like this, we may seem to leave too much on one side or leave out altogether the rules and the vocabulary which are certainly essential; without which we could not be speaking a common language, and without which we should not understand one another. I think they are essential. But if they are necessary to a common understanding, they are certainly not sufficient.

There is a difficulty through all this of whether one is thinking of the connexion between what is said now, what someone is telling you, and other things that have been or may be said; or whether it is something like a formal law, or structural connexion. I am thinking of the kind of thing that Wittgenstein talks about when he is speaking of language games; and of the interrelations which are between them – which he is wont to describe in terms of 'family likenesses'. These are thought of as games that *could* be played. And this may leave out of account the kind of connexions that there may be between things that are actually said.

I did say earlier that the description, or determination of what these relations are between what is said here and what is said on other occasions, is very difficult. In other words it is very difficult to make definite what you do mean by 'saying it in the language' or 'in a language'; to give any single account of this. And this is just part of the difficulty of giving an account of what saying something is, or what language is. And it is because of this kind of difficulty that Wittgenstein introduced the suggestion of language games in the way in which he did.

This matter of what we might call the structural as against the historical connexions is related to the distinction between learning to speak and learning to use the vocabulary and syntax. Wittgenstein wanted to emphasize that there is no development of propositional or grammatical forms, for instance, which a language must have. (This was one of the reasons for speaking of 'complete systems of communication'.) And when I say that if you can understand what someone says now, you must be able to understand other things on other occasions, I do not want to deny this point of his. On the other hand, it seems to me that Wittgenstein is inclined to treat the language games which he mentions as too self-contained, and to neglect the sort of interdependence that there is among them, even though there is not that kind of system by which one implies the other. I suspect that he is led to this partly by neglecting the difference between learning to speak and learning the mastery of a technique.

If you think of a language game as rather self-contained, or if you suggest as Wittgenstein does that there might be a language consisting only of orders given in the field of battle, then you are reducing language to a notation or technique – in a way which I think Wittgenstein was trying to avoid. At any rate, you have got away from the distinction between learning to use the words and follow the rules on the one hand, and speaking on the other.

Perhaps at this point one would have to bring in the matter of the various standards that are relevant to discourse between people; which makes it possible for them to understand one another. It is important to notice that we may always use the same language in pretence or deceit. (There is not any distinction of this sort in playing a game; and this is one of the chief reasons why carrying on a conversation is not like playing a game.) Genuineness and deceit. The possibility of this distinction belongs to what we mean by speaking: saying something, telling one something. Another point (still in the connexion of the conversation with the rest of language) is the relevance of the kind of things that people say. If you are to get the point of a remark that someone has just made, you may have to be familiar with the sorts of things that people say; otherwise you will miss it. It is important to recognize anything like irony that there may be in the remark a person is making. In the interpretation of a cryptic remark, there is not a close distinction between the way in which the familiarity with the sorts of things that people say is relevant, and the way in which the possibility of using language in pretence is relevant. (This ought to be worked out.)

If we are speaking about the generality of language, we must take account of the difference between speaking the language as you might use a notation or do exercises in it, and saying something. If language were like a notation it should be possible to speak the language without saying anything at all. One must also take account of the general character of understanding correctly. There are certain important differences between understanding a remark that is made, and understanding a conversation; although for some purposes there may be analogies. When you understand the conversation, what is important is what you get out of it; and people may differ in this. To what extent can you say something similar about the understanding of remarks?

v

(4.9.58–14.2.59)

If it is difficult to see what language is, then – for this is the same point – it is difficult to see how language hangs together. It is difficult to see why 'saying something' and 'saying something in a language' are exactly the same.

We emphasize that the connexion with other things said is in some sense or other internal. And then the trouble is that you cannot by any sort of analysis establish what the connexion is. You cannot by any sort of analysis establish even with what other things this remark is connected.

The point of a remark lies in the way in which it comes into the conversation. It depends also to some extent on the sense of the conversation itself. You have to learn to understand this kind of thing, if you are to understand and if you are to be able to speak. But it is also the kind of thing of which you cannot give any general account. And it is only partly a matter of what the meanings of the expressions which are used in the remark are, and of the grammar of the remark itself.

On the other hand, it *is* partly that. And this is what makes the account of the matter so difficult. The difficulty lies very largely in trying to see the connexion or the relation between the meanings of the words and the grammatical construction of the remark – the relation between all this, which is in a way general, which could be learned by someone who was learning the language; which could be understood in the course of the sorts of exercises which he might perform – and the point of the remark as it occurs in the conversation which is not something that could be learned in this way. On the other hand, the relation of the remark to the rest of the conversation does depend on the general meanings of the expressions used in it; this is undoubted.

There are other points which are of importance when one is

considering the relation of the remark to the rest of language: how language hangs together. And these lie, for instance, in the fact that what you say in earnest could be said as a joke or in some sort of pretence. This distinction between a genuine remark and a pretence and a sham is again something of which we might say that it is *internally* connected with the understanding. One does not want to speak of an external connexion here. One wants to say that if there were not this connexion between what is being said and other things that are said and that may be said, in other words, if it were not the case that when he says something he must be able to say other things, or that when he understands something he must be able to understand other things: if it were not absurd to speak of using language only for one particular matter or one particular task or job, then it would not be speaking or understanding or using language at all. This is why we feel like saying that it is an internal connexion. Now: internal connexions, as we ordinarily speak of them, are what we call timeless connexions. And this one is not.

There are other difficulties about speaking of it as an internal connexion; difficulties which recall some of the things that people used to say about the concrete universal. It might suggest that you would not really understand anything that is said unless you understood every way in which it was connected or every kind of connexion that could be relevant to the understanding of it. That would be absurd. It would lead to suggestions that no two people ever both got the same point or understood what is said in the same way; perhaps that no two people ever really understood one another. It might suggest that you cannot understand what is meant unless you understand the reason for saying it. This is sometimes true, of course, but very often it is not. (It might lead to the suggestion that each person understands everything in his own way – 'I know what *I* mean by it – but of course this cannot be quite what anyone else means by it.' This might lead to some suggestion of private languages. Anyway, it would make discussion and conversation impossible.)

Compare the discussion which Wittgenstein gives of understanding the proper name 'Moses' (*Philosophical Investigations*, §§ 79, 87). It does not matter what the person had in mind; it depends on how he uses it. This is the reason for putting the emphasis on 'how he uses it'; and on the distinction between correct and incorrect usage, and what goes with this: the distinction between understanding it correctly and not understanding it correctly, or misunderstanding it. This rules out the idea that no two people can understand what it means. You do not have to have in mind everything that belongs to the correct usage at the time when you are using it; or cross all bridges before you come to them.

'You have to understand what he is talking about.' Temptation to think of this as 'You have to understand the system.' (Cf. recognizing the formula.) 'You have to know something about medicine.' 'You have to have travelled the continent.' 'You have to know what has been happening in politics or in boxing.' In the last two cases, anyway, it is not like understanding a system. (Not a matter of knowing how to go on, for instance.) 'Is it a matter of knowing what he is alluding to, then?' Sometimes. But probably more important is seeing the kind of thing he is saying. Getting the sense or point – not the allusion – of his remark.

If you are not familiar with Marxist discussion, it will mean nothing to you when he speaks of the Marxist conception of ideology. But what is more important is familiarity with the kind of question, the kind of issues, with which people are concerned in this discussion. What anyone is likely to be concerned about, when he is talking on the subject. And this is in large measure similar to understanding people who are talking about their personal difficulties.

This is why the notion of a game, and of understanding a game, seemed plausible. If it is chemistry – 'You won't understand what they are saying unless you know a bit of chemistry' – thus it may be more like formal knowledge. To some extent, the trouble is that you do not know the meanings of the words and formulae. But also you have to know certain fundamental experiments. You have to know elementary laws (at least) and the evidence on which they are based. What you study when you study a subject. This is a conception which comes up often. Here it may seem more like knowing your way about the town: 'I know where I am'; 'I don't know where I am.' (Ich kenne mich nicht aus.) (I don't know my way around.)

The people who speak the language can go about among one another. And this is much more fluid, we might say, than simply fulfilling a particular role which one may have. Of course, if one is speaking of a common language with other people, this does not mean at all that one has any particular role vis-à-vis those other people. And this going about with one another does not seem to be like the ability to play a game either. And I do not see that you can give an account of it by reference to the interrelations of different games. We might say that if you tried to do that, you could lay too much emphasis on 'making up the rules as you go along'. But also, if you are speaking about 'various games' – it is bizarre that none of them seems to be finished; at least, most of them never are. Also, it is often not clear whether you are still playing the same game or whether you are not. But I criticized that notion especially because it suggested that it would be conceivable that there were only one game that was ever played. And that seems to me to leave out what is essential in the idea of being able to speak and understand.

Obviously when you learn to speak you do not learn a way of expressing things. I do not believe you could say that you learn a way of looking at things either. (Partly: that way of looking as opposed to what? It is the kind of suggestion which seems to be in place only where you might have a different way of looking at things.)

Inventing language games: inventing different kinds of calculus. Tribes which did arithmetic differently. This is especially valuable in bringing one to look on *mathematics* in a different way. ('Perhaps our mathematics has a contradiction. Perhaps we have not really been drawing mathematical conclusions; perhaps we have been doing mathematics all wrongly.' 'The logical foundations of mathematics.' 'Is mathematics a game?' Etc.) Perhaps especially to emphasize the connexion between mathematics and what you do with it. Or throw light on the relation between mathematics and reality.

But is it the same with language? with speaking and understanding? You come to mathematics when you can speak already. It is something within language. And the idea of 'how you look at it' may be different for that reason. The chief difference is that in speaking there is not the same emphasis on 'do it this way', 'this is the correct way to do it'. 'Understanding what he means' is not a matter of being able to do it correctly, except perhaps in the case of orders.

And for this reason it is less easy to imagine a game in which people 'did it differently'. You can imagine people who *use expressions* differently, of course. And Wittgenstein used to imagine different ways in which *pointing* or *arrows* might be understood. (I think he took these as 'different ways of following a rule'.) But does this mean that the conception of *understanding him correctly* would be different in these cases? Or that *learning to speak* would be different? As Wittgenstein thought of learning mathematics, I suppose learning to calculate *would* be different if you learned a different procedure; if the rules you were taught were different. (I am not sure about this.) But one of the points about learning to speak is that it does not matter so much *what* it is that you learn to say or understand. Certainly no one would begin by trying to talk with young children about international law. What they learn to speak about has to do with things in which they are interested, or things which they are doing. And this itself is important and different from mathematics. This is connected with the emphasis upon understanding other people, understanding what he is saying. This does not come into mathematics (at least that is not part of what you are being taught there), and the emphasis is wholly upon procedure.

'If you represent (or imagine) people speaking with one another differently, then you represent them as understanding one another differently. There may be different ideas of what makes sense, for instance: of what is a sensible reply or what kind of reply would make no sense at all.' This is not so easy to work out in detail. (The light which Samuel Beckett's dialogues may throw on our ordinary conversations.)

Certainly I do not want to suggest that there is anything like an act of understanding which is the same wherever there are people speaking together. (What is the analogy between 'act of understanding' and 'acts of seeing'? Cf. 'understanding is not something that happens all at once.' 'How do you tell whether he has understood? How do you tell whether you yourself have understood?') There are circumstances which make it hard to say. But is this the kind of thing that enters when one is *learning* to speak? Would this come in when you are trying to decide whether the child can speak or not?

What it is that makes it possible for the child to understand more now than it did a month ago. I was emphasizing that it is not a question of greater mastery of a technique. It is not like being able to play more things on the piano than he used to. I think I would say that it is not like being able to read more complicated things either. This would be a matter of knowing a greater vocabulary and perhaps being familiar with more complicated grammatical structures and turns of phrase, and so forth. We speak of this independently of whether he understands the particular subject that is being talked about. (Note that this holds in considerable measure of understanding what you read and of understanding what is being said.) In some ways it might seem more natural to call this sort of thing greater familiarity with the language. Almost like being familiar with the ways in which people say things; rather than being familiar with the sorts of things that people say.

And yet, what has that to do with the matter of want of understanding? And is that really what one does mean when you say of the child that is learning to speak, that he can understand now? This is the point where the parallel between being able to speak and being able to read does not hold very well.

There are ways in which you have to speak to children if they are to understand you. In particular, the ways in which you have to try to explain things to children, if they are to understand you. This is the kind of thing that anyone training to become a teacher has to learn. That point about explaining things is important here. One of the points is that you have to avoid a vocabulary that they are unfamiliar with. Don't use long words, and so forth. But that is not the only matter. Making yourself understood is especially a matter of getting the point across. This is connected with being able to follow a conversation, and in that way being able to understand what people are saying.

This does come in even when one is talking about reading. If you ask 'Can he read?', I might reply 'Do you mean "Can he read anything"?' If you were to give him a passage from a complicated legal argument, the objection would be 'Well no, that is much too difficult for him to read.' What would this mean? Would it mean that he could not read it aloud to you? (The trouble for him would be partly that he just did not understand the words – did not know the words. And this would be the same trouble whether he was trying to read or whether he was listening to someone who was saying this. So being able to read, is being able to understand what you read; being able to understand what is written there.) Perhaps it is like this when I cannot understand the parts of finance acts dealing with income tax. Does this mean that I cannot *read* them?

Any school primer would begin with very simple things, and go on to more difficult ones. And the more difficult ones are . . . well, is this a matter of being able to recognize words when you see them? Being able to read that, or being able to understand it if someone were to read it to you – generally these are not the same; or at least they are not the same in the exercises which the child has to master in his school reading book. The child would understand 'The boy throws the ball to the dog' when you said it to him, even though he may find it hard to read.

Understanding what he is saying. Understanding what you are reading. 'What you are reading' suggests that in some sense or other you can read it, if only in the way which Wittgenstein called that of a *Lesemachine* (reading machine).

As regards the 'ich kenne mich nicht aus' ('I don't know my way around'), that would apply much more to a perplexity in connexion with mathematics. A matter of not understanding the working of the language, in the sense in which you might not understand the working of a notation. The logical paradoxes would in a way illustrate this. 'I don't see how this arises when the deductions are all perfectly valid. I don't see what is wrong.' But whether this is characteristic of the perplexity about 'thing' and 'thinking', or about 'language', for the matter of that, is not so clear.

If I ask about a child of 18 months 'Can he speak?', you may reply, 'Well, he can speak a little.' And later on you may say that he can understand quite a bit now, more than he used to. But I should not say anything like this about a normal child of 4. And yet it is clear that there is a great deal which the normal child of 4 could not understand, if you were to say it to him. Even more obviously there is a great deal which the normal child of 4 could not tell you, or could not explain to you; even if it is a question of explaining to you what has happened, something that he has seen. You might add 'because he does not understand it'. It means nothing to him.

Speaking and understanding. Being able to speak and being able to understand. The difficulty of putting this in terms of 'being able to understand the language'. Once again, perhaps the influence of being able to understand mathematics. Also perhaps because of the propositions of logic in connexion with understanding, and the special perplexities in connexion with logic and the logical paradoxes.

I may come upon a puzzling construction in Latin or in Greek; and I may ask you how you would construe it. It may be easy enough for me to read Caesar or Ovid, and I may find it very difficult to read Tacitus. Notice, by the way, the difference between 'Can he read?' and 'Can he read Latin?' (or French). The point about the difficulty with Tacitus is of course not that I could not understand the sorts of things he was saying; and I am inclined to add 'if I knew Latin well enough'. (But what does 'well enough' mean? It would be hard to give an account which did not include being able to read Tacitus; or something equivalent to this.)

It will not help if you try in English to make me familiar with the sorts of things that Tacitus is writing about. If the difficulty were one of understanding a German work on chemistry, for instance, then such an explanation in English might have helped. But it is not that sort of difficulty. And we come back to the point that I do not know enough Latin. But what is that – 'enough Latin'? 'I should get what he was talking about if I knew Latin well enough.' Part of my point is that this is not the kind of situation which ever arises in connexion with the child who is learning to speak. It is not a matter of his being able to understand more when he knows the language better.

'Knowing Latin well enough' has to do partly with vocabulary, of course. But it is more a matter of being familiar with idioms and constructions – would you use the dative in this kind of case? Could the dative be used to mean so and so here? One generally uses a relative clause there, but you need not always, you can also use something else. It is partly a matter of knowing other constructions that are equivalent to those that I have been used to. All this kind of comment is at home in translation.

I think this a point where the matter of being able to appreciate differences in style also comes in. Also, even having a *nose* for the language; so that when he is using a turn of phrase that I have not met before, or making a new use of a construction, I can say 'Oh yes, I see what he is doing.' I can go along with him. I expect that is very important. (Understanding James Joyce or Samuel Beckett.) And it is the sort of thing that comes with familiarity with the language and not otherwise. It would be impossible to say just what you have to know in order to be able to do that. How do you *teach* anyone to follow you in that way – when you use a metaphor, for instance?

VI

Generality and the unity of language. Tarski insists that it is necessary to speak as though there were only one language. In one sense I would say this too. But in one sense the different notations of which he is speaking are not languages at all (though they are *systems*).

There is often something queer about speaking of 'language'. And so similarly of 'belonging to language'. As when we are asking about the relation of language to reality; or if we are asking what understanding is, and what intelligibility is. (I dare say Austin would dismiss all these questions.) 'When would the general concept of language be used? Language, as opposed to what?'

'You cannot say (in language) what it is that language does.' What is wrong in all this is the idea of 'showing you how language does its stuff'. And the suggestion that when a proposition has meaning, or is understood, this is like having a kind of effect or influence. If you could *observe* language having its effects, and performing its functions, then you ought to be able to distinguish between language and what you observe, and what you show about it. (Just as you could if you were speaking of the operation of an electric circuit.) If the demonstration were *in* language, you could not distinguish then between the language and its function. 'You cannot say (in language) what it is that makes it language; what it is that makes it have meaning.'

'The way in which the different remarks are connected – this gives what we mean by "language".' But what of the question: 'What is it that makes them all *language* games?' Wittgenstein avoids this trouble by emphasizing that 'having meaning' is not one sort of thing (like magnetism or radiation). Just as *understanding* is not one sort of thing.

One of the difficulties is that the discussion always has (apparently) to be in *analogies*. And when you are arguing in analogies it is always a matter of 'more or less'. (This may have been part of what Russell was complaining about in Wittgenstein.) 'If all you are looking for is more or less satisfactory analogies, then it does not really very much *matter.*' The importance of these analogies – and of the 'anthropological' view – is precisely to get you to look on the 'relation to reality' differently.

Whether we should speak of 'language' or simply of this or that language. One of the tendencies we meet in philosophy is just this tendency to speak of 'language'; the principles of language; discourse; ideas about the relation of logic and language; the principles of intelligibility. Which shows something about the kind of puzzlement; the kind of perplexity about language and about understanding there is in philosophy. The way this is different from the feeling that I shall never be able to understand Welsh or understand French or what it may be.

Russell had hoped for great things from the application of logical analysis. This seems to have been a matter of bringing out the precise significance of the statement; and also of bringing out its logical form. But Wittgenstein's idea – which he took from Paul Ernst – of misunderstanding the logic of our language, and the idea that the apparent problems of philosophy come from this source, seem to be something different.

One way of pointing to the difference is to bring out the different attitudes of Wittgenstein and of Russell towards the idea of what a *solution* to any philosophical problem would be. Russell seems to have been interested in showing the falsity or the untenability of certain views, rather than with showing that the question itself springs from a misunderstanding of the logic of our language.

All this hangs together with the question of what can be said. I am not sure how far Russell ever took or perhaps even grasped Wittgenstein's notion that logic cannot be said. (Alle Sätze der Logik sagen dasselbe, nämlich nichts.) (All the propositions of logic say the same thing, namely nothing.)

If you misunderstand the logic of our language, you do not see clearly what makes it possible for an expression to have sense, and what rules it out. You do not see how the very form of certain 'questions' would show that they are not questions at all; that they 'try' to ask or say what cannot be said or asked.

One of the difficulties which has led people to doubt whether there can be any science of philosophy – or any such study as philosophy – is that we seem to be asking about the reality of investigation. Cf. the question whether there can be a theory of logic. In this the difficulties concerning an account of what speaking is may be analogous.

'You know what to do when you are trying to teach him how to speak. And you know what you are trying to teach him. Where is the difficulty? If I can tell whether he can speak or not, then I know what speaking is. And if you ask me *how* I can tell, I can explain.'

How is it that you *do* recognize when he can speak? This is like 'How do you recognize it as a proposition?' Feeling that the reference to the criteria you use in practice does not really meet the question. Those would be much like the criteria you would use to tell whether someone has understood what you just said to him. And in this case you are taking for *granted* that he can speak.

'Are you sure he can speak?' 'Certainly. You can carry on a

conversation with him.' 'What about?' 'Why anything – anything that children of that age can understand.' 'How do you tell whether he can understand?' By the sort of replies he makes, partly. And this is not the same as seeing whether he does something *correctly*.

Does this bear on ideas about generality? And on ideas about 'belonging to language'? Does the idea of 'belonging to language' (intelligibility) imply some formal criterion of 'what can be said'? Well, and are you then thrown back on 'and so on'? 'And things of that sort'? ('The generality of language.') A rule for continuing. Following a rule.

But continuing to speak is not a matter of following a rule. Certainly it is not continuing with the rule for the application of a particular expression, like '+2'. But it is not continuing in a particular game either. 'No, but with games.' But what does this mean? And *would that* be something like following a rule?

This is where this explanation of generality does not work. It will not do for what one might call 'the generality of language'.

CHAPTER 13

Philosophy, life and language
(30.10.57–30.4.58)

I

If philosophy is concerned with language, this is because it is concerned with understanding. (I think it would be wrong to say that it is concerned with the various features of a technique.) Philosophy is concerned with what you learn when you learn the language, or when you learn to speak.

What is the relation between understanding what is said, and appreciation of style? The difference between saying one thing and another is not the difference between one way of saying it and another. So understanding what is said is not just an appreciation of style.

It was understanding of style that seemed to have analogies with understanding human behaviour or human lives. And if that is different from understanding what is said – or understanding language, in the most usual sense of that expression – it might seem that since the chief concern of philosophy is with language and the understanding which belongs there, therefore the interest of philosophy or the subject of philosophy is something different from the understanding of lives or from the understanding of life.

I do not think one can draw that conclusion. For one thing, 'understanding life' is not the same as 'insight into the course of human lives' or 'understanding why human lives go as they do'. The understanding which a great artist shows is certainly more than that, otherwise he has nothing to say. If an artist can show the sense of the lives that the people of whom he writes are leading, that is something more than appreciation of style; it is something more than seeing the point or the force or the terribleness of the things they do and say. Understanding the sense of their lives is not the same as understanding the sense or the point of their remarks and actions.

Something analogous goes for the understanding that is sought in philosophy: the difference between that and appreciation of the differences between the grammars of various expressions – as though perhaps that were a perception of the differences between techniques which might at first sight seem similar; or of the ways in which grammars might mislead one – and so on.

One way of bringing that out is to show that the main problems of philosophy, or the main forms of philosophical perplexity, are concerned with the possibility of sense or understanding or language altogether (or the possibility of philosophy altogether), and not with the puzzling features of a particular expression. Suppose we said that the 'point' of language or of speaking was intelligibility, or understanding. That that is what you learn when you learn to speak. The philosophical difficulties expressed in scepticism seem to call all that in question; call in question the possibility of *learning* anything in that sense – the possibility of understanding people. The possibility of saying anything. The possibility of learning or of growing wiser. The possibility of the growth of understanding. It is in *this* sense of doubting whether it makes any difference what you say – not doubting whether there is any difference in meaning between one statement and another. That is rather important. Whether it makes any difference what you say – whether there is any point in it anyway; whether there is any point in saying anything anyway.

Somehow this is connected with the difference between learning how you would say so and so – learning how it is done, knowing how to use it – and learning to speak with people and to understand people. The kind of difference it makes – what it is that you learn. (What it is you gain in philosophy.)

Not that philosophy teaches you the correct answer – as though it were something you could take away. The understanding that you gain as you learn the language. Not something that is given in the books or in manuals. 'What is it that you have, when you have achieved it, then?' You are able to speak and understand people. That does not mean: you are master of a technique. The language – what you understand when you understand the language – is not something apart from understanding people and speaking with them. It is not something different from carrying on with them. Something which makes that possible. The understanding that you have when you understand a discussion.

My question concerning philosophy and the understanding of life.

But for that reason I have to ask something about understanding altogether.

I was considering the difference between understanding the depth and force of what is said, and understanding what is said. (This was partly because it seemed to me at first that understanding life was something that belonged to art rather than to philosophy.) It is obvious that there is a difference there. But I think there is a connexion too, although it be less immediate than some have taken it to be.

This leads to the question of what it is you understand, when you understand what is said. And what it is you understand when you understand the language. In this connexion I was discussing the relation of philosophy and language – whether for instance there are certain principles or forms which are implicitly recognized whenever there is understanding of what is said. The conditions of the possibility of discourse; or the conditions of the intelligibility of discourse. And whether these are the subject matter of philosophy.

What the intelligibility of the language (or of the remark?) depends on. 'That is how we do it' – can we let it rest on that? Or must we say that there is some reason why our actual languages have the form or the grammars that they do? The connexion of language with logic: 'At any rate, there could not be a language which did not conform to the elementary principles of logic.'

The way in which language hangs together: not in virtue of a formal or systematic connexion. Any more than it is some fundamental form that is the condition of its intelligibility; or of the intelligibility of what is said in it. Yet there is something in the notion that the intelligibility of language depends on the way it hangs together.

The idea that there is some essential form of language had been connected with an idea of the relation of language to reality. (The intelligibility of language depends upon the nature of reality. Cf. also: the world is what makes it possible for language to have sense.) The idea of being responsible to some reality. As though there could not be any distinction between sense and nonsense otherwise. Cf. the relation of logic and reality. Almost, the reality of logic. The necessity of the force of logic. What makes it *logic*. Gives it its claim. So that it can rule out anything else.

If we make it a matter of convention or convenience or way of living, then the form or the grammar does not seem to have the same sort of significance about it; does not seem to show 'the reality of things' in any way. As though we could not speak in the same way of the reality of the distinction between sense and nonsense. (Is this because if something else is always possible – and apparently just as good – there seems to be nothing specially binding about this one? This is just the way in which people happen to speak with one another. They do not speak with one another in this way *because* they want to be intelligible; because they recognize that to be intelligible they must observe this distinction.) We have found out something about the possibility of language, when we have seen that it corresponds to some reality.

Could we say that we had found out something about the possibility of language when we found that it went with a way of living – one way of living among others? How could that be when we admit that there can be so many various ways of living? When we admit that there is no way of speaking which *could* not be sensible?

This seems to raise the question of what we mean by the intelligibility of language; and perhaps by the intelligibility of what is said. 'That the distinction between sense and nonsense is not just an arbitrary one.' That is a very obscure remark.

And life? The reality of life. But we are still not clear what the intelligibility of life depends on. Or rather, before that: what we *mean* by the intelligibility or the sense of life. Better: what we mean by understanding life. Still better: what we mean by recognizing that there is or can be some sense in life. Whether 'understanding life' is of a piece with 'understanding the lives of people', somehow.

An artist could hardly understand the lives of individuals unless he were familiar with 'the way they lived'; with the way of living. (Perhaps in analogy with the need to understand the language before you can understand what is said in it. But the 'before' is difficult in the case of language, and perhaps in the case of life also.) You would not get the significance of the things they do; any more than you would get the significance of the musical phrase if you could not understand the music. 'He might just as well have done anything. What he is doing means nothing to me. I cannot read it.'

'That the distinction between sense and nonsense is not just an arbitrary one.' I suppose certain of the distinctions between good and bad grammar would be called arbitrary; like 'U' and 'Non-U'.

But these do not seem to affect *intelligibility* in any very fundamental way. Even if you cannot understand people who speak in 'uneducated' grammar, you can easily learn to. Whereas if people 'put signs together in a wholly unintelligible way' – especially if they uttered nothing but contradictions and other logical absurdities – then you would not even know how to learn to understand them. It would be like a foreign language which could not in any circumstances or by any method be translated into our own.

So there is something about language that is arbitrary and there is something which is not (did not Boole say something like that?). Well, if we say that there are certain things which *could* not make sense, I suppose this is what we should mean by saying that any intelligible language corresponds to some reality, or that it is responsible to reality.

Was this the sort of thing Plato was trying to emphasize? That the forms, or whatever else we are to include among the conditions of the possibility of discourse, may seem to be in some sense 'intellectual', in the sense that they do not belong to the physical objects which we see and handle. But on the other hand they are not products of our intellects or imaginary webs we weave in the air. They are not *idle* or *empty* principles – even though we cannot point to physical happenings in confirmation.

We can distinguish between fact and fiction, because facts are 'hard' and they do not depend on us. They are what they are whether we like it or not. With the principles of grammar, what makes the difference between sense and nonsense, we might want also to say that we are concerned with what is fact and not fiction. At any rate, it would seem that 'we cannot just say anything we like' any more than we can just say anything we like about physical objects.

And yet there is something wrong about speaking of these as matters of fact, just as there would be something wrong in suggesting that we discover them or that we investigate to find out what they are, in the way in which we should investigate to find out what the facts are. When we ask what the facts are, we are asking whether something or other is or is not. And if we find out that it is, well all right, that is interesting and it might have been different.

It is not that kind of distinction here. (Nonsense is not fiction. That is the whole point. And incidentally it goes with the point that in these principles we are not saying anything.) So it is a different kind of reality (from the reality of facts) and a different kind of correspondence. 'Something which *could* not be talked about in any other way' – though as a matter of fact you are not really talking *about* it – 'in any other way, because if you tried to you would be simply uttering nonsense and not saying anything at all.' But for the same sort of reason, it seems absurd to suggest that anybody *decided* to make this sort of distinction between what has sense and what has not. That distinction is presupposed in the whole notion of making a discussion of any kind. Cf. the idea of 'choosing our logic'.

When 'what we say corresponds to the facts' that seems almost like the correspondence of a map with the countryside, or the correspondence of a picture with what it is a picture of. Correspondence of your description with what you describe. But in such a case you might wonder whether it really did conform; or how accurately. Whereas there would be no sense in asking that about the principles of logic or of grammar. You might ask whether the principles were clearly expressed, but not whether the principles themselves were trustworthy. And *yet* we cannot say that it does not make any difference whether you trust them or not – you can please yourself.

What the intelligibility of language depends on. Not on the 'content' of what you say. So it must be on the form? On the way it is put together? On the way it hangs together? Plato would have held to the latter, but he would not have said that that connexion was just a matter of the *form* of the language. (That it is the forms which make it a proposition.) Not the content. Because if you had said something else it would have been perfectly intelligible. Only you must have *said* it. (That is something which holds no matter what you say.)

It must belong to a dialogue. I do not know how far it is possible to give an account of that. The reality of the distinction between sense and nonsense. Whether it can be understood. What it is that you learn when you learn to understand people.

The distinction between form and content is not like the distinction between one thing and another. Just as there is not quite the sharp distinction between grammatical propositions and empirical ones. This is what is brought out when we consider what belonging to a language is. And what it is that we learn when we learn the language, or when we learn to understand. There is the form, or the way we speak, certainly. But that is not something which you learn before you learn to understand. And it is not something that can be set over against the intelligibility of the dialogue or the conversation.

Wittgenstein's distinction between explanation and training is important when one is distinguishing learning to speak and learning to understand from being familiar with a notation. We may 'imagine a different language' in the sense of a different way of speaking. And this is something different from 'imagining that we replace our present notation by a different one'; for that need not bring any considerable change in our way of living. But to imagine a different way of living, is to imagine a general sort (as the term 'way' indicates).

And what is the relation between different language games – especially when they belong to the same language? Simply one of *likeness*? If you are asking what they have in common, or what is the relation between a form of one language game and another, you may well speak of family likeness. But that does not answer the question 'what makes them all language' or 'makes them all *this* language'. Any more than the relation of a statement and the answer to it – what makes them part of the same conversation – can be put in terms of a common form or a similar form; or having a common grammar either (for they could have that if they were not in the same conversation). (Which makes me wonder, incidentally, whether the notions of 'a different grammar' and 'a different language game' are really equivalent. 'It is a different grammar – we are playing a different game now.') It is not as though each had a role in the calculus, and so had a bearing on one another in *that* way. Perhaps they must have something like that logical bearing on each other *as well*.

But even the time at which it is said is important – for most discussions anyway. (And that is something different from its place in a formal argument or calculus.) It depends upon what other remarks have been made, and this is nothing like the logical completion of a system. ('Understanding its place in the system of the language' is surely *not* what is important. Or anyway, that is not what 'understanding the point of the remark' is.)

The special difficulties that the other person is bringing forward. Why he happened to raise just that point. His difficulties in understanding what was said earlier perhaps. The matter of clearing away misunderstandings. All that would be left out of a calculus.

But it is not just that difference either. 'Their bearing on one another' – that is important, and it includes their logical bearing, though it is not only that. No consideration of a calculus, and no consideration of their logical forms, would tell you whether this statement *did* bear on that, whether they had to do with the same question, or had anything to do with one another.

I suppose this is one of the things that distinguishes this from moves in a game – even though for the bearing of one move on another, the *time* of the move is important. (Wittgenstein did not want to say that the various *games* are related to one another as moves in a game.) All the same, the different moves in a game do not bear on one another by having to do with the same subject. (That is why they do not contribute to understanding.) They bear on one another because they are made in the same game. And none need be a move that would mean anything in any other game. I suppose that is important, especially when we consider the relation of the language games to each other. All you have to understand is the game. You do not have to understand what it is about. If you ask 'what move it is', or perhaps even 'what the point of it is', then the reference to the role might be an answer. The idea of 'the *course* of the game' – that is different from 'the course of the discussion' just because there is no parallel to 'what the discussion is about' – what they are trying to understand, which would not come in if it were simply a contest. But then, understanding one another would hardly come in then either. Because understanding what someone is saying in the conversation (cf. being able to speak) is not just a matter of understanding the move he is making in a game or in a contest. And I wonder whether Wittgenstein ever brought these clearly together – even made clear how they are related. Much the same goes for thinking of language as an *institution*. In some ways better than the game simile, because an institution belongs to the lives we lead as a game does not. But once again: what of 'understanding what he said'? That is not just recognizing its role in the work of an institution; nor just 'recognizing what he is up to' either.

II

'The way in which we use language.' Can you speak of using language in one way or another? You can speak of using a given expression – and also a given construction, perhaps – in this way or that. But that seems to be within language and to presuppose it.

Can you say anything about the practice of language? You cannot say that it is intelligent or unintelligent, anyway. (Cf. 'an ideal language would . . .') But could you say anything else? Could you say what you do with language, for instance? Could you say anything else except that you speak it? That does not mean anything much, except that you speak a particular language, and it would always be conceivable that you had spoken some other. There is the further point that you speak a language which is also spoken by those to whom you are speaking. But that is something which belongs to the idea of speaking altogether; and it would be out of place to think of that as something added, when you have already said that you speak.

Learning to speak is learning to understand what is *said*. Or at least that is a large part of it. This is one reason why the reference to *Abrichtung* seems to me misleading or a misplaced emphasis. (It leaves out, or it does not reach, what is the most important part of learning to speak.) Wittgenstein introduced it because he wanted to get away from the suggested parallel between understanding and explanation: that I have told you what understanding the meaning is if I have told you what explaining the meaning is. But it still seems to go with the idea that you must explain understanding in terms of something that is *done*. Perhaps this is to guard against the idea that understanding is a meta-logical concept. The idea of 'operating with words', 'reacting to words', etc. Were it conceivable that you should train animals to do this? Just as you might train them to play a complicated game? If that were all there were to it, then it would not seem to have any special connexion with the lives people lead. That is *why* it does not seem straight off inconceivable that animals should do it. Or more to the point: that one should be able to construct machines that would do it. (Grant for the moment, anyway, that one can construct machines that play chess.) If it is a question of making reactions to rules, why should one not have machines that 'speak' just as truly as one can have machines that 'calculate'?

Machines do not have lives and do not grow. And the fact that they do not understand what is said – that they do not *learn* the language, however they may be adjusted and set for it – gocs with that. But this is also why I do not think that learning the language or learning to speak is simply a matter of *Abrichtung*. Cf. the importance which Wittgenstein used to place on 'the role which it plays' (when he was pointing out the *defects* of behaviourism and formalism). Only it will not do to think of the role which it plays in a game simply. That does not bring out the important sense in which speaking is something which people do together. And it does not bring out the important sense of 'belonging to a language'. Role which it plays in *what*, then?

A machine does not carry on a discussion. And this is connected with the fact that a discussion is not like a calculation. *It is not like a game of chess either.* A machine does not give an explanation of why it said so and so. Any more than it tries to understand your difficulty. A machine can carry out instructions, though; or something more nearly like that.

Wittgenstein's account of language in terms of games grew from his criticism of his earlier view that there is some fundamental form of expressions which is a condition of their intelligibility. This determined what could be said and therefore it must underlie the possibility of any relation between language and reality. 'Belonging to language' – or to *our* language? – must lie in some sort of relation to that form. (Otherwise what you have is not a proposition.)

This was rather like the way of deciding whether an expression belonged to a calculus or not. You decide that by reference to the formal or logical relations of this expression or proposition to other propositions in the system. (What was queer, of course, was the notion that one might in some such way decide whether an expression was a proposition at all; or even, perhaps, whether a mark or sound was an expression at all. How is one going to look to its logical relations without assuming that it is a proposition to begin with? So perhaps we should say simply that we can see that it *has* the form of a proposition – cf. the question 'How do you recognize that something is written there?' – but that for this reason it must have logical relations, or it must make sense to ask about its logical relations, to other propositions.) The idea of the unity of a calculus is the unity of a system. The connexions between the different expressions – part of a system of proofs. The notion that the intelligibility of the statement in the calculus lies in its connexion with the others – lies in its proof, possibly. (How is that to be reconciled with the idea that the intelligibility is already present in its form? One of the big questions would be the question of what you are going to mean by 'form' – '. . . in virtue of its form alone'.)

But that would be misleading if you were wanting to say, for instance, that the intelligibility of anything that is said in the language lies in its relation to the rest of the language. Yet it must have certain connexions with other things that are said. And perhaps the most important matter that I am trying to decide is the question of the kind of relation that there is there. In what way does the intelligibility of the statement being made now depend on its relation to other things that are said? What sort of *dependence* is there?

There are two things that I seem to have been saying here. One is that the connexion which various remarks in the *discussion* have with one another is important; things that are said in a language are related to one another. But this seems to get one into difficulties, because obviously you cannot say that all the people speaking the language are engaged in a common discussion, just because they are speaking a common language. And somehow the intelligibility of what is said does depend upon this idea of a common language.

But *another* thing that I have been saying is that this connexion has to do with the way in which people are carrying on their lives; with their living. And I suppose that this has to do with the fact that they *learn* from what is said (cf. understanding the point of the remark). And this may allow some account of the matter I have just mentioned – that not all people who speak a common language are engaged in a common discussion. And at the same time it may allow one to treat the discussion as in a way typical of the kind of relation there is in what we call 'leading a common life'.

At any rate, one of the things I am wanting to emphasize is that to understand what people are saying, you have to understand more than just the language. And this goes together with the point that if you are going to understand the discussion, you have to understand what is being talked about. The matter of leading a common life and understanding one another is what Plato was emphasizing. I suppose I wanted to suggest that the way in which the various parts of the man's life are connected, especially when we talk about his learning – that this has something to do with the way in which the different parts of the language are connected, and with the idea of belonging to a language.

There is a connexion between discussion and relations between people. (Or perhaps: between conversation, and relations between people.) And this has to do with the way in which what is said belongs to a language. What we might call the unity of a discussion – the bearing of the different things that are said on one another – seems in some way typical of the unity of language.

Discussion and the relations between people: I have been talking about understanding what is said as illustrated especially by understanding the remark that may be made in a discussion (or conversation). And that seems to depend in so many ways on the relations between people. Children learn to speak from the people with whom they are living. And it would seem impossible that they should learn in any other way.

This is one of the ways in which learning to speak is unlike learning the rules or learning to carry out orders. Learning to speak is not simply learning how to do something. Not even learning how to go on with a particular sort of procedure. Confusion of learning to speak and learning a foreign language. As though when you taught a child to speak, you taught him the language. Wittgenstein sees the falsity of that in his criticism of Augustine in the *Investigations*. But he thinks it comparable to training one in reactions to words or reactions with words. And this does leave it too similar to learning how to operate a machine.

If you are to understand what people are saying, you have to be familiar with more than the language. This has to do with the point that language in some way goes all through one's life. And that one would not be saying anything if one uttered things only in connexion with one specific activity, like that of building. Learning technical terms in connexion with building is not learning to speak. The point that building is not the only thing that they do. They are not simply parts of an organization. 'If they speak there, they are certain to speak elsewhere.' This is because speaking is not simply the exercise of a special technique. If it were simply a question of understanding orders, this might be confined to one set of special circumstances. (The way the horse understands the orders of the ploughman.) But *giving* orders is already something different. Cf. 'telling him what you want'. This rather than that. It is not simply like saying 'full' when the water reaches the level, though even that is something you could not train an animal to do. As you might train him to bark when his name is called; or to 'speak for it'. Deciding what to say and deciding when to say it. If you can say 'full' when it reaches the point, then presumably you can say 'not yet' when you are asked.

You can of course construct a machine to show when water reaches the mark, instead of posting a man there to tell you. But that does not mean that the man is behaving like a machine when he does tell you. And it is still true that he could not tell you that unless he could tell you other things. You would be thinking of the man as part of a machine if you thought he never did anything else than that. (Or if he were a machine that had to be set for that. So that he would not be 'doing' either in our sense at all.) The fact that he does and can do other things, and that he is kept doing this not by being set – this goes with the point that what he says may be true or false. The machine may be out of order, but it does not make a mistake, and it is not careless or stupid. I do not think the man could make a mistake, or be careless or stupid, if this were the only thing he ever said. He would not be using words in this connexion, if he never used them in any other. Though he might make the sounds, just as a machine might.

III

When we speak of the development or of the history of an institution or of institutions – this goes commonly with the working out of problems: problems which people have in their lives and their affairs. I want to emphasize that idea of 'working out problems' which is so much of what we call 'life' for human beings, and has much to do with what we call history. Probably the notion of 'initiative' goes with that.

Anyway, they are problems concerning what people are doing together, in some way. The term 'problem' may lead to misunderstanding, if it suggests something like theoretical or scientific problems and the solution of them. (Problems in engineering, for instance: 'social engineering'.) That would leave the road open to demands that experts should be put in charge. But that is not what I mean – any more than I mean that all discussion is scientific discussion. The idea of 'difficulties', and of a 'solution' to them. This is often a matter of difficulties in getting along with people; and there is no question of a scientific solution to that. For all that, they are problems that arise from the nature of *human* intercourse, and they would not have any parallels, for the most part, in the lives of animals.

Neither is it simply a question of overcoming obstacles in the carrying out of an instinctive procedure, like migration of birds or the building of dams or nests. Animals may deal with problems of that sort, but those are not problems of living together. Such problems or difficulties have to do with 'the way things are in our lives'. Also more generally: attitudes towards gambling; towards divorce; towards suicide; towards the observance of the sabbath;

towards the rights of individuals; the inviolability of the domicile; the whole conception of public opinion: 'the feeling in the country'. Questions regarding 'the position of women'. Or the position of people of different race. The general question of enfranchisements. But it concerns also attitudes and a good deal of what we call morality.

The question of understanding the life we are leading. The importance of the study of history for this. (Perhaps in more primitive societies the teaching of myth takes the place of that.) Why is it that in the social life of animals there is no question of understanding in this way? I suspect that this is because there are not problems in the life of animals or of animal societies, and that is hardly more than another way of saying that there is not language or discourse.

I want to suggest that there is some important connexion between understanding the life we are living and understanding the language (we are speaking). This is open to objections if we leave it there, since we seem to be able to understand languages, like Latin or Sanskrit, without ever having participated in the life of the people by whom those languages were spoken (note that we do not count ourselves, in this context, as among those by whom the languages were spoken). The medieval men of learning spoke Latin, but then it was medieval Latin that they spoke, not classical Latin. And the Latin which they spoke was spoken in the problems of the life they led. Even the rather restricted life of academic activities – even giving lectures – is full of the practical problems of education, for instance, and of research. This is nothing like trying to decipher a text. Is it a different sense of 'understanding the language', then? I think it is a different sense of 'what you learn when you learn the language', anyway.

Understanding a living language, and understanding a dead one. The question whether you could have learned to speak in that language. It is only the understanding of a living language that is relevant to this question of 'learning to speak'. And here the point is that it is learning to speak it in the way it is spoken by people who live and have the sorts of problems that human beings do. *That* is the most important part of the *way* in which it is spoken, I should think. At any rate it seems to be important for understanding the point of a remark. (The difference between this and learning the phrases of a foreign language which are appropriate for travelling, or the phrases which are needed for shopping, or the phrases that are needed in the kitchen, or the phrases a salesman needs.)

To understand a science, you need special training. And similarly with understanding the problems of historical research or of law. You need 'a long and difficult course of education' in order to try to answer these. It is not like that in connexion with human difficulties; nor, I imagine, with understanding people or understanding what they say. It might be said that you need 'experience', but not what is commonly meant by education.

Certainly educated people are no less liable to difficulties, or no more skilled at solving them, than others are. If Plato thought that education was the answer to the troubles of human relations, it was only because he thought of those relations in a quite external way, really as relations between crafts or occupations. Yet I am suggesting that difficulties of that kind belong with language and with speaking with one another; and that this is why it does not make sense to speak of anything of the sort in the lives of animals. I seem to have suggested, too, that you would not understand the language, in the sense of being able to speak with people in it, unless you understood such difficulties – were familiar with them, knew what they were. This went with the idea of learning to speak at all. And it even went with the idea of having to understand 'things' – in order to know what was being talked about. It had to do especially with the idea of understanding people and what they were saying – and with the differences between that and understanding a process or understanding a technique or a game. Why is it that to imagine a language is to imagine a way of living?

Rush Rhees: a biographical sketch

Rush Rhees (1905–1989) was a remarkable person. He was a pupil and a close friend of Ludwig Wittgenstein. Rhees edited many of Wittgenstein's works and was one of his literary executors. In his biography of Wittgenstein, Ray Monk refers to Rhees' 'incomparable knowledge of Wittgenstein's work'.[1] Some of Rhees' published papers became classics: for example, his contribution to a symposium with A. J. Ayer on 'Can there be a private language?', and his paper, 'Wittgenstein's Builders'. Most of his work, however, remained unpublished during his lifetime. The Rush Rhees Archive at the University College of Swansea contains work by him on every aspect of philosophy. For him, philosophy was one subject, not a collection of specialisms. In this sketch, I hope to provide a brief glimpse of Rhees' background and of the style which made him so distinctive as a person and as a philosopher.

Rush Rhees' great-great grandfather, Morgan John Rhys (1760–1804), was a Welsh radical preacher and pamphleteer who wrote tracts on the abolition of slavery, the disestablishment of the Church, and other reforms he thought desirable. He was prominent in promoting free elementary Sunday schools at which the illiterate poor were taught to read and write. In 1791, wanting to witness the fruits of the French Revolution at first hand, he went to Paris with an American officer, Major Benjamin Loxley of Philadelphia. During the political upheaval which followed the Revolution, Rhys, fearing arrest, fled to America in 1794.

In America, Rhys married Loxley's daughter, Anne, a powerful supporter of all his future endeavours. After emigration, the family surname changed to Rhees. In 1796, along with eminent Philadelphians, Rhees organized the Philadelphia Society for the Infor-

---

[1] Ray Monk, *Ludwig Wittgenstein: The Duty of Genius* (London: Vintage 1991), p. xii.

mation and Assistance of Persons Emigrating from Foreign Countries. He became acquainted with the philanthropist Benjamin Rush, a signatory of the American Declaration of Independence. Rush helped Rhees in founding a Welsh colony in the Alleghenies. Such was the latter's gratitude and admiration that he named his second son Benjamin Rush Rhees.

The distinguished history of the Rhees family is to be found in *Rhees of Rochester* by John Rothwell Slater.[2] The book concentrates on Rush Rhees' father, sometime Professor of New Testament Interpretation at Newton Theological Institute who, in 1899, became President of Rochester University. This is not the place to speak of President Rhees' distinguished term of office, marked by his remarkable collaboration with the University's chief benefactor, George Eastman. The Rush Rhees Library stands as a memorial to his achievements.

Rush Rhees, author of the papers in this collection, was born on 19 March 1905 in Rochester, New York. He attended the Choate School in Wallingford, Connecticut. From there he went to Rochester University in 1922, where he studied for two years. His stay there was not a happy one. In his book, *A History of the University of Rochester 1850–1962*,[3] Arthur May writes that Rhees' sudden departure from the university was due to

a head-on clash between Professor George M. Forbes and Rush Rhees Jr, Class of 1926, younger son of the President. 'Radicalism of Rochester President's Son Causes Professor to Bar Youth from Class' read a startling front-page headline in the *New York Times*. The accompanying story related that Rhees, a youth of 'advanced ideas', had been dropped from a philosophy class because he presumed to refute everything Forbes taught and was guilty of shallow thinking and inordinate conceit. Professing allegiance to anarchism, Rhees was quoted as saying, 'I am radical. Dr Forbes is not. That is why I am debarred . . . From a Puritan I have revolted into an atheist.' Certain undergraduates reproached Forbes on the ground that the expulsion of Rhees violated the principle of independence of thought. President Rhees was abroad at the time of the expulsion on campus, and his biographer is wholly silent on his reaction to this bizarre incident.

In an interview granted to the Rochester campus magazine, some time after his retirement from the University College of Swansea in 1966, Rhees said:

[2] New York and London: Harper and Row, n.d.
[3] University of Rochester, 1977.

When I left Rochester I went directly to Edinburgh to continue study . . . I wrote to my father and said that a certain professor suggested that I might not be suited to study philosophy, but that I hoped to stay on in philosophy long enough to think coherently. He wrote back and urged me to do so, saying that 'the very best thing education can give a man is the ability to think coherently'.

It is this high value based on a liberal education for which Rush Rhees Jr would like his father to be remembered.

When Rhees went to Edinburgh in 1924, the chairs of philosophy were occupied by A. E. Taylor and Norman Kemp Smith. Rhees made quite an impression on the latter. In the course of a letter to Baron von Hugel, Norman Kemp Smith wrote:

Among the American students here this year is a *very* picturesque youth, called Rush Rhees – of rather distinguished parentage, on the side both of his mother & of his father. He is quite a picture, like the young Shelley, & rather lives up to it – tho' quite a nice & simple youth – wearing his shirt collar loose & open at the neck. Why he has been sent over to Edinburgh, I can't quite make out: he is taking undergraduate courses, & is in my big class. I cannot help thinking that he must have got into some kind of youthful trouble at Syracuse [sic] University where he was studying & where his father is President. He came with an introduction, so I feel some responsibility for him. Asking him whether in his work here he wanted discipline or mainly stimulus, he replied, as I expected, very definitely the latter. He aspires to be a poet (I have not seen any of his verse) but conceals this high ambition under the very thin disguise of journalism.[4]

Late in life, Rhees told me of his encounter with Norman Kemp Smith. When he told his teacher that he wanted inspiration from his studies, Norman Kemp Smith replied, 'You won't get it without discipline.' Returning an early essay by Rhees he described it as full of promiscuous feeling and in need of reworking, adding: 'It is as difficult to get a student to return to his essay as it is to get a dog to return to its vomit.' Rhees said to me, 'That was a good remark, and I needed it.'

In 1928 Rhees graduated with an excellent first class honours in Mental Philosophy, and was awarded a Vans Dunlop Scholarship, one of the highest distinctions the Philosophy Department could bestow. In the autumn of the same year he was appointed Assistant Lecturer in Philosophy in the University of Manchester, a post he

---

[4] *The Letters of Baron Friedrich von Hugel and Professor Norman Kemp Smith*, ed. Laurence F. Barmann (New York: Fordham University Press), 1981, pp. 275–6.

held for four years. J. L. Stocks was the Professor of Philosophy at Manchester, and Rhees was his only assistant. In a reference, dated July 1931, he testifies to Rhees' wholehearted commitment in teaching a wide range of courses, but says: 'It is rather early to say on what lines he will develop as a philosopher.' Writing in 1936 of his main interests while at Manchester, Rhees says: 'My principal interests . . . during this time were the study of the philosophy of Fries and L. Nelson, and the independent investigation of certain questions in ethical theory.' Typically, Rhees adds in his statement: 'But I did not, during the whole of these four years, succeed in producing anything fit for publication.'

In 1931, A. E. Taylor notes Rhees' achievements at Edinburgh in a brief reference. In a letter to Rhees, he regrets that he could not say more, but says, 'it is difficult when one has no published work to go on'. The major influence on Rhees at Edinburgh, however, had been neither Taylor nor Kemp Smith, but John Anderson, who was to become Challis Professor at Sydney. Although Rhees became critical, later, of Anderson's views on logic, his influence on Rhees in social philosophy remained a powerful one. Rhees was deeply attracted by certain aspects of anarchist thought in political philosophy, while being realistic about the problems posed for them by the emergence of advanced industrial societies. In the forties, Rhees told Wittgenstein that he felt he ought to join the Trotskyist Revolutionary Communist Party: 'I find more and more that I am in agreement with the chief points in their analysis and criticism of present society and with their objectives.'[5] Monk tells us:

Wittgenstein was sympathetic, but tried to dissuade him on the grounds that his duties as a loyal party member would be incompatible with his duties as a philosopher. In doing philosophy, he insisted, you have got to be ready constantly to change the direction in which you are moving, and if you are thinking as a philosopher you cannot treat the ideas of Communism differently from others.[6]

Rhees published some articles in the journal *Freedom*. When I asked Rhees, late in life, for details of these publications and any others he may have written, he replied by saying that it was better to leave them buried.

The Manchester post was a temporary one, and in the summer of

---

[5] Monk, *Wittgenstein*, p. 486.
[6] Ibid., pp. 486–7.

1932 Rhees left Manchester to study with Alfred Kastil at Innsbruck. Kastil was an authority on and editor of the work of Franz Brentano. The principal aim of Rhees' visit was to acquaint himself with Brentano's philosophy. His interests soon centred on Brentano's theory of relations, and more particularly, on how it related to issues concerning continuity. Rhees returned to England in the autumn of 1933, but, up to 1937, he returned to visit Kastil, retired in Vienna, for periods of a month or six weeks for further discussions. In a remarkable reference, dated Easter 1935, Kastil writes: 'I must confess that I looked forward to the hour of our meeting each day with eager curiosity in expectation of the new material which he would bring. For the relation of teacher to pupil had become inverted. I was chiefly the receiver.'

In 1933 Rhees applied to enter doctoral studies at Cambridge and Oxford. In his reference, Norman Kemp Smith refers to the fact that in view of the quality of Rhees' honours' work, his Vans Dunlop Scholarship was renewed in 1928 for a further three years. In the event, Rhees went to Cambridge where G. E. Moore was his supervisor for two years. By Christmas 1934 his research had concentrated on questions connected with continuity. Yet, in 1936, at the end of his period of study, Rhees wrote in a statement concerning himself:

Notwithstanding the opportunities that were furnished me and the time I have allowed myself, however, I have succeeded neither in preparing anything for publication nor in completing a thesis for a PhD. Nor can I say that I see any great likelihood of my doing so.[7] Since I came to Cambridge, I have applied for positions as lecturer or assistant lecturer in Bedford College, the University College of Swansea and the University College of Bangor. At Bedford I was interviewed and dismissed. Swansea and Bangor saw no need for an interview. My latest employment has been as a shop assistant in Messrs Deighton, Bell and Co's book shop.

In 1938, Rhees wrote to Professor Emery at the University of North Carolina at Chapel Hill enquiring about the possibility of a junior post in philosophy there. His application not only included the frank statement concerning his PhD prospects and the absence of any publications, but concluded as follows:

In conclusion perhaps I ought to say that I have some serious doubts about

---

[7] Some of the fruits of his reflections, no doubt revised over the years, can be found, I believe, in his paper 'On Continuity: Wittgenstein's Ideas, 1938' in *Discussions of Wittgenstein* (London: Routledge & Kegan Paul, 1969), pp. 104–57.

my competence in the sort of post I am applying for. I like teaching and am interested in philosophy. But I have not made an unqualified success of either, and I do not grow more sanguine with time. But I cannot resist a wish to go on with them (altogether this may be bad psychology, but it seems to me an accurate description of my mental condition nevertheless). And I find myself hoping that a start in new conditions might prove more fruitful.

The candour of these applications would make them unusual at any time, but in the present practice of providing references laden with superlatives, they would be unintelligible.

The incongruence between Rhees' assessment of himself and the opinions of J. L. Stocks and Alfred Kastil of him will have been noted. In May 1935, G. E. Moore wrote in a reference for Rhees: 'I regard him as exceptionally well qualified to lecture on philosophy in a University. There are few, if any, of the pupils I have ever had whose ability I should be inclined to rank higher than his.' By the end of the second year of supervision Moore wrote: 'I have now an even higher opinion of his ability than I had then . . . I feel still greater confidence in recommending him as a teacher of philosophy.'

When Rhees informed Moore that he would not be submitting a dissertation for a PhD, Moore wrote to him on 19 August 1936:

I am writing exceedingly sorry to hear that you have not been able to write anything that you thought worth sending in as a dissertation; and still more sorry that your failure to do so has been due to your feeling so incompetent and confused since the beginning of June. Don't you think that this feeling may have been mainly due to your having become more conscious of the difficulties of your subject? In any case, I hope you will soon feel able to work again.

I do not think the time I have spent in discussion with you will have been wasted, even if it should turn out to have been of no ultimate benefit to you; for I think it has been of benefit to me. I only wish I could have been more helpful to you.

In 1937, Rhees returned to Manchester as a temporary replacement for J. L. Stocks who had left to become Vice-Chancellor of the University of Liverpool. He taught courses on the history of philosophy, Descartes to Kant; a course on the history of political theory for the ordinary degree; an introductory course on Russell's *Problems of Philosophy*; and honours courses on logic and the theory of the state, with a course on Greek philosophy for Classics students.

Rhees counted John Anderson, Alfred Kastil and G. E. Moore

among the teachers who influenced him, but, above them all, he put Ludwig Wittgenstein. He began attending Wittgenstein's lectures during his time at Cambridge. In 1939, Wittgenstein wrote the following reference for Rhees:

I have known Mr R Rhees for 4 years; he has attended my lectures on philosophy and we have had a great many discussions both on philosophical and general subjects. I have always been strongly impressed by the great seriousness and intelligence with which he tackles any problem. Mr Rhees is an exceptionally kind and helpful man and will spare no trouble to assist his students. His German is very good indeed.

In 1940, Rhees was appointed to a temporary assistant lectureship at Swansea. At the time of his appointment he was a welder in a factory. A. E. Heath was the foundation professor of philosophy at Swansea. His previous appointments had included R. I. Aaron, Alfred Ewing and H. B. Acton, but, now, his most recent appointments, Karl Britton and W. B. Gallie, had gone off to the war. At Swansea, Rhees taught pass degree courses in psychology, logic, Plato's *Republic* and the history of philosophy from Descartes to Hume. He gave honours courses in logical theory, Greek philosophy, and Kant. In 1944 and 1945, Rhees applied for a Fellowship at University College, Oxford, and a lectureship at University College, Dundee, respectively. Wittgenstein and Heath were his referees for the Fellowship, while Moore was a third referee for the lectureship. The applications, as usual, ended with the words: 'I have published nothing and I have not written anything that might be published. It is not likely that I ever shall. I have had opportunity enough.' Rhees was now forty years of age without a permanent post. In his reference in April 1946, praising Rhees as a teacher and colleague, Heath mentions that efforts would be made, now that Britton and Gallie had returned to the department, to create a permanent position for Rhees. These efforts were successful. Rhees taught at Swansea until he took early retirement in 1966. Throughout his career he declined all promotion. When J. R. Jones was to come as professor in 1952, Heath persuaded Rhees to accept a senior lectureship to assist the new man. During his first year as professor, Rhees asked Jones, casually, whether he had settled in well. On being told that he had, Rhees promptly relinquished the senior lectureship before the date of its commencement. Rhees had an enormous influence on staff and students, not only within the department. There was great respect for him in the College from the Principal to the porters. Nevertheless, there were many occasions during his time at Swansea when Rhees worried over whether he should resign his post. Rhees' influence was at its height from 1952 to 1964 when he had J. R. Jones, R. F. Holland and Peter Winch as his colleagues.

Rhees was an inspiring teacher. He did not use notes, although they were invariably at his side. He wrestled with philosophical problems before the class as if for the first time. He had a great love of Plato's dialogues. Throughout his time at Swansea he introduced them to first year students, lecturing on the later dialogues to honours students, after first giving a course on the Presocratics. He also taught a course on philosophical logic. In all the courses he taught, Rhees conveyed a sense of the unity of philosophy. He drew intriguing parallels between Wittgenstein's concern with language and Plato's *Parmenides* concerning the conditions for the possibility of discourse. In any branch of philosophy, from logic to aesthetics, the question of what it means to *say* something, of whether one can distinguish between appearance and reality, was never one far away in Rhees' deliberations. From his early interest in Brentano, philosophical logic was central in Rhees' interests. In 1952 he edited George Boole's *Studies in Logic and Probability* and wrote a substantial Note in Editing.[8]

Ever since his days at Cambridge, Rhees had discussions with Wittgenstein. During the vacations Wittgenstein visited Swansea for these discussions, exclaiming invariably on his arrival from Cambridge, 'Man, am I glad to be here!' He was in Swansea from March to October in 1944 going on almost daily walks with Rhees. Monk states: 'The prospect of daily discussions with Rhees was not the only attraction of Swansea. Wittgenstein loved the Welsh coastline, and, perhaps more important, found the people in Swansea more congenial than those in Cambridge.'[9] Wittgenstein said to Norman Malcolm in 1945: 'I know quite a number of people here whom I like. I seem to find it more easy to get along with them here than in England. I feel much more often like smiling, eg, when I walk in the street, or when I see children, etc.'[10] Rhees attended Welsh classes in a vain attempt to learn the language. At a meal in a Welsh-speaking home, those present turned to speaking English with each other in

---

[8] George Boole, *Studies in Logic and Probability* (La Salle, Illinois: The Open Court Publishing Co, 1952), Note in Editing, pp. 9–43.
[9] Monk, *Wittgenstein*, p. 459.
[10] Ibid.

deference to Wittgenstein's presence. He insisted that they should not stop speaking Welsh to each other.

Rhees was one of the three literary executors who made over Wittgenstein's papers to Trinity College, Cambridge, in 1969, and one of the principal editors of his work. He edited *Ludwig Wittgenstein: Personal Recollections* (1981), and some of his own penetrating essays on Wittgenstein appeared in his collection, *Discussions of Wittgenstein* (1970). After his retirement from Swansea, Rhees was made an Honorary Professor and a Fellow by the College.

On coming to Swansea in 1940, Rhees founded the Philosophical Society which has met weekly ever since. Until retirement, Rhees dominated its discussions. He would almost always ask the first question, a question which took one to the heart of the paper being discussed. Often, a general theory propounded by a speaker would be seen to collapse once the question was asked. Rhees would show great patience with any question, however simplistic, if the questions were genuine, but his reactions to sham and pretence could be fierce. After discussions, it was not at all unusual for the person giving the paper, or for someone who had made a particular contribution to the discussion, to receive long typed letters from Rhees which were philosophical papers in themselves. Some of these appeared in his collection *Without Answers* (1969). I had been instrumental in convincing Rhees that he had enough material to publish two collections of essays. Having edited *Without Answers*, I found, to my amazement, that Rhees had instructed Routledge to pay all the royalties to me. Naturally, I refused to go along with this arrangement. The publishers were confronted by refusals from an author and an editor to accept money. I then suggested to Rhees that he might want to establish prizes for students with the royalties. He was delighted with the suggestion, saying that it would never have occurred to him.

On leaving Swansea after 1970, Rhees lived for some years in London. He gave seminars at King's College where Peter Winch held the chair of philosophy. Later, he lived in Cambridgeshire, but still had weekly discussions at his home with Peter Winch, Norman Malcolm and Raimond Gaita. Late in life, Rhees returned to Swansea, giving his time as liberally as ever to discussions with students. He had been liberal with them in other ways too. When grants were not forthcoming, many students, over the years, received financial help from Rhees, with no question of a loan. It was clear on Rhees' return, however, that his health had deteriorated. Although he attended every meeting of the Philosophical Society, his contributions to discussion were few. Rhees concentrated his energies on his weekly graduate seminars. Even though he was a shadow of his former self, he won enormous respect from his students. Such respect had always been forthcoming from his first students in 1940 to these, his last.

During his final stay in hospital, Rhees said, 'Discussion is my only medicine. When that is finished, so am I.' Once he was unable to conduct his weekly discussions his decline was rapid. He died at his home on 22 May 1989. Rhees had been told that a Festschrift in his honour was in the press. The volume, *Wittgenstein: Attention to Particulars* (1989), was edited by Peter Winch and myself. In a critical notice of the volume, David Hamlyn wrote: 'I myself did not know Rhees well, but I met him on more than one occasion and was impressed by that combination of philosophical percipience, directness and modesty which was the man.'[11]

After Rhees' death, the A. E. Heath Memorial Fund enabled the Department of Philosophy to purchase his papers. At various times, I had offered to help Rhees to consider the possibility of gathering his papers in collections. His reply was always the same: thanks for what he described as the generosity of the offer, together with an assurance that he had nothing, absolutely nothing. From what I had seen, I knew this could not be true, but even I was not prepared for the 'nothing' to turn out to be sixteen thousand pages of manuscript. It became obvious that Rhees, who published little during his lifetime, wrote almost every day. Sometimes, he wrote for himself, but, more often than not, in correspondence with friends and acquaintances, or in response to papers heard or read. His writings range widely in their subject-matter: Greek philosophy, philosophical logic, philosophy of mathematics, moral philosophy, political philosophy, philosophy of religion, aesthetics, Wittgenstein, Simone Weil, and subjects which do not fall easily into designated categories.

At the end of his life, Rhees expressed a desire that his papers be kept at Swansea, the one place he said he regarded as home. He was prepared to leave questions concerning publication to others, as he had done, in effect, with the two books published in his lifetime. In all his writings what we see is a philosopher truly exercising his vocation; a rarer occurrence than one might suppose.

---

[11] *Philosophical Investigations* vol. 14, no. 4 (October 1991), p. 342.

Index